better together

I love the First Place 4 Health staff and members, so I am happy to add *Better Together* to my quiet time. The First Place 4 Health program is not just about weight loss but also focuses on the whole person through Bible study, Scripture memorization and encouraging fellowship. This is the perfect program for those of us leading stressful lives.

Sandra P. Aldrich
Author of *From One Single Mother to Another*

The women in my First Place 4 Health group have become trusted friends during the past two years. I cannot imagine life without their prayer support, encouragement, spiritual wisdom and inspiration to grow and change. Truly, we are being rebuilt from the inside out through this Christ-centered program. I can't wait for us to use this devotional. It's a true gem.

Virelle Kidder
First Place 4 Health Member, Author and Conference Speaker

Carole Lewis has touched thousands of people with her writing and speaking ministry, encouraging them to live healthy lives physically, mentally, emotionally and spiritually. *Better Together* will inspire others on a daily basis to put Christ first in their lives and to love one another.

DiAnn Mills
2010 Christy Award Winner (www.diannmills.com)
Author of *Pursuit of Justice, The Fire in Ember* and *Under a Desert Sky*

Have you ever spent time with a group of friends where the conversation covers every subject imaginable and the encouragement is so sweet you never want the time to end? *Better Together* is like that, only better. These friends share how God has changed health issues and mental and spiritual struggles to blessings and joy. Spend a year reading daily devotions from these new friends and be renewed and filled. You'll see how we really are better together.

Karen Porter
Christian Author and Speaker

better together

*helping, encouraging and supporting one another
on the journey to a healthier, better life*

CAROLE LEWIS

GENERAL EDITOR | NATIONAL DIRECTOR, FIRST PLACE 4 HEALTH

Regal

From Gospel Light
Ventura, California, U.S.A.

Published by Regal
From Gospel Light
Ventura, California, U.S.A.
www.regalbooks.com
Printed in the U.S.A.

Library of Congress Cataloging-in-Publication Data
Better together : a First Place 4 Health daily devotional / First Place 4 Health.
p. cm.
ISBN 978-0-8307-5958-3 (hardcover)
1. Christian women—Prayers and devotions. 2. Devotional calendars.
I. First Place 4 Health (Organization) II. Title: First Place 4 Health daily devotional.
BV4844.B43 2011
242'.643—dc22
2011008404

Rights for publishing this book outside the U.S.A. or in non-English languages are
administered by Gospel Light Worldwide, an international not-for-profit ministry.
For additional information, please visit www.glww.org, email info@glww.org, or write
to Gospel Light Worldwide, 1957 Eastman Avenue, Ventura, CA 93003, U.S.A.

To order copies of this book and other Regal products in bulk quantities,
please contact us at 1-800-446-7735.

The title of this book gives credence to the dedication.
We are better together with so many who have been instrumental in
helping the First Place 4 Health program grow and thrive since 1981, when it was
first birthed. Our 30th anniversary year is a fitting time to thank you all.

I will be forever grateful for the 12 men and women who dreamed,
planned and created the original program. Who could have known the impact
this program would have on thousands of lives around the world?

To Houston's First Baptist Church, I am especially thankful for making the
program a ministry of the church and giving it a home from 1981 to 2009.
I am grateful for the leadership of Gregg Matte, senior pastor, and David Self,
executive pastor, for the church's encouragement to become an independent 501c3,
and for ensuring a smooth transition of the move to our own offices.

I would be remiss if this dedication did not include the thousands of First Place 4 Health
leaders and members around the world. We have, without a doubt, the sweetest and most
committed people in the world. You all make it such a joy to serve you.

To the great people at Gospel Light, who have gone above and beyond
to make our program the finest it could be, a great big thank-you. We are sincerely
grateful for the conscientious way you work to make all our planning and writing
into the finished product that changes so many lives.

We love you all,

CAROLE LEWIS AND THE
FIRST PLACE 4 HEALTH STAFF

contents

acknowledgments

A special thank you to every First Place 4 Health member, leader, networking leader, board member and staff who join together to create this successful ministry. Because of your love, prayers and commitment, First Place 4 Health is celebrating 30 years of changed lives.

My deepest gratitude and appreciation to all of you who have volunteered your time and talent to write these wonderful devotionals and inspirational testimonies for *Better Together*. They are a lasting reminder of the faithfulness of our God, and they are sure to bless many people for years to come.

We truly are better together.

introduction

You've heard the story about the little boy who was scared to be left alone in his room at bedtime. Over and over he was assured that Jesus was with him and that he was safe. One night, after several assurances from his parents, the little boy said, "I know Jesus is with me, but I need someone with skin on."

The First Place 4 Health program provides people "with skin on," and what a blessing those people are to all of us.

The First Place 4 Health ministry was birthed in March 1981, so this is our thirtieth year of ministry. The idea for this book was birthed out of the many friendships that have formed between people who participate in the First Place 4 Health program.

The community that we have found in First Place 4 Health has been a key component to our success in giving Christ first place in every area of life. First Place 4 Health people are, without a doubt, the best people in the world. They are present to pray, encourage and pick us up when we stumble. These same people are our greatest cheerleaders, and their cheering and prayer support spur us on to victory.

Cindy Secrest McDowell, a Christian writer, speaker and First Place 4 Health leader, who lives in Wethersfield, Connecticut, has written a new Bible study, titled *Better Together*, which goes along with the theme of this book. The Bible study will include a Scripture Memory CD and is sure to be a great addition to the inspiration you find in the pages of this devotional book.

how to use this book

This 260-day devotional book has been designed for use by anyone seeking inspiration and growth through a daily time of fellowship with God.

The book is divided into 12 sections, one section for each month of the year, with inspirational stories in each section. The writings are based around 52 key Scripture verses, and many are the "One Another" verses in keeping with our *Better Together* theme. We have written the book so you can read five devotions per week.

To help you absorb and meditate on each verse before moving to a new one, we have offered several devotionals around a single verse, exploring it from different angles. The verses were carefully selected to encourage and inspire a closer walk with the Lord and with other people.

If you are involved in a First Place 4 Health group, you will also enjoy using the Bible study *Better Together,* which contains most of the verses chosen for this devotional book. The memory verses for each of the 10 weeks of the Bible study are used as the first verse in each of the first 10 sections.

We believe you will enjoy this devotional book even if you are not participating in a First Place 4 Health group at this time. The 260 daily devotionals and 12 inspirational stories are sure to inspire you to seek a closer walk with God and will help you develop closer relationships with family and friends. *Better Together* is for anyone wishing to gain inspiration and strength in the following areas:

- Weight loss
- Prayer
- Journaling

You will notice throughout the devotional that contributors mention terms that may be unfamiliar to you, such as "Tracker," "Live-It Plan," and so on. These are descriptions of some of the components of the First Place 4 Health program. The program is designed to help people draw closer to the Lord and become stronger and healthier in every area of life—comprising the mental, physical, emotional and spiritual.

Many blessings to you as you allow the scriptural principles contained in this book to strengthen you, and as you allow the words of personal wisdom gained from God's Word and His Holy Spirit to inspire you.

We truly are *better together* as Jesus Christ becomes first in our lives.

MONTH 1

LOVE

1

when God is pleased

*And this is his command: to believe in the name of his Son, Jesus Christ,
and to love one another as he commanded us.*

1 JOHN 3:23

The verse just before this one tells us that we will receive whatever we ask from God if we obey His commands and do what pleases Him (see 1 John 3:22). And then the Bible tells us what pleases Him. It pleases God for you and me to love one another as He commanded us.

It is easy for me to love people who are lovable. There are many people like this in my life. The problem is to love people who are unlovable. I believe that God places unlovable people in our lives to teach us more about His character—*God is love*. I learned many years ago that it is impossible for me to love unlovable people in my own strength. The secret is to ask God to love that person through me.

As a First Place 4 Health leader, I have met a few women who have come to our class as less than lovable. I can see it in the first meeting; they have put up high walls around their hearts and they are full of anger and despair. I call this kind of person EGR (Extra Grace Required). I look at a woman like this and know that God has trusted me with her precious body (at this point, she is only interested in the physical aspect of her life) and that He wants to work a miracle in her. How does He work the miracle? He uses love—unconditional love—that keeps on giving even when love is not returned.

Little by little, the walls start coming down and I find that there is a very special child of God inside that hard outer shell. Love is the medicine we all need. Sometimes when we reach out and hug someone, it is the only human touch she or he has received for a long time. A kind word, gesture or touch is a gift that keeps on giving.

Action Item: Today, ask God to transform any unlovable people in your life by loving them through you. Look for ways to show them God's love, and watch Him work a miracle in their lives.

Carole Lewis
First Place 4 Health National Director
Houston, Texas

2

love back at you

And this is his command: to believe in the name of his Son, Jesus Christ, and to love one another as he commanded us.

1 JOHN 3:23

Several years ago, my husband and I were going through a very emotional time of grieving and change. My 49-year-old sister-in-law was dying from brain cancer. Our college-age sons both made major decisions that same summer. Ben, our youngest, was going to be married that August, and our oldest son moved out of state. This move was one that brought us to a place of testing and trusting God. Nate's move was prompted by an admission that he was homosexual. We were devastated, yet clearly knew that God calls us to love unconditionally. By His grace, we have been able to maintain a relationship without compromising God's truth.

I have been blessed to attend the annual First Place 4 Health Leadership Summit in Houston, and that particular year, I was needy for love and reassurance. My sisters in Christ ministered to me and loved me without judgment. The Lord gave me that time to come away with Him and He embraced me through a community of faith. Carole, Vicki, Becky and Meagan were the Lord's hands and feet. They spoke His words of encouragement and did a lot of listening. That time gave me the strength I needed for the days and weeks ahead.

I can remember many times over the years when my First Place 4 Health group *was* the family that ministered to me in a way that no one else could. With Christ at the center of those relationships, there is a unique and lasting bond between us. First Place 4 Health is about loving and being loved—loving our Lord Jesus Christ, loving others and learning to love ourselves through His eyes. It's about receiving the love others have to offer, not feeling the need to do anything in return. And for all of this, I am eternally grateful.

Action Item: Are you opening yourself up to the love and support offered through First Place 4 Health? Are you learning to express your love to others?

Prayer: *Heavenly Father, thank You for Your perfect love, and for loving us through others. Thank You for giving us the opportunity to love in Your Name. Amen.*

Jenn Krogh
First Place 4 Health Networking Leader
Kewaunee, Wisconsin

3

the missing link

And this is his command: to believe in the name of his Son, Jesus Christ,
and to love one another as he commanded us.

1 JOHN 3:23

I was 53 years old and felt burdened with many doubts of insecurity about my salvation. Although I continually sought to be accepted and approved of by those around me, something was missing in my life. I could not get close to the Lord, no matter what I did.

One night, when I was attending my First Place 4 Health class, we were discussing the apostle Paul's imprisonment. I felt like I was in prison too. I felt as if I could go no further. All my friends and family assumed that I was born again, so I was embarrassed to even allow myself to think that I might not be a Christian.

My Bible study leader brought out that we all have dirty hearts that we need to give to the Lord to cleanse. She added that if we had any doubts that we had ever done this, we should drive a metaphorical stake in the ground and just do it. I stood up. I wanted to do this immediately. My leader and another member of the group stood with me, and I prayed to receive Jesus into my life. At that moment, it was like singing the hymn, "Heaven came down, and glory filled my soul. My sins were washed away, and my night was turned to day."[1]

Now all things have become new. I want to start my day in His presence and in His Word, which speaks to me like never before. I want to obey Him. I want to love others unconditionally, just as He loves me. I want to be around His people. I want everyone to have what I have—Jesus Christ.

Prayer: *Lord, I have a dirty heart that needs Your daily cleansing. I need You as my Savior and Lord. I want You more than anything else in this world, and I surrender my whole life to You!*

Rachel Aranda
Houston, Texas

4

loving others

And this is his command: to believe in the name of his Son, Jesus Christ, and to love one another as he commanded us.

1 JOHN 3:23

I came to believe in the Lord as a preschooler at the First United Presbyterian Church in a small steel town in Pennsylvania. I had a wonderful Sunday School teacher, Mrs. Powney, who had the patience of a saint. Mrs. Powney played the piano and taught us songs like "Jesus Loves Me," and she told us all the Bible stories using felt board people.

Back then, I really felt special because "Jesus loved me." As I grew older, my childlike enthusiasm waned. In college, I turned from the Lord for many years. It wasn't until I was an older adult, moving to a new city, that I realized it was Jesus who had brought me there, leading one of His stray sheep back into the fold. I came to know and love Jesus in ways that I had never imagined before.

As I began studying His Word, I realized that I didn't really know His character or what He asked of me. I was in awe that He could love a "wretch" like me. But as I grew to know Jesus, I learned that He didn't just want to know me; He wanted to make me His own and teach me His ways.

The hardest thing He asked me to do is to love others as God has commanded us. It's easy to love the people I like, and even folks around the world I don't know. But there are always some people who just aren't lovable. Loving them is really hard.

But God is faithful, and He led me to First Place 4 Health and a whole community of people with whom I could interact. Through these people, He showed me unconditional love in action. Some have experienced severe tragedy and loss, yet they are able to love those individuals who have been the source of their pain. I have met people who forgave the unforgivable and comforted those who harmed them.

God has blessed me through His use of others to teach me about the depth and breadth of His love for us. Each day, I thank Him for renewing my life.

Action Item: Are you living out God's command to love others? The more we understand God's love for us, the easier it is to love one another.

Prayer: *Father God, help me to see others as You see them so that I may love them too.*

Deb Stark
San Antonio, Texas

5

God at work!

And this is his command: to believe in the name of his Son, Jesus Christ,
and to love one another as he commanded us.

1 JOHN 3:23

In my family, we just had the opportunity to "live" this verse. We recently lost my mother-in-law, a precious believer, who lived 91 years of faith. She lived a healthy life physically until the last few weeks, when our family came together to love her through the last part of her journey. During those weeks, our family members, who "believe in the name of His son, Jesus Christ," were able to lovingly speak the truth of eternal life through Christ to other family members who were open to listening.

We sang hymns, prayed, read Scriptures and had open conversations about what it means to believe in Jesus. I know the Holy Spirit gave us this opportunity, and the Lord also gave us clear guidance in how to "love one another" during this time. We hugged and cried together. We ate dinner together every night, reminisced about old times, laughed together and listened to each other. We simply spent time together, nurturing our family relationships, and we could tell that God was at work in all of our hearts.

Looking back, I can see clearly that while Grandma lingered in this world, God was at work creating this atmosphere of love, which allowed truth about Him to be spoken to softened hearts already nurtured by the love that was being expressed. It was hard to see her fading slowly, but we sensed that she knew better than us what God was doing; and when she finally passed into His presence, she was peaceful, and so were we.

When you face a hard time, perhaps the passing of a loved one, look to these two commands—believe in the name of Jesus, and love one another—to get you through. Cling to what you believe, and reach out in love to those around you. Know that God is at work, and He will see you through it.

Action Item: If you know someone who is facing the loss of a loved one, share this verse with him or her. Encourage that person to follow the command by shining the light of his or her belief in Jesus and also nurturing love relationships with friends and family who are caregivers. Then watch God at work!

Jeannie Blocher
President, Body & Soul Fitness

6

purifying truth

*Now that you have purified yourselves by obeying the truth so that you have
sincere love for your brothers, love one another deeply, from the heart.*

1 PETER 1:22

Purification makes something usable. Take water, for example. Dirty water becomes useful to drink after being purified. I believe this verse is saying to us that
we, as believers, are purified by obedience to the truth we have learned in God's
Word. The verse seems to be saying that it is impossible to have sincere love for our
brothers until we have been purified by obedience to God's truth.

What are some characteristics in you that need to be purified? Are you hot-
tempered, rude or unforgiving? Are you jealous or mean-spirited? Are your hurts
so deep that you are inwardly focused, making it impossible to love others sincerely? Do you make critical and negative comments? All such characteristics
spring from a heart that needs to be purified.

Recognizing your need is the first step to purification. Ask God to show you
personal characteristics that need purifying. I promise that He will do it. You have the
Holy Spirit living inside of you, and "He will guide you into all truth" (John 16:13).

Purification happens as we learn what the Bible says about the negative traits
we all possess. Use the concordance at the back of your Bible to find Scriptures
that speak to the specific areas in your life that need purifying. Write down those
verses and read them every day. It is so helpful to memorize Scripture that speaks
to our need so that the Holy Spirit can bring them to mind when we find ourselves acting out in an un-Christlike way.

After you learn what the Bible says, it is up to you to obey the commands you
have learned. But also realize that obedience is impossible without God's super-
natural help. Many traits that need to be purified have been with you a very long
time; but God, in His grace and mercy, wants to heal you and purify your heart so
that you are able to love others deeply, from the heart.

Action Item: Record some characteristics in your journal that keep you from loving others deeply. Look up Scriptures that can help you change and spend some
time in prayer. Ask God to purify your heart so He can receive glory from your life.

Carole Lewis
First Place 4 Health National Director
Houston, Texas

7

leading in love

Now that you have purified yourselves by obeying the truth so that you have sincere love for your brothers, love one another deeply, from the heart.

1 PETER 1:22

It was a strange place to meet—she was coming out of the restroom as I was going in. We were in a hotel in Houston, attending a First Place 4 Health conference. Her nametag said she was from Shreveport. "What church do you attend?" I asked.

"Broadmoor," she said.

"That is where my son and his family go!"

She looked at my nametag and said, "You are Emily's, Rebecca's and Victoria's grandmother!" Need I add that I fell in love with the beautiful, blonde Barbara Clark?

I was living in Houston, but soon moved to San Angelo, my hometown. God had blessed me with many great leaders in First Place 4 Health in Houston, and I was concerned about whether any groups would be available. Although I was attending a small country church, I was able to join a group at First Baptist Church in San Angelo. But they were not going to meet the next session. Help! I called Houston and asked if there were any other groups in the area. Yes, Glen Meadows Baptist Church, and the leader was Barbara Clark—the same Barbara Clark whom I had met in Houston at the First Place 4 Health conference. I enrolled!

At the first meeting, Barbara gave us two verses that were not a part of the regular study. "Then you will call upon me and come and pray to me, and I will listen to you. You will seek me and find me when you seek me with all your heart" (Jeremiah 29:12-13). Little did I know at the time how profoundly the verses would impact my life. Barbara always woke early to spend time with the Lord, and she prayed for our group. Her love for us showed through her leadership. Although she had severe health problems, she never let on. She encouraged us, led us and loved us.

The verses she gave us became a strong support I could cling to as my husband became ill with cancer. When Ray went home—the verses remained. Although the Clarks were called to another church, what I learned through her teachings and love remain with me still.

Action Item: List some practical ways that you can encourage others in your small group, and begin right away.

Betha Jean McGee
Wall, Texas

8

prickly pear people

Now that you have purified yourselves by obeying the truth so that you have sincere love for your brothers, love one another deeply, from the heart.

1 PETER 1:22

We all have "prickly pear" people in our lives that are hard to get along with—people who spit criticism and sport an aroma of arrogance. What I have come to discover is that these people are actually warm-fuzzy folks who have chosen to wear their prickly exterior instead of taking it off and letting out that warm-fuzzy person who lives inside.

We can call them insecure, insensitive or self-centered, but what they need is an extra dose of love. This can be a challenge. Who likes being riddled with thorns when you reach out to embrace them? Jesus was surrounded by prickly pear people. We see through Scripture how He interacted with them and loved them deeply from the heart.

The key to loving others from the heart is that we have to be made clean ourselves by obeying the truth, which is God's Word. We are following Jesus when we choose to put God's Word into action. Then we are able to love each other, even the prickly pear people God puts in our path. When we ask God to help us see someone through His eyes and not our own, it changes our perspective.

Philippians 2:3-5 says, "Do nothing out of selfish ambition or vain conceit, but in humility consider others better than yourselves. Each of you should look not only to your own interests, but also to the interests of others. Your attitude should be the same as that of Christ Jesus."

Prayer: *Lord, help me to see others through Your eyes and not my own; and forgive me of my sin when I have put on my prickly pear coat. Help me to love others the way You love, deeply, from the heart.*

Connie Welch
First Place 4 Health Networking Leader
Keller, Texas

9

a blessed act of obedience

Now that you have purified yourselves by obeying the truth so that you have sincere love for your brothers, love one another deeply, from the heart.

1 PETER 1:22

We all have had them. Those people who come into our classes with a tremendous amount of need. We call them EGR—*extra grace required.* Such was the case with Linda (not her real name). She came from another denomination that did not place value on Bible reading. Therefore, she was continually unprepared to enter into any discussion of our study. Not only that, but she also seemed to find a way to argue with me on most every point! I was really getting annoyed and finding myself thinking not so good thoughts about her.

As we closed the class one evening, I led in prayer. The Holy Spirit prompted me to pray out loud for her. I resisted initially, but finally obeyed and called her name out loud to the Lord. I thanked him for sending her to us and asked Him in Jesus' name to bless her. I finished my prayer and dismissed the class. As usual, everyone quickly made an exit—it was late, after all. But Linda hung back, which was very unusual for her. She lived in a neighboring town and had quite a drive ahead of her.

As I was gathering my things, I looked up and noticed that she was silently weeping. I quickly went to her and asked, "What's wrong? Are you okay?"

She looked up at me, drying her tears, and smiled. "Yes, I'm okay," she said. "I am so moved!"

"Moved by what?" I asked.

"Your prayer; it's the first time I have ever heard my name called out loud to God in a prayer!"

I have never been the same since. God blessed me with sincere and genuine love for Linda from that moment on. That small act of obedience on my part was a bigger part of God's plan for Linda. Her faith grew and so did our friendship; and I now love her deeply, from the heart.

Action Item: Ask the Holy Spirit to reveal to you who needs to hear words spoken out loud to the Father on their behalf. Then obey, bless the person and be blessed.

Vicki Heath
First Place 4 Health Associate Director
Edisto Beach, South Carolina

10

miraculous love

*Now that you have purified yourselves by obeying the truth so that you have
sincere love for your brothers, love one another deeply, from the heart.*

1 PETER 1:22

When I started in First Place 4 Health, in the spring of 2002, I expected to lose
some weight, and I desperately hoped to find some balance. But I never enter-
tained the thought that God held some miracles in store for my life!

In this verse, Peter tells us that we purify ourselves by obeying the truth *so that*
we have sincere love for those around us. I just never believed that it could extend
to my husband. For years, our marriage had been in shambles—a mere decision of
the will. Love had died. While at the First Place 4 Health Wellness Retreat in
Round Top, Texas, the speaker for the morning spoke on the romance between
Adam and Eve. What kind of message was that for a health conference? It was perfect—perfectly ordained for me!

This was the first step on my journey toward becoming the kind of wife the
Bible teaches I should be. When my attitudes and actions were viewed through
the lens of the Word of God, I realized how sinful they were. Though it was daunt-
ing at first, I began praying and applying Scripture after Scripture to the issue of
how to be a godly wife. I poured all that I had into obeying the truth. *And the truth
set me free!*

A sincere love began to burn in my heart for my husband. Our Creator created
love where there had been none left. The shambles of our marriage was redeemed
by our Redeemer! The God who kept our covenant purified us so that we could
love one another deeply, from the heart!

What about you? What did you expect when you started your own First Place
4 Health journey? There are miracles on your horizon, but it's going to take some
obedience. Are you ready?

Action Item: Who is that person (or persons) in your life who seems too difficult
to love? What truths does the Word share with you about those individuals? Begin obeying that truth today so you can have a sincere love for others—loving
deeply and right from your heart.

Karrie Smyth
Brandon, Manitoba, Canada

real love

This is the message you heard from the beginning: We should love one another.
1 JOHN 3:11

Learning to really love another person takes time. I thought I really loved Johnny when we married in 1959. Looking back, I realize that I knew very little about real love. In 1 Corinthians 13:4-7, the apostle Paul tells us that real love is patient and kind. Real love compels us to help others for no other reason than the fact that we want to make their lives better—it is not envious, boastful or proud. Real love means forgiving others and not keeping any record of wrongs that another person has done against us. When we truly love others, we don't give up on them, for true love always protects, always trust, always hopes and always perseveres.

In 1997, when Johnny was diagnosed with stage 4 prostate cancer, we finally began the process of learning how to really love each other. By this time, we had been married 38 years! You would think we would have mastered the art of loving each other completely, but this had not yet happened. What made the difference?

I think that most of us believe we have plenty of time to become completely loving. When we are brought up short to the reality that we don't have all the time in the world, it changes everything. Today, 13 years after Johnny's initial diagnosis of only one to two more years of life, we don't waste a single minute practicing behaviors that aren't loving. Life is precious, and our marriage is precious. We no longer take each other for granted. We kiss hello and goodbye every day. We have learned how to persevere through this time of cancer, and both of us count cancer as a blessing in our lives. Do we want Johnny to have cancer? Of course not! Has God used it for good in our lives? Absolutely! We have already had 11 more years than predicted, and we thank God for every minute we have to love each other.

Thank God today for the people He has given you to love. Quit taking for granted that you will have forever to show love to them. Life is short, and we are not promised tomorrow. Start really loving those people today; you will never be sorry.

Prayer: *Dear Lord, You have given me people to love. They are precious to You and precious to me. Help me learn what it means to love each one unconditionally. I want to live my life with no regrets; so I'm asking You to change me and make me love them like You do.*

Carole Lewis
First Place 4 Health National Director
Houston, Texas

1 2

a higher love

This is the message you heard from the beginning: We should love one another.

1 JOHN 3:11

Most Christians, if they have been a believer for any length of time, know that the greatest commandment is to love the Lord God with all your heart, mind, soul and strength; and the second is like it—love your neighbor as yourself. However, Jesus says in John 13:34-35, "A new command I give you: Love one another. As I have loved you, so you must love one another."

Whoa! This loving our neighbor as we love ourselves is hard enough; but Jesus is now saying don't just love like we love, but love like Jesus loves! John, who was in the room when Jesus revealed this new command, emphasizes it again in the verse above.

This love is not a brotherly love, but an *agapao* love—a God-like love. It is a love that looks out for the best interests of the one being loved and is sacrificial by its very definition. It is a love that is impossible for us apart from the work of the Holy Spirit.

There are seven questions we can ask ourselves on a regular basis that will give us an idea of whether or not we love as God would love. First, *do I show compassion?* This is the ability to connect in a caring way with the feelings of another, usually at their moments of greatest need. Second, *am I available?* This is the decision to value people simply because of their inherent value, and to seek ways to spend time with them for the purpose of serving them. Third, *do I forgive?* This is the willingness to relinquish our own pursuit of justice. Fourth, *am I an encourager?* This is the commitment to instill hope in others. Fifth, *do I honor those around me?* This is the readiness to direct applause toward others. Sixth, *am I accepting of others?* This is the choice to value and harmonize with other people who are different than us. And finally, *do I submit?* This is the capacity to defer to authority or the needs of another person instead of demanding the lead position or preference.

So, how are you doing in this new command?

Action Item: Take one of the questions each day and live out that trait. At the end of each day, journal how the Holy Spirit empowered you to love as He loves.

Becky Turner
First Place 4 Health Speaker
Houston, Texas

it's all in the delivery—or is it?

This is the message you heard from the beginning: We should love one another.
1 JOHN 3:11

I wish we could hear John's tone of voice in the written Word of God recorded in 1 John 3:11. Was he imploring, reinforcing or correcting? Was he discouraged, exasperated or excited? I wonder if he had his head in his hands when he said it, gloomily shaking it back and forth, the words coming out muddled from in between his fingers, maybe even warbled through tears? Or how about this image: hands on hips, wagging his head from side to side, saying his version of "If I've told you once, I've told you a thousand times!"

My big brother loved to call me "thickhead" when he had to tell me something more than once. It was usually preceded by his face getting red and the veins in his neck starting to pop out. And it was usually accompanied by something like, "How long is it going to take for you to get it through your thick skull?" It was usually followed by his turning and walking away in a huff. I know he loved me; it was just our way to flavor everything with sarcasm.

I would hope that John was a little kinder and gentler than my brother. But no matter *how* he said it, nothing changes the simple fact that we really *should* love one another.

Action Item: Can you think of someone who is difficult to love? Write a letter to God, asking Him to soften your heart toward this person.

Prayer: *Lord, please help us to keep it as simple as You meant for it to be and just love one another. As simple as Your message is, we still seem to mess it up. That is why we so desperately need Your Spirit to work through us. Help us, Lord. You know we are just a bunch of thickheads. Thank You for loving us anyway.*

Jeanne Deveau Gregory
Chatham, Virginia

14

a friend to all

This is the message you heard from the beginning: We should love one another.
1 JOHN 3:11

Attending church is not about me and it's not about you. It's about Him. Each Sunday, when you enter your church, remember that each and every person you meet, greet and encounter is bringing with them the wounds of their past, the struggles of their present and the unspoken anxieties of their future. What people want to know is whether you will love them just as they are, even if they don't fit the mold or change as quickly as you would like them to change. Most people are shy, distrustful and relationally impaired. Our mandate is to make friends out of them, not just benchwarmers and financial contributors.

Jesus told His disciples, "I have called you friends" (John 15:15). Take the opportunity and privilege on Sunday to be a friend to everyone you meet. Be the one to extend your hand first, to smile first, to lean in and offer a warm, welcoming hug.

Scan the people in your congregation and whisper a silent prayer to the Lord. Ask Him to show you anyone who may need an extra-special moment of your attention. You'll be amazed at how quickly people respond to your question, "Is there anything I can pray for you during this upcoming week?"

It's about Jesus. He has called us to love one another. He wants us to be vessels through which He can express His love to others.

Action Item: On Sunday, don't think about what you are going to get at church or how you are going to be affected by the message. Think about who you are going to touch and how they are going to be affected by the love you show them. You'll be fulfilling the Lord's command and you'll end up being the one who is most blessed.

Prayer: *Loving Shepherd, I will spend much of my time today with people. Some of them know You, but many do not. Please give me wisdom to say things that lead people closer to You. Give me words of help and hope for the broken; words of tenderness for the faint of heart; words of direction for the confused. Father, I pray that whatever words I say today may reflect Your will and bless others. In Jesus' name I pray.*

P. J. Bahr
Rapid City, South Dakota

15

the face of love

This is the message you heard from the beginning: We should love one another.

1 JOHN 3:11

My friend and I had no idea what we were walking into when we arrived at the First Place 4 Health Wellness Retreat event on October 7, 2010. From the moment we arrived in Houston and managed to find others headed to the same event, we were immediately friends in Christ. As we waited for the shuttle, we started to get acquainted; and by the time we arrived, several of us were buddies, and friendships were developing.

This is the way it should be when God's people come together. We should have love one for another. That is what my friend and I found with every person we met, with each conversation and with each encounter with the leaders and staff. We had several opportunities to be in different groups and to choose between several different activities. In each of these, we found that the love of Christ was evident in the lives of the people we met.

The spirit of the First Place 4 Health participants was an amazing thing. The Holy Spirit was so present in the people and the place. And as the schedule unfolded and the days passed, many commitments were made to each other and to God. Better together? Absolutely!

Action Item: Reflect on how you experience the love of Christ in your life. When you do, it is not only possible but easy to love one another. If, on the other hand, you are living in the flesh instead of the Spirit, then it will be difficult if not impossible to love one another.

Prayer: *Dear heavenly Father, fill me with Your Holy Spirit that I may love as You have commanded. Help me to be more like You, more Christlike in my daily walk. In Jesus' name I pray.*

Jewel DeWeese
South Boston, Virginia

16

love shows

Love is patient, love is kind. It does not envy, it does not boast, it is not proud.
1 CORINTHIANS 13:4

The last phrase of this verse strikes me as odd. Patience, kindness, envy and boasting are external behaviors that are easy to spot when they are present or absent. I can easily pinpoint in myself or someone else when patience or kindness is lacking or when envy or boastfulness is present. But that last one, pride, is something that is not as easy to discern. Pride is insidious and destructive, and it is usually hidden deep inside our hearts, which keeps us from loving others deeply.

I believe that a prideful person usually has a low opinion of their own worth to God, and it manifests itself in two ways. We can think too highly of ourselves or too little of ourselves—both are indications of a prideful heart.

Proverbs 16:18 says that "pride goes before destruction, a haughty spirit before a fall." I quoted this proverb often to our daughter, Shari, when she was a teenager. Shari was our middle child between Lisa and John. Middle children often have a hard time coming to terms with who they are in the family structure.

When Shari became a teenager, she wanted name-brand clothes and shoes that were very expensive and more than we were able to spend at the time. She even went to work while she was a full-time high school student so that she could buy her own clothes. Shari didn't understand that it was a manifestation of pride; and I know she felt that I was being unreasonable when I would quote Proverbs 16:18.

As Shari grew and matured in Christ, she let go of the tangible trappings of pride. She still loved beautiful things, but she learned to create them instead of buying them. She learned to sew, and she made beautiful smocked dresses for her three girls. She also decorated her home beautifully without spending a lot of money.

Shari has been in heaven since November 22, 2001, when her life was taken from her by a drunk driver. I am so grateful that our Shari learned the art of loving God and others to such a degree that her husband and girls are still drawing from that deep well of love today.

Prayer: *Lord, show me areas of my life where pride is present. Root out pride wherever it lurks in my heart so that I can love You and others deeply.*

Carole Lewis
First Place 4 Health National Director
Houston, Texas

17

what love is not

Love is patient, love is kind. It does not envy, it does not boast, it is not proud.
1 CORINTHIANS 13:4

Envy . . . pride . . . competitiveness. These are words that sadly but perfectly described me and my beliefs about others prior to my First Place 4 Health journey. I'd never been very comfortable around women. As a young adult, I'd experienced more than my fair share of blistering betrayal from women who proclaimed unconditional friendship and love but had said and done things that hurt me deeply. They weren't the only ones doing the betraying, though. I, too, was more than capable of acting in the "mean girl" mode.

It was as if the female population had created their own private competitive sport where the cutest and cattiest were crowned winners. Who looked prettier? Who attracted the cutest guys? Who had the nicest wardrobe? Whoever best answered these questions was declared a success. To make matters worse, honest and meaningful sharing often resulted in ridicule and gossip. We'd banter and brag about our wonderful, womanly wiles at the expense of those we called friends.

So, when I finally gathered the courage to walk into my very first First Place 4 Health meeting, I was met by a group of smiling women. Unbeknownst to me, I'd found a group with only female members. *Just great,* I thought. *I won't be sharing any secrets with them.* However, by the end of that first meeting, I was let in on a huge secret: True love is all about kindness, patience, encouragement and honest-to-goodness unconditional friendship as modeled by Christ and the group participants, who made it a top priority to follow His loving example.

The women God strategically placed around that table were not like the ones I'd learned to distrust. Rather, they truly loved and cared about one another's success. It wasn't about competition, but about compassion; not about envy, but about encouragement; not about pride, but about purpose.

I embraced the evidence that disproved my false beliefs about love and friendship, trading them for these eternal truths: *Love is real. Christ is Love.*

Action Item: Take time to read and rejoice over Paul's words in 1 Corinthians 13:4-13. Is there someone you know who is afraid to love or be loved? How can you demonstrate God's love and friendship to that individual, starting today?

Carol Van Atta
Troutdale, Oregon

18

for others' sake

Love is patient, love is kind. It does not envy, it does not boast, it is not proud.

1 CORINTHIANS 13:4

When it comes to our weight-loss journey, we can be our own worst enemy. We do not always use the tools that lead to success—the Live-It Plan, exercise, or even keep up with recording daily food intake in our Tracker. We can rationalize our actions better than we can adjust our actions. We can be so damaging to our own success; but God is not like that.

God meets us where we are. He shows up when we feel horrible after we have made a poor choice and are still sitting in the guilt and shame that follow. He patiently loves us no matter what. God is also gentle and kind in correcting us. Often He will show up as a still, small voice, reminding us of our commitment to wellness and the successes we've had along the way—no matter how small.

What can prove to be most difficult is seeing success around us that is much quicker than our own. If you have more than 100 pounds to lose, like I do, you know what I'm talking about. You can become so envious of people in your group reaching their goal weight that you are unable to celebrate with them. It can also be difficult when you have the smallest success and want to shout it out and boast about it.

But if we respond in love to our fellow sojourners, we will be able to appreciate their successes as proof that we can do it as well. Loving others like Christ loves us is so important as we seek to be an encouraging group member. We need to take time to support each group member and celebrate each other's successes. Loving each other is no simple thing; but it is something God expects from us.

Prayer: *Lord, help me to love others like You do. It can be so hard to be patient while restoring health to my life, but I thank You for showing me what love is. In Jesus' name, amen.*

Emily Ardolf
Fairmont, Minnesota

19

live loved

Love is patient, love is kind. It does not envy, it does not boast, it is not proud.
1 CORINTHIANS 13:4

"I want you to live loved today," God whispered in my ear during quiet time.

His words echoed in my heart until I asked Him to show me what He meant. The Lord told me to write down what would be different in my life if I lived as though I was loved today.

I reluctantly obeyed, not wanting to face the lesson I knew He was setting before me. "I would be more joyful," I wrote, "and feel somehow lighter. I would have more peace, more to give, and I wouldn't have to be so in control."

The Lord revealed to me that I wasn't living loved because I had a hard time trusting love. I desperately needed to know about His kind of love. My childhood years had left me believing the lie that I was not lovable and that I was incapable of loving anyone—to admit that I needed love was to admit weakness. I had this lie buried so deeply in me that only the truth of God's Word could free me to live the way He desired.

Love is patient and longsuffering. God would not quit on me. He was in it with me for the long haul. Love is kind, gentle and understanding. God wouldn't push or force me. He was not harsh or hard with me.

Love does not envy, does not boast and is not proud. God would meet me right where I was; I didn't have to be something I was not. And this is the best part for me: I didn't have to do it on my own. I was never meant to do anything without Him! We would do it together!

God has brought me so many precious people in First Place 4 Health to be able to live loved more easily. First Place 4 Health has been a safe place to grow and experience God's unconditional, patient, kind and selfless love. This year's Wellness Retreat was the culmination of living loved for me.

Prayer: *God, thank You for people who show me Your kind of love. Thank You for living and loving me through First Place 4 Health. Help me to live loved today, so that I may be someone who can help others to live loved.*

Donna Roberts
Houston, Texas

20

imagine love like that

Love is patient, love is kind. It does not envy, it does not boast, it is not proud.
1 CORINTHIANS 13:4

We love our families. We love our pets. We love our homes. We may even love spaghetti! But what is love—really? The answer can be found in this passage in 1 Corinthians 13:4. It is an amazing list of attributes. But that is not the end of it. The description of love continues in the next few verses: "It is not rude, it is not self-seeking, it is not easily angered, it keeps no record of wrongs. Love does not delight in evil but rejoices with the truth. It always protects, always trusts, always hopes, always perseveres" (verses 5-7).

Imagine what it might be like to be married to someone who loved like that—loved with patience and kindness—someone who did not ever delight in evil. What if you worked with someone who loved like that—someone who didn't keep a record of wrongs? Or think about your neighbor for a minute. Would your life be different if your neighbor loved like that—always protecting, trusting, hoping and persevering?

I have one more question, and it is the most important one: Are *you* willing to love like that? Are you willing to be patient and kind, to refrain from envy, boasting and prideful behavior? How about honoring others without seeking honor yourself? Or tempering your anger and refusing to keep score of the wrongs committed against you?

That amazing list of attributes can be your goal as a follower of Christ. With God's help, you can continually move in the right direction to become an example of what love truly is.

If that is your desire, ask your heavenly Father to help you become the family member, co-worker, neighbor who loves like that—who loves just like Him.

Action Item: Write out the words to 1 Corinthians 13:4-8a, substituting your name each time the word "love" appears. Then begin to make the changes that God directs so that you can be a living illustration of what love really is.

Kendra Smiley
Christian Author and Speaker
East Lynn, Illinois

if I can do it . . .

I started toying with the idea of doing something about my weight in May 2006, after I got stuck in the ticket turnstile at Busch Gardens, Williamsburg. I don't know who was more humiliated, my daughter or me! I began to have negative thoughts, spiritual doubts about my salvation and even about the truth of God's Word.

Then, during a work camp project, I became too sick to finish the week from a combination of heat, exhaustion, obesity and diabetes that had become unmanageable. This really scared me. My mother and grandmother had both died of complications from diabetes, and I was particularly scared of going down that same road.

I had one of those "groanings that cannot be uttered" moments with God, and I begged Him to help me know what to do to fix my life.

The next morning, Karen, the wife of one of our church elders, called and said she had picked up a First Place 4 Health Leader Kit at a Christian conference. She wanted me to help her get the program started at our church. It only took a

BEFORE

AFTER

few minutes of reading through some of the program's scriptural values to know that God was answering my prayer for help with my negative thoughts and doubts, as well as the physical part of me.

A few days later, Karen asked if I'd be interested in attending the First Place 4 Health Leadership Summit meeting in Houston, Texas. During the conference, I was repeatedly convicted that God had directed this path for me and I had joined a supportive nationwide family of godly men and women.

I remember how excited I was when I made it one mile around the local track after struggling to walk to the mailbox. I have since worked up to four miles. My original weight-loss goal was 50 pounds in one year, but it took one year and a week. The extra week is significant because I believe God wanted me to remember that this was on His timetable, not mine. I have lost a total of 68 pounds and maintained it for over three years.

I can now buckle my own shoes and keep up with my two-year-old grandson. I can also run and play with the preschoolers at my job as a teacher's aide

One of the best physical benefits has been the near-disappearance of my diabetes symptoms. But I am most thankful to see my spiritual transformation, especially in the area of a quiet time with God. And He continues to help me every day to see the positive side of things.

I am currently taking a correspondence course in nutrition and have an interest in helping families develop better lifestyle habits in order to improve the childhood obesity statistics in our country. I know that it is the strong Christ-centered element that will help us all find balance in our lives, regaining our health and becoming the people God created us to be.

Jeanne Deveau Gregory
Chatham, Virginia

Note
1. John W. Peterson, "Heaven Came Down," 1961.

MONTH 2

SERVICE

21

good at your gift

Each one should use whatever gift he has received to serve others,
faithfully administering God's grace in its various forms.

1 PETER 4:10

Our First Place 4 Health staff recently traveled to Brookings, South Dakota, for a Hope 4 You event. Cris Engen is the leader of a couple of groups in the church that hosted the event. We knew the event would be a good one because of the excitement in Cris's voice every time we spoke with her during the planning process.

When we arrived on Friday afternoon, we observed a beehive of activity in every corner of the church. One group was decorating tables in the gym for lunch on Saturday. Each table hostess was asked to decorate her table as she desired, so all the tables were beautiful, but different. On Saturday, the table hostess served each of us at her table and kept our conversation lively the entire meal.

It was obvious that Cris has the gift of administration, because every detail was covered. Cris had organized a dinner at the hotel where we stayed on Friday night for all the First Place 4 Health leaders attending the Hope 4 You Conference the next day. One of the ladies in the group cooked a fabulous dinner and brought it to the hotel for us to enjoy.

I had to laugh when Cris told me she had come to the church on Thursday to work, but none of her friends were there. She said she couldn't do a thing without her friends there, so she walked all over the church for three hours, praying over each room we would use during the event. On Friday morning, when her friends showed up, they were finished with all the work in three hours.

God is honored and others are blessed when we use the spiritual gifts He gave us. Using our gifts allows the Body of Christ to work in harmony to accomplish His work in our world.

Action Item: Romans 12:6-8 provides a list of some of the gifts God gives us. What are your spiritual gifts? Are you using them to benefit others?

Prayer: *Dear Lord, as I serve You, help me to use my spiritual gifts today to serve others well.*

Carole Lewis
First Place 4 Health National Director
Houston, Texas

22

specifically gifted

*Each one should use whatever gift he has received to serve others,
faithfully administering God's grace in its various forms.*

1 PETER 4:10

In 1981, when God created the First Place program through 12 men and women at Houston's First Baptist church, He began to bring in people to serve as leaders. Dotty Brewer orchestrated the production of the material and the beginning of groups at the church. When God called her home, he brought Carole Lewis in as the director of the program, and working through her gifts, the program is now changing lives worldwide.

Throughout the years, God has brought people who have served alongside Carole with their many gifts and talents. At times, He has sent specifically gifted people for a season to help in times of need. Bruce Barbour came when First Place was in need of a new publisher, and he helped establish our partnership with Gospel Light Publishing. He is still a dear friend and mentor today. David Taylor, a partner in a Houston law firm, has been invaluable in many ways at different times to the ministry. Art Nicholson is in commercial real estate in the Houston area and has recently been of great value in the search for a new home office for the program. Art and David served on the First Place Council for many years and both continue to serve as board members today. These are only a sampling of the specifically gifted people that God has led in service to the ministry.

God is still bringing forth people to serve Him. The First Place 4 Health staff now consists of a variety of gifted and talented people who love God and are committed to serving Him through this program. Romans 12:4-5 says, "Just as each of us has one body with many members, and these members do not all have the same function, so in Christ we who are many form one body, and each member belongs to all the others." We do not all have the same function, but through Christ, we serve Him as one body, and we are definitely *better together.*

Prayer: *Lord, thank You for Your wonderful plan of gifting Your people and sending them to various ministries for use of their talents in service to others. Help us to always be aware of the gentle voice of the Holy Spirit directing our lives for our good and Your glory.*

Pat Lewis
First Place 4 Health Assistant to the National Director
Houston, Texas

2 3

a godly network

Each one should use whatever gift he has received to serve others,
faithfully administering God's grace in its various forms.

1 PETER 4:10

We have a leadership team in Ohio called FOCUS, which is made up of First Place 4 Health leaders from all over the state. God put this team together and is using them to network and reach others for His work. This verse in 1 Peter reminds me of their gifts and their willingness to use them for His glory.

Ann Quillen has been a part of our leadership team for many years. She can plan, prepare and serve a wonderful tasting, healthy meal for 25 or 250, spending the least amount of money of anyone I know. Melody Lutz has a keen business knowledge and keeps us in line as we plan events. She is our fitness coordinator and a valuable asset to our team. Shirley Anneken is our promotion coordinator and does the entire computer work, along with contacting everyone before the event. Pat Warfield helps cook, greet everyone with a smile and helps me in all the details. Crystal Davidson works the bookstore and also helps wherever needed.

Our church, New Hope Baptist, hosted the Ohio Hope 4 You event in September 2010. As the Ohio networking leader, I coordinated the event with the First Place 4 Health national staff. As I observed the day of the event, I was reminded in a beautiful way that God has given each leader on our team spiritual gifts, and they were using them as God directed them to help the people who attended the conference, and the speakers. They made my job a breeze! They all worked together, using their individual gifts to make the event one of the easiest and smoothest running that we have ever done.

The comments from those who attended showed that they saw Jesus in the lives of our workers and He received the praise for a successful event. Our team is truly better together. I praise God for the faithfulness and love these leaders display as they do His work to further the First Place 4 Health ministry in Ohio.

Action Item: In what area of your sphere of influence are you using the spiritual gifts God has given you? What will you do today for His kingdom?

Janet Kirkhart
First Place 4 Health Networking Leader
Loveland, Ohio

24

"various forms" of grace

Each one should use whatever gift he has received to serve others,
faithfully administering God's grace in its various forms.

1 PETER 4:10

We were preparing for our very first victory party in November 2006. First Place 4 Health staff member Vicki Heath had graciously offered to come from Charleston, South Carolina, to our little church in Virginia to speak. I wanted her to stay at my house, so I turned myself into a basket case trying to get everything perfect. I had literally turned my house upside down to get everything off the carpets so they could be cleaned, but the clock was ticking faster than I could restore order—and I still had to wash the floors, get the prizes, decorate the hall, fix the refreshments, take a shower, change the sheets, print the certificates, fill the gift bags . . . My group members could see that I had that deer-in-the-headlights look, so they showed up on my doorstep—sweet Dawn even dragging her own vacuum.

I'm sure that Jane knew Vicki wouldn't see the cobwebs on the plastic tree behind *my* bed, but she helped me drag it outside to clean it anyway. I'm sure Mildred knew that Vicki wouldn't care that I hadn't hung decorations on my kitchen wall, but she helped me put them up in just the right place anyway. I'm sure Rita knew that I would never get the errands run in time, so she did them for me. I'm sure they *all* knew that I would never get to the hall in time, so they took care of that too.

I don't know if Vicki sensed any of the behind-the-scenes hysteria that had gone on, but if she did, she played it cool. I learned that there *are* people who really do just come to visit, encourage and love you, and they don't judge your housekeeping ability or anything else. I sure learned that Vicki Heath is one, and I also learned what this First Place 4 Health family is all about.

By the way, we had an awesome victory party!

Prayer: *Father, thank You for teaching me that I can humble myself and let my Christian sisters see the "dirt behind the bed" and know that my secrets are safe with them. Thank You for giving them a heart like Yours. Even though they have seen me at my absolute worst, they love me just the same. Thank You for helping me see how silly it is to worry about what people think when I need to focus on pleasing You.*

Jeanne Deveau Gregory
Chatham, Virginia

always a good gift

Each one should use whatever gift he has received to serve others,
faithfully administering God's grace in its various forms.

1 PETER 4:10

As a child, I looked forward to my birthday for weeks preceding the actual *big* day. I would spend countless hours imagining what type of gift I might receive from my parents. They always knew exactly what gift would best suit me. I didn't always get everything I wanted, but inevitably, what I did receive was something I liked. I don't ever recall tearing through the wrapping paper and opening the box only to exclaim, "How could you! Give me another gift!" I knew that I could trust that whatever my parents had for me was a good gift.

Granted, we don't always receive the presents we dream about. I've heard enough regifting stories to know that some things belong better with another person. However, when it comes to the gift or gifts God gives, we can trust He got it right the first time. He knows us better than any parent, spouse, child or best friend. We'd be wise to joyfully accept whatever special treasure He's bequeathed us.

Too often, like immature children, we compare our gifts, wishing we had been given the gift of hospitality instead of the gift of prophecy, or this gift rather than that one. Instead of analyzing our gifts, we'd be better off learning how to best use them to serve others. After all, whatever God has given us is meant to be shared, not hidden away.

Children are encouraged to share their gifts. As a parent, I battled against my children's desires to keep their gifts all to themselves. I understood that in the end sharing would have a better result. The same is true with the spiritual gifts God so generously and perfectly provides us. Let us make the absolute best of whatever we've been given and start spreading God's grace-filled gifts around.

Action Item: How can I use my gift(s) to serve someone in a practical way today?

Prayer: *Lord, thank You for the gifts You have given me. May I use them in a way that best serves You and others.*

Carole Van Atta
Troutdale, Oregon

26

washing feet

Now that I, your Lord and Teacher, have washed your feet,
you also should wash one another's feet.

JOHN 13:14

I have been a part of two actual "foot washing" events. The first was one of the scariest and most humbling experiences of my entire life. Scary, because I had never before experienced it, and humbling because of how God used it in my life and in the lives of others that day.

It happened on a Saturday morning at a beach house in Galveston, Texas. My dear friend Beth Moore had graciously agreed to share a message with our 12 First Place leaders at our leaders' retreat. This was in the mid 1990s, and Beth was our keynote speaker for most all of our First Place events (before she became *Beth Moore*).

I thought it was odd when Beth got out of her car with a huge bowl, pitcher and a towel, but I never gave it another thought until it was time for her to speak to the group. Beth filled the pitcher with warm water and brought it to the center of the circle of leaders. She asked each of us to take off our shoes and then began to go around the circle washing each of our leaders' feet. This, in itself, was a moving experience for our leaders; but what happened next was what really drove Beth's message home.

She placed me on a chair in the middle of the circle and asked each of our leaders, as the Lord led, to come forward and wash my feet. I don't think I have ever been more filled with emotion. As my feet were washed by the leaders, my tears led to a complete breakdown of walls, and things were shared in that circle that had never been shared with another person.

You may never have been to an actual "foot washing," but there is great spiritual significance in the act of washing another's feet. We "wash feet" in many ways: reaching out to others in need, being there for someone during illness or grief, and by serving without recognition. As you continue to love one another in these ways, God will open up more opportunities than you could ever imagine.

Action Item: Write in your journal a time when someone literally or figuratively washed your feet. Then write about a time when you did this for someone else.

Carole Lewis
First Place 4 Health National Director
Houston, Texas

precious connector

Now that I, your Lord and Teacher, have washed your feet,
you also should wash one another's feet.

JOHN 13:14

You just never know how your Bible study classmates are going to minister to you. I had one precious woman in my First Place 4 Health class who unwittingly assisted God with my healing—for a time. My chief health concern right then was chronically aching feet, and I knew the extra weight was making it worse. Betty asked me if she could do something special in class. She wanted to follow Jesus' example in John 13 and serve her classmates by washing their feet.

The afternoon of the meeting, she brought out bowls and towels, and we held an old-fashioned foot washing. The humorous part was the different reactions from the ladies—from huffing off in aggravation to running behind a screen to eagerly remove panty hose—all absolutely acceptable since we waited until the end of class to spring it on them. As we randomly knelt and washed someone's feet, we prayed for each other.

The next week I was thrilled to testify to God's amazing mercy. For three days my feet were blissfully pain-free for the first time in recent memory. Then the constant ache came back. I told them that God spoke in my spirit, "See, I can heal you, but I want you to do the work." I believe the prayer-covered foot washing precipitated the healing, along with the message, and I was so grateful to Betty for her obedience. I was very encouraged by the experience, and it fueled my waning motivation for the program. Without realizing it, Betty was the connecting piece between me and my Lord.

Action Item: Think of someone who has helped you "hear" from God, and ask Him to renew the message to your heart.

Prayer: *Dear God, thank You for people in my life who will act as connectors to You. Bless them mightily for their obedience. Show me when, where and how I can do the same, even bringing someone to my mind today.*

Beth Serpas
Houston, Texas

28

a true valentine heart

Now that I, your Lord and Teacher, have washed your feet,
you also should wash one another's feet.

JOHN 13:14

Every Valentine's Day since our marriage more than 30 years ago, my husband and I have done something special to celebrate. But Valentine's Day of 2006 proved to be very different. My father-law had come to live with us because of dementia with sundowner's syndrome. Due to his sundowning, he would wander around the house all night. We had to watch over him 24 hours a day. My husband worked from our home and was able to watch over him during the night, and I watched over him during the day. His living with us changed our entire lives. It was our privilege to care for him, but it was very stressful as well.

We found ourselves trying to figure out a way to celebrate Valentine's Day that was in keeping with the changes in our home. My husband surprised me that morning about 6:00 A.M., the time when I usually got up and my father-in-law was still asleep. Still in my pj's, he sat me down in the chair in our bedroom and began to wash my feet and pray over me.

I was shocked, first that he even thought to do that, and second because he was the one I felt was making the biggest sacrifices and I should be washing his feet. He humbled himself before me to let me know how much he loved me, and how he appreciated my rearranging our lives to care for his father. It felt like Jesus was standing right there in the room in the form of my husband.

It was the most special Valentine's Day I've ever had. Jesus said, "Now that I, your Lord and Teacher, have washed your feet, you also should wash one another's feet" (John 13:14). This is the way we should live toward our fellow believers.

Action Item: Ask God if there is someone in your life before whom you need to humble yourself.

Prayer: *Lord Jesus, please show me anyone in my life that I need to humble myself toward so that I might do as You have done to Your disciples. In Jesus' name, amen.*

Karen Ferguson
Houston, Texas

29

water, bowl and towel

Now that I, your Lord and Teacher, have washed your feet,
you also should wash one another's feet.

JOHN 13:14

In Jesus' day, there was no lower rank of servanthood in a household than the one who washed people's feet. Let's face it, it wasn't an appealing job. Feet got dirty and sweaty in those sandals and needed tending to as people entered a house. Jesus—the very Son of God—humbled Himself and willingly served His disciples in this servant role.

Our spiritual "feet" get pretty dirty too. It can be a long, hard road at times, with slippery shoulders dropping off to muddy ditches. Perhaps, like me, you've found your way into quite a number of ditches and stand amazed at the cleansing ministry of the Savior.

Just like the disciples, Jesus loves us so much that He washes our "feet." All of the dust and grime that cover us as we journey through life, He washes away. He ignores the stench. He sees our need and ministers to us . . . and I have learned to *let* Him.

Simon Peter initially said, "You will never wash my feet!" To which Jesus replied, "If I don't wash you . . . you don't really belong to me" (John 13:8, *CEV*). That caused Peter to quickly change his tone. Jesus told them that if their "Lord and Teacher" had washed their feet, they should do the same for each other.

What does that look like? How do we follow Christ's example and pass on the ministry we have received from Him? Many around us are tired and worn out from their journey. They could use the refreshing touch of the Savior, and He wants to use our hands to do it. Despite the dirt and the grime, He asks us to humble ourselves and minister to *one another.*

Action Item: Is the Lord showing you someone right now who is in need of His refreshing touch? What can you do today to show that person the love of our Savior? Are you willing to humble yourself and reach out of your comfort zone?

Karrie Smyth
Brandon, Manitoba, Canada

30

bless me, feet

Now that I, your Lord and Teacher, have washed your feet,
you also should wash one another's feet.

JOHN 13:14

It was a drastic change to leave Houston to live on a farm! The scenery was different; the lifestyle was different; the pace was drastically different; and even the food was different!

We were living in the old farmhouse where I had spent many happy hours playing with my favorite cousin as children. Next door was a precious lady, my Aunt Vi. She was in her nineties and still able to get around when we first moved there. She had her garden, and I enjoyed helping her while she reminisced about the "old days."

We talked about food and how much better the fresh fruits and veggies were compared to the canned ones. I told her some of the things I had learned in First Place 4 Health. We talked about recipes and the ones we liked to fix the most. Her kitchen usually smelled like a dream, especially when she was making bread!

One day, I went over to her house, and she was sitting in her chair in the living room, soaking her feet. She seemed discouraged. I asked what was going on, and she said she was getting crippled so that she could not trim her toenails. Without thinking, I got down and started washing her feet and trimming her toenails. She had big feet for a woman and nails as tough as the ones you have to hammer in wood. I found it to be a humbling experience. As I finished, I gently massaged lotion on her feet and put her slippers on. To me, Aunt Vi was already a saint just waiting to go to heaven!

She tried to thank me, but I told her I really should be thanking her, because I was able to do for her what she could not do for herself. So many times in my life the shoe had literally been on the other foot.

Jesus told us to wash one another's feet, and it is a privilege you do not want to miss.

Action Item: The next time you visit someone in the hospital or in a nursing home, ask for their bottle of lotion and gently massage their feet. You are in for a blessing!

Betha Jean McGee
Wall, Texas

31

help when you need it

*You, my brothers, were called to be free. But do not use your freedom to
indulge the sinful nature; rather, serve one another in love.*

GALATIANS 5:13

I will never forget the day when I was driving with Vicki Heath to look at a conference center where we planned to have a Wellness Retreat. The conference center was about halfway between Charleston, South Carolina, where Vicki lives, and
Savannah, Georgia.

Vicki was driving when my cell phone rang. The call was from our precious
daughter-in-love (law), Lisa, telling me that her dad, George Gerdes, had died.
George was only 71 years old. He had died from an abdominal aneurysm.

We were all in shock; George had not been sick and he was driving home from
work when the aneurysm struck. I flew home immediately, and we all pitched in
to help plan the service and the dinner afterwards at the church.

Lisa and I both lead First Place 4 Health classes at noon on Tuesdays at Houston's First Baptist Church, and I was really trying to lose weight that session. Anyone who knows me knows that sweets are my downfall, and that stressful day at
the luncheon was no different. I was standing at the dessert table, looking at a
piece of Italian Cream Cake, when I heard a voice behind me say, "Step away from
the cake!"

Lisa had lowered her voice to sound like a stern policeman, and we both had
a good laugh. Our family helped to serve Lisa's family in love during this sad time,
and Lisa had served me in love when I was being tempted by that piece of cake.

We are always better together. God didn't intend for us to go through life living like the Lone Ranger. He designed us to work in community to serve one another in love. Remember, one kind deed is worth many kind thoughts.

Action Item: Is there someone you know who needs a kind word or a kind act today? God will surely bless you if you will serve that person in love.

Carole Lewis
First Place 4 Health National Director
Houston, Texas

32

easing the hard work

You, my brothers, were called to be free. But do not use your freedom to indulge the sinful nature; rather, serve one another in love.

GALATIANS 5:13

When I asked my daughter how she liked the first few days of her freshman year in high school, she said, "I love it! It's like summer camp!" A few months later, the hours of homework were beginning to pile up and grades beginning to weigh on her. She still loves the friends and the extracurricular activities of high school, but doing the actual schoolwork is hard!

Isn't that how it is when we join First Place 4 Health? We're revved up and determined to lose some weight and start exercising and eat right. We fill out our food and exercise Tracker. We start walking with a friend three days a week. We do our Bible study every morning. But then, a few weeks later, our friend gets sick, so we don't walk. We get too busy to do our study. Our friend has a birthday, so we share some cake with her. The next thing you know, we've had fried chicken for dinner, and who even knows where our Tracker is. We still love seeing our friends each week at the group meeting, but making healthy choices every day is hard work.

In my First Place 4 Health class, we all share in the work of making healthy choices. Nancy brings a healthy cookie for us to try. Dolores brings a new wrap she found in the grocery store. Kathy shares her tips for getting enough fiber in her diet. Diane tells us how she has turned a corner in a difficult relationship. Each of us brings something that helps the others in the hard work of staying on track. We all serve one another in love so that the hard work is made a little easier.

Action Item: Are you in a First Place 4 Health group? If not, find a friend to participate with you to make the health choices easier. If you are in a group, what can you share with them this week that might help others in the class? A strategy for success? A newfound food? A recipe? Let's serve one another in love.

Lisa Lewis
First Place 4 Health Director of Events
Houston, Texas

excuses turned into service

You, my brothers, were called to be free. But do not use your freedom to indulge the sinful nature; rather, serve one another in love.

GALATIANS 5:13

"All grandmas are fat!" Those were the words of my five-year-old son one day when he came home from kindergarten. He was talking about his overweight teacher. He said those words with a loving, matter-of-fact tone in his voice. He liked his teacher.

Twenty years later, as a grandmother myself, those words came to mind as a way of rationalizing my overweight figure. However, all around me there were plenty of friends who were trim grandmas. That's when I decided to start a First Place 4 Health group at my church. I asked the Body & Soul exercise instructor there to help me. We decided to hold our First Place 4 Health class after her Body & Soul class right there at the church.

We shared the class together. I took care of the weigh-ins while she wrapped up the Body & Soul class. She helped the First Place 4 Health attendees with the fitness side while I led the Bible study part, as well as taking care of the class administration. The Lord raised up a young dietician who helped the class to understand good nutrition as she read each one's food Tracker. I lost my weight, but better than that, I was ministered to by the other class members and encouraged in ways that would have never happened if I had believed a kindergartener's words that were rattling around in my head. In God's economy, we are blessed when we give to others. Think about it. Everything in nature only receives when it first gives.

"Make sure that you don't use this freedom as an excuse to do whatever you want to do and destroy your freedom. Rather, use your freedom to serve one another in love" (Galatians 5:13, *THE MESSAGE*). We are free to indulge ourselves, but what joy and personal encouragement come when we step out and serve others! We almost always benefit more from serving others.

Action Item: What lies are you listening to in your head? What rationalizations or excuses are you making for your situation in life?

Prayer: *Lord, help me to turn excuses into service. Show me where You would have me serve others.*

Nan McCullough
Reston, Virginia

super-size *that*, please

You, my brothers, were called to be free. But do not use your freedom to indulge the sinful nature; rather, serve one another in love.

GALATIANS 5:13

You're ordering at the drive-thru window when you hear the words, "Would you like to super-size that?" Your old nature screams, "Yes, and hurry!" as your new nature urges you to pretend you didn't hear and drive through quickly.

Every day is a battle. The temptation of the food industry's lure and the desire to make healthy choices is a constant clash. Most of us have the luxury of well-fed bodies. But our spirits are starving. That unsatisfied feeling in us is the new nature craving to be fed with the Word of God.

Think about it. Who loves you more? Who will not lie to you—the billion-dollar food industry that deceives us with colorful packaging and the promises of advertising, or God who loves us so much that He gives us the freedom to choose?

Feeding our new nature isn't difficult if we do not give in to the sinful desires of the old, sinful nature. Eating without planning, spur-of-the-moment food shopping and habit eating are all ways of giving control back to the old nature. One cookie leads to two, then three; and soon the package is half empty. The old nature is happy but not content. The new nature whispers, "What about me?" Guilt arrives and we finish off the cookies. It's okay to have a cookie; however, when you reach for another, grab a Scripture verse instead. You can have as many helpings of God's Word as you desire.

Yes, super-size when it comes to feeding your spirit. As you grow inside and learn of God's will for your life, you will make wise choices. And the outside results will be amazing.

Action Item: Love your new nature and others enough to stop urging second helpings. And tuck a Scripture verse in the napkin or on the plate with the smaller slices of chocolate birthday cake. Your family and guests will leave the table feeling fully satisfied and comforted.

Linda D. Derck
Shamokin, Pennsylvania

the beauty and tragedy of free will

You, my brothers, were called to be free. But do not use your freedom to indulge the sinful nature; rather, serve one another in love.

GALATIANS 5:13

William Wallace's story, portrayed in the movie *Braveheart,* tells us that he was strapped down on a plank of wood in the shape of a cross and was about to die for what he believed in. You knew that the credits would soon roll, but you hoped the movie would not end that way. As he filled his lungs for one of the last times, he cried out, "Freedom!" and moments later the executioner's axe was on his neck.

As I read Galatians 5:13, I can't help but believe that when Jesus was hanging from a cross, looking down the corridor of time, He saw me and cried, "Freedom for you!" His death paid for my freedom, and with it all things are permissible but all things are not beneficial. How I use this freedom—how you use this freedom—is up to us. It's both the beauty and the tragedy of free will.

Free will gives us the ability of choice to use this dearly bought freedom to indulge our sinful nature and our fleshly desires. The paradox is that when we do choose to indulge ourselves, greater bondage is created rather than greater freedom. The more we feed the flesh, the less we feed the Holy Spirit of God. The Spirit is still present and fully available to empower us to say no to ourselves and yes to godliness, but He will not impose Himself on us.

But, oh my, if we do choose to use that freedom for righteousness and ask Him to empower us and fill us with His Spirit, He will dive into that pit of our own making and lift us out onto solid ground! In the process, we will not only experience greater freedom, but we will also be able to love and serve others like never before. Our choices will either appease the flesh (for it is never fully satisfied) or bring glory to God. How will you choose today?

Action Item: Are you walking in freedom that indulges self or glorifies God? Are there areas of bondage in your life brought about by your own choices? Journal your confessions and ask the Holy Spirit to fill you so you can walk in freedom.

Becky Turner
First Place 4 Health Speaker
Houston, Texas

36

total commitment
to God's lead

Whoever serves me must follow me; and where I am, my servant also will be.
My Father will honor the one who serves me.

JOHN 12:26

Jesus' words in John 12:26 make me think about the boss/employee relationship here on earth. Have you ever worked with fellow employees who served but did not follow management? Yes, they did their job, but their allegiance was definitely not to their boss. Instead of following the leadership of the boss, they talked about their boss in a disdainful way. They tried to get other employees to see that their ideas were much better than the ideas of the boss. They disagreed openly in meetings and constantly tried to go around the commands of their superior.

Jesus is saying that if we want to serve Him, then we must learn what it means to follow Him. Just three weeks before Hurricane Ike hit land and destroyed our home and furnishings at Galveston Bay, I had begun writing *Give God a Year*. I had written six chapters in three weeks because I was sticking close to Jesus every day. Our lives were turned upside down after Ike, but I soon realized that if I was to finish the book, I would have to stay "up close and personal" for the entire year. That year was one of the worst yet best years of my life!

God became more real during that year than He had ever been before. Someone said, "When He is all you have, He is all you need," and I found those words to be true. Jesus is telling me in this verse that life will be good if He and I do it together. He wants us to always be where He is, not trying to do it our way, but His. The most beautiful part of this verse is the promise at the end: "My Father will honor the one who serves me." Jesus is the best boss we could ever have. Let's serve and follow Him with great joy!

Prayer: *Dear Lord, I don't want to be the kind of worker talked about in this devotional, always trying to do everything my way instead of taking Your instructions. Help me today to obey You and stay close to You.*

Carole Lewis
First Place 4 Health National Director
Houston, Texas

37

total commitment

Whoever serves me must follow me; and where I am, my servant also will be.
My Father will honor the one who serves me.

JOHN 12:26

When I hear Jesus' words "follow Me," I undoubtedly think of John Denver's words and tune from his famous song by the same name: "Follow me where I go, what I do and who I know. Make it part of you to be a part of me. Follow me up and down, all the way and all around. Take my hand and say you'll follow me."[1]

This refrain encompasses what Jesus wants from us: total commitment. He wants us to follow Him wherever He leads through the storms, deserts, valleys and mountains of life—even to the pit of hell, if necessary. And He doesn't want us just to follow His footsteps but to also model His character in our habits, faith and obedience.

It's a nice incentive to cling to the promise that when we follow Christ we will be honored by the Father, but that shouldn't be our only motive. Another verse from John Denver's song states that one of the benefits of being in a relationship is that there is always someone there with whom we can fellowship when no one else is around. This is the privilege we have been given—that we have the opportunity not only to follow our Savior but also to have a personal relationship with Him.

When we follow Christ where He leads, we connect with Him in a deeper way and grow in our faith as a result. This is what makes Christianity the one and only way to the Father.

Action Item: Where do you find it most difficult to follow Jesus? Write a prayer asking Him to reveal what needs to change in your life to make this happen.

Prayer: *Dear Lord, thank You for loving us enough to die on the cross for our sins and to heal us with Your lifeblood. We can never do enough to deserve Your grace and mercy. Thank You for wanting us around.*

Betha Jean McGee
Wall, Texas

3 8

follow into the darkness

*Whoever serves me must follow me; and where I am, my servant also will be.
My Father will honor the one who serves me.*

JOHN 12:26

In fall 2008, my faith community became concerned about the human slavery issue. We heard of the many young girls and women sold into prostitution. What was happening in our community in this regard? A group visited the strip club in town while others remained home and prayed. Compassion filled our hearts, and we began a ministry to the young women who danced nude, taking them gift bags and words of love. My role was to provide gifts and to pray for those making the visits.

"Those who serve Me must follow Me," Jesus said to my heart. My excuses began to pile up. My husband would not like it; I would be too embarrassed; I could never go into a place like that. "I will be with you," my Lord reminded me, and the excuses began to seem flimsy.

How I prayed for Jesus to walk with me as I entered the dark gentlemen's club! Was Jesus really in this place? I felt His presence as a bubble around me. We walked into the bar, loud with music and dimly lit. No one was in the bar. No one was dancing on the stage, as there were no customers. The bartender greeted us warmly and led us back to the dressing room. Six young women met us, eager to see what we had brought (brownies, lotions, cards). Scantily dressed, they were so young (18 to 24) and seemed too vulnerable to be doing what they were doing. Conversation was easy, as they proudly showed pictures of their babies (three were moms) and even shared personal struggles. Their names and faces were burned into my mind and my heart.

On each successive visit, we know that Jesus has gone before us. Sometimes my eyes see more skin than I am comfortable with, but His compassion removes the sting and I feel His love for each one of these girls. He is there, in this very dark place.

Action Item: Where is Jesus calling you to follow Him? When it is outside your comfort zone, are you willing to trust His presence and go?

Prayer: *O Lord, be the guide of my life. I want to follow You wherever You lead, for then I know You are with me. Amen.*

Jan Blankenship
Medford, Oregon

39

follow Jesus where He leads

Whoever serves me must follow me; and where I am, my servant also will be.
My Father will honor the one who serves me.

JOHN 12:26

When we follow Jesus, our lives are forever changed. I have heard it said that He loves us just the way we are, but He loves us too much to leave us that way. Following Jesus means walking in His footsteps. We take this action by modeling His actions. This is not just a physical act, but also one that involves our whole being. Jesus was asked in Mark 12:28, "Of all the commandments, which is the most important?" We see His reply referenced in verses 30-31: "'Love the Lord your God with all your heart and with all your soul and with all your mind and with all your strength.' The second is this: 'Love your neighbor as yourself.' There is no commandment greater than these."

Loving others as yourself evokes loving them like Jesus does. When we live this out in service to others, we walk in His footsteps. It doesn't matter what our job is, our calling is the same. Every job is important. We surrender all of our being and the control of our lives to Him. When we do this, we become the instrument He uses to minister to others.

We need to be attentive to listening to His voice and walking in His Word. Then we will become His hands, His feet and His voice. His Holy Spirit lives in us and through us. One of my favorite verses to pray is Philippians 2:3-5: "Do nothing out of selfish ambition or vain conceit, but in humility consider others better than yourselves. Each of you should look not only to your own interests, but also to the interests of others. Your attitude should be the same as that of Christ Jesus." This verse is the road map to following in Jesus' footsteps of service to others.

Action Item: Walk in His Word daily and memorize Scripture; this allows you to think His thoughts and pray to have a servant's heart like Jesus.

Prayer: *Lord, help me to do nothing out of selfish ambition or vain conceit, but in humility consider others better than myself. Help me to look not only to my own interests, but also to the interests of others. Make my attitude be the same as that of Christ Jesus. Amen.*

Connie Welch
First Place 4 Health Networking Leader
Keller, Texas

40

bucket list encounter

Whoever serves me must follow me; and where I am, my servant also will be.
My Father will honor the one who serves me.

JOHN 12:26

I relaxed in the lounge chair, my feet dangling in the swirling and soapy warm water. I was having a pedicure, one of the things on my "bucket list." I had never allowed myself the luxury of this treatment until now. I remembered that Sue, a member of my First Place 4 Health class five years ago, had a small business and we had prayed for her. I took my toes to her shop.

The pretty dark-haired woman hugged me as I came in the door. It was good to see her and her unique shop. "My life has changed so much since those classes, and things are better," she told me. Her self-esteem and attitude were positive. Her business had grown. She told me how the Bible study and fellowship had brought her closer to God. She was attending church regularly and said God was blessing her business.

The phone rang, and Sue had a cancellation. Five minutes later it rang again—this time, someone wanted to come in today if they could. Sue smiled and said, "It seems that when I get a cancellation, I don't need to worry; God sends a replacement."

I looked at a chart on the wall that had a thermometer pointing out her goal to raise funds for a mission trip to Guatemala. "I am going with Linda," Sue said. Linda had been one of the teachers in our class.

Sue's goal was three-fourths met, and she had six months to save. I watched Sue as she carefully dried each of my toes and then painted them a bright color and added flowers! "I hope you become addicted," she said, and laughed.

"It would be easy," I replied, as I hugged her and handed her an added bonus toward her missions fund. First Place 4 Health touches lives by serving others in many ways—this was just one. I never dreamed that someday Sue would wash my feet. Next she will be serving in Guatemala.

Prayer: *Thank You, Lord. You have shown us how to be a servant. Lead me where I need to serve. Amen.*

Beverly LaHote Schwind
Fairfield Glade, Tennessee

maintenance in the process

There I was—50-plus pounds overweight again. At least, this time it was only 50, not 80 or 90. When a couple started First Place 4 Health at our church, I signed up. This time was a bit different, because my husband, Charles, could attend with me.

It was great the first two weeks. I couldn't wait to weigh in. That was my good/bad meter. But when the new wore off, and I had to be weighed at each weekly class, I cringed every time. When they began to talk about calories and food choices, it gave me a sick feeling. All I heard were things I had done in the past that didn't work.

Charles and I never wrote down our food or learned the memory verse. The only thing we managed to do was the Bible study, which I now realize is what we needed. The Bible study was the common denominator that brought us closer together. This lasted for a few weeks; but then our leaders had an unexpected move and class was cut short. The leader left me the material to lead the remainder of the session.

BEFORE   AFTER

Life went on for a while without First Place 4 Health. I was now past 40 and needed to get busy. So I mentioned to our associate pastor that I might want to start another class. My husband agreed to be my co-leader, even if it meant he was only there for moral support. A couple of months went by and I didn't hear a word about whether we could start the class. Just as I was beginning to think I would get out of this obligation, our associate pastor called.

God knew before I did that I belonged there. He knew that if I wasn't leading the class, I would find a way out. God did the same with Charles. I told him up front that I would not do this without him, and he loved me enough to come to every class. The best part of this journey with God and this class is that I now have a closer relationship with my husband of 25 years.

It's interesting how when you are in the process, you miss the small accomplishments and goals. I had begun the habits of the program, and it didn't bother me to track my food or plan exercises anymore. I looked forward to it. How quickly a year passes. I had soon dropped the 50 pounds. This past year, I participated in two 5k runs and loved it. I'm now looking forward to running a 10k.

Before starting First Place 4 Health, I didn't know how to maintain. Did you know there is a whole article on "maintaining" in the First Place 4 Health material? I never saw that section before. I was always on my way up or on my way down. I told my friend that I was a little apprehensive with the thought of maintaining. She quickly reminded me that I was already doing it. God had brought me there, and it was so easy. I can now say, "I'm a maintainer!" Yes, there are days when I get off track, but it takes a lot less time to get back on track. Praise God!

I have watched our church friends, close friends and even our daughter, Kelly, lose weight. In this past year, they have shed a total of approximately 250 pounds. Charles, after some reluctance, has lost more than 30 pounds and is still working on his goal of 45 pounds. I have seen him go from a *churchgoer* to a *God-doer*.

Beverly Cody
Bastrop, Texas

Note
1. John Denver, "Follow Me," (1970), *John Denver's Greatest Hits*, © 2005 Sony BMG Music Entertainment.

MONTH 3

PATIENCE

winsome living

Be completely humble and gentle; be patient, bearing with one another in love.

EPHESIANS 4:2

Loving parents have all the characteristics mentioned in this verse. We are *humbled* that our union could produce a perfect little human being. We are *gentle* beyond words, never yanking an arm or leg, and always speaking in soft soothing tones. Our *patience* is sometimes tested when we are up all night with our little one, but we don't want them to feel or sense our impatience, because we know it's not their fault they are being fussy. Why do we treat a baby with such love and care? The first reason is because this is our baby, and we love him or her.

The second reason is that we know this is a baby and not a mature adult. Paul is saying that we should treat everyone the same way we treat our much-loved child. These four qualities—humility, gentleness, patience and love—are powerful. They will make a baby smile and laugh out loud before he or she even knows what laughter really means. These qualities will also draw others to Christ because they are so foreign to our twenty-first-century world.

What if these qualities were ever present at work, in the grocery store line, at the cleaners and with our spouse or friends? People would flock to us to learn the secret we possess.

I will never forget the last three years of my mom's life on this earth. She came to live with Johnny and me at the age of 86 and was suffering with arthritis in her spine and dementia. She was in a wheelchair, and much of the time she was confused about so many things. I found myself praying daily that I would always be gentle, patient and loving with my mom, as she had been with me every day of my life.

Without the Holy Spirit's power inside us, we cannot live out this verse. But when we ask for His help, He will live it through us.

Action Item: Write the words "humility," "gentleness," "patience," "bearing with each other in love" on a card and carry it with you today. Ask God to help you be this kind of person in every interaction you have today. Tonight, write in your journal all the things God was able to do because of your obedience to His commands.

Carole Lewis
First Place 4 Health National Director
Houston, Texas

42

a work in progress

Be completely humble and gentle; be patient, bearing with one another in love.
EPHESIANS 4:2

One of the wonderful things about First Place 4 Health is that the program focuses on the whole person—the physical, the spiritual, the mental and the emotional. Promoting health, wellness and balance in all of these areas transforms you into the person God created you to be.

It all begins with a humble heart. Sometimes I feel like I need to hang a sign around my neck that says, "Caution, work in progress. Please be patient with me; God is not through with me yet." For many years, I convinced myself that I was not a patient person, nor was I wired that way. I had a misguided thought that others should accept that flaw in me as well. This was a prideful, blind attitude that needed transformation.

Very important aspects of First Place 4 Health are the commitments to daily Bible study and memorizing Scripture and the weekly reading assignments in the *Members Guide*. I had no idea how much light the Lord would shed on the dark areas of my life to bring about the deep healing I so desperately needed. He bore with me patiently, lovingly and gently as He walked me through eye-opening revelations about how I related emotionally with food and with others. I allowed my emotions to be in control of me instead of allowing these areas to be under the Holy Spirit's control.

Bible study, Scripture memory, prayer support and First Place 4 Health lessons all worked together in concert to bring me health and clear vision to see into the various areas of my life. Through the program, I have lost more than 40 pounds, but I have also gained a new life on the inside. Now I am able to relate to others differently, in a healthy way. I am still a work in progress, but I am thankful for His patience and for not giving up on me when I had given up on myself.

Prayer: *Lord, help me to relate to others with a humble, gentle heart, being patient and loving with them like You are. We are a work in progress, and You see us not only as we are but as who we are in Christ.*

Connie Welch
First Place 4 Health Networking Leader
Keller, Texas

43

bear with me

Be completely humble and gentle; be patient, bearing with one another in love.

EPHESIANS 4:2

The benefits of being humble, gentle and patient are generally understood, but rarely do you hear someone talk about the benefit of bearing with another person. We can all recall comments made about bearing with others that imply what a hassle or burden such an action generates; but seldom do we consider how precious it is to have people in our lives that will bear with us in love. Thinking back over the past five years since I joined First Place 4 Health, the faces of those who participated in those sessions with me come to mind, warming my heart and reminding me of how God always provides what we need.

While it's true that learning to make healthy food choices and building exercise into my life has been important, it is the people and the relationships I've built over the past several years in First Place 4 Health sessions that have nurtured my soul and given me living examples of what bearing with one another in love looks like in real life.

Some people have come in for a session and drifted off. Others have come and stayed for several seasons, committed to making their health—spiritual, mental, emotional and physical—a priority. We have laughed together and cried together. But more importantly, we have prayed together. We have prayed for our families, for our jobs, for guidance; and we have prayed for each other.

I'm doubtful that anyone in our group anticipated that we would grieve together, but we have grieved through the loss of a spouse and the death of a son. Over and over we have seen that God is faithful and always provides. And sometimes He uses the arms of those in my group who are willing to "bear with me" to give me a hug and offer comfort and an encouraging word.

Action Item: Developing patience requires careful cultivation and frequent practice. Ask God to help you see people as He sees them and seize opportunities to share with them the love and comfort He has given you.

Prayer: *Thank You, Lord, for my First Place 4 Health group and the encouragement they have shared with me. Bless them for their kindness to me, and help me to follow their example.*

Sandy Matthews
Houston, Texas

44

called to win

Be completely humble and gentle; be patient, bearing with one another in love.

EPHESIANS 4:2

My First Place 4 Health story is one of learning perseverance and patience. God has changed me in so many ways. He has changed my heart and made me a different person from the inside out. He has worked in my spirit, emotions and mind to make me more Christlike. But I must tell you that the physical area has been the most difficult for me! (Not for God, just for me.)

My journey has been one of losing, gaining and beginning again. God has always been there, ready to forgive my disobedience and give me another chance. My walk with my God has proven to me that I can trust Him and that even though I lose a battle or two, and believe me I have, we will win this war!

There have been several times when I have wanted to just quit, give up and take the easy way out. As a First Place 4 Health leader and networking leader, I felt unworthy. I felt I was not being a good witness or testimony for my Lord.

In fact, I tried several times to tell Carole Lewis that I could not continue to be a leader. Carole and I would talk on the phone as she drove from Houston to the bay where they used to live. She would remind me that God had called me and He had other plans!

One year at Wellness Retreat in Round Top, Texas, God spoke very plainly to me. He said, "I have called you, and I will win this battle for you, if you will continue to trust Me and obey My plan for your life." After this encounter, and with Carole's and the First Place 4 Health family's encouragement, I now know that God has called me to First Place 4 Health and the wellness ministry. I refuse to allow Satan to stop me as I seek God for strength and power for the victory.

God and I are now on the winning side of the weight-loss battle. I have reached my ideal weight goal—the one God and I set many years ago.

Prayer: *Thank You, Lord God, for being so patient and for loving me. I thank You, Lord, for the wonderful friends and First Place 4 Health family who love me for who I am and who continually pray for me.*

Janet Kirkhart
First Place 4 Health Networking Leader
Loveland, Ohio

45

lessons from an elephant

Be completely humble and gentle; be patient, bearing with one another in love.
EPHESIANS 4:2

This is such a sweet verse, but that word "completely" always trips me up. After losing weight, following the First Place 4 Health program, I never thought I would envy an elephant, but the other day in preschool we watched an old favorite: *Horton Hatches the Egg.* How my feathers were getting ruffled at that selfish mama bird! I wanted to give her a piece of my mind! I would have told her what to do with her egg. How lucky it was that she bumped into Horton before she bumped into me!

Now, I have certainly been in situations where I found myself saying yes when I really wanted to say no. I even managed to say yes nicely. But it wasn't because I was being *completely* humble and gentle, or bearing with one another in love: I felt intimidated . . . but I kept my word because I felt guilty.

Now, take our friend Horton. Honest. Sincere. Gentle. Longsuffering. I don't know how Jesus would like being compared to an elephant, but Humble Horton probably would blush if he knew I was comparing him to Christ. He (both of them) is just sweet to the core. If cartoons *do* get saved, I'm sure Horton is at the front of the line.

"An elephant's faithful 100 percent," said Horton. It seems to me I recall making some sort of promise to Jesus to be faithful to Him and "follow Him all of my days." I think that includes being *completely* humble and gentle, being patient, and bearing with one another in love. I'm not an elephant anymore, the last time I checked, but I do have a Helper, and He is a whiz at this kind of thing. I know His motives are always pure, and He is fully capable of mastering that "completely" part. And if He sits on me long enough, hopefully I'll come out in His image.

Action Item: Where has God surprised you lately? In what areas do you need to be more alert to His presence?

Prayer: *Father, I thank You for meeting us where we are and showing up in a simple thing like a child's video during a normal work day. Thank You for the element of surprise and the freshness You bring to Your Word. Thank You for ears to hear Your voice from a cartoon elephant. Help us always to be looking anywhere and everywhere for signs of Your presence. Amen.*

Jeanne Deveau Gregory
Chatham, Virginia

46

sleep on it

A patient man has great understanding, but a quick-tempered man displays folly.

PROVERBS 14:29

Most of us know what it's like to have a quick-tempered person in our life. Whether this person is a relative, friend or someone we work with, you can never be sure what will set them off. Quick-tempered people almost never take responsibility for their actions and can easily place the blame on another person for setting them off.

I have a great "Better Together" story that involves me and my assistant, Pat. I don't have a quick temper, but I can get angry. Pat and I have been friends for over 30 years, and she knows me as well as almost anyone. We have worked together in First Place 4 Health for more than 15 years, and early on we devised a method for me to rein in anger.

When I get angry and write an email that is less than kind, I always run it by Pat to make sure it is not harsh. Pat will invariably say, "Why don't you sleep on it tonight and we'll look at it in the morning." What great advice! Most of us, if given a little time, will not want to react in an angry manner.

The Bible has a lot to say about the tongue and the disastrous effects it can have on other people. Patience is a fruit of the Spirit, and I believe it is a skill we must all learn, usually through doing or saying something foolish.

When our grandson, Hunter, was about six years old, all the family was at our home for New Years' Eve. We had two big sliding glass doors, and the kids were all outside shooting fireworks. Twice, when Hunter was running back into the house, he slammed into the closed glass door. After the second time, he said through tears, "Why can't we just leave the door open?" Most of us have to hit the wall a number of times before we learn not to run "full steam ahead" with our mouth or our actions.

Prayer: *Dear Lord, I want to learn patience. Help me today to rein in my tongue and speak only what You would want me to say.*

Carole Lewis
First Place 4 Health National Director
Houston, Texas

avoid gravel groveling

A patient man has great understanding, but a quick-tempered man displays folly.

PROVERBS 14:29

I like to organize, but I dislike stepping on anyone's toes, unless, of course, I am having a mood swing, in which case I just stampede over everyone's feet and worry about it later. When I directed our Vacation Bible School a few years ago, I had many such opportunities to stampede and took advantage of every one. It took me a long time and lots of hand cramps to write personal apologies to eighty-plus volunteers. I love each and every one of them; and when I came to my senses (after it was over and I had slept the entire following day), I realized I had a lot of forgiveness to seek. I am glad I got to do my groveling on the carpet and not the gravel or I'd still be spitting rock fragments out of my mouth.

I am oh so glad I am part of a church family where they don't take the title of Christian lightly. Almost without exception, they live and breathe it. They were so patient with me and so understanding—when I couldn't even understand myself. I know many of them were offshoots from our First Place 4 Health classes, so they had the treat of working with me before, and *still* agreed to volunteer!

I recently read in Beth Moore's book *So Long Insecurity* that I was not a fool. That was news to me. I have so many folly stories that I have convinced myself that the whole book of Proverbs is about me (no wonder I am reading about insecurity). However, I do know without a doubt that I have a quick temper. God and I have been working on that for about two years now. I believe that "in all things God works for the good of those who love him" (Romans 8:28), and I know I do love Him, so I expect to see results any time now. What time do you have?

Action Item: In what areas do you need to display more patience? In what areas do you have the most problems holding your temper?

Prayer: *Lord, this is a vicious cycle in my life—praying for patience and understanding to avoid losing my temper and displaying folly. I trust You to keep working on me until we can cross this character flaw (sin) off my list. Thank You for the patience and understanding You always show me. I truly want to be like You. Help me to believe the truth You say about who I am.*

Jeanne Deveau Gregory
Chatham, Virginia

48

please don't quit!

A patient man has great understanding, but a quick-tempered man displays folly.
PROVERBS 14:29

One of the most common reasons people give up on exercise is a lack of immediate results. It takes time for change to take place in our bodies. Developing patience with and proficiency in the area of exercise may be one of the biggest challenges for us, but it is well worth the effort.

I recall one dear lady in my class in Charleston, South Carolina, who had decided she was going to work diligently at her commitment to exercise. She walked faithfully every day for one week, and when she got on the scale to see how much weight she had shed, she had stayed the same. She immediately began to cry and said, "It's no use—I am just going to quit. I won't be back next week."

We all have had the same experience. I gently reminded her that the scale cannot measure everything that is going on in her body. It can only measure what she has on—her bones, blood, skin and major organs. Furthermore, it takes time for our bodies to really get in shape, more than just one week! It's not reasonable to think that the weight we put on in one year can all come off in a matter of weeks.

I encouraged her to be patient with herself, gain some understanding about the human body, and remain faithful. She did, and she lost more than 40 pounds in two sessions! How foolish we are when we forget that success is in the process! I am reminded that it takes time in all four areas in my life—mental, emotional, physical and spiritual—for my life to change, and I praise God that He is not quick-tempered and impulsive with me!

Prayer: *Dear God, grant me this day patience and understanding from Your Holy Spirit, and keep me from impulsive foolishness!*

Vicki Heath
First Place 4 Health Associate Director
Edisto Island, South Carolina

patience and wisdom go together

A patient man has great understanding, but a quick-tempered man displays folly.

PROVERBS 14:29

My earthly dad modeled patience for me. He grew up in a home with parents who fought continually, and when he and my mom married, he said, "Our home will never be like the one I grew up in."

I remember so many instances while growing up where I would try a saint's patience, but my dad never lost his temper with me. I remember a Sunday morning when I kept talking during the worship service. After we got home from church, my mom was in the kitchen making lunch, and my dad had me in the bedroom for a talk about my behavior during church. He calmly pointed out the words on the bottom of the Sunday bulletin, "Meditation, not conversation," and asked me if I understood what that meant. After our little talk, he simply said, "I know you won't do it again next Sunday," and that ended my time of correction for my misdeed.

When my dad was dying from congestive heart failure, he endured a four-hour ordeal of his mom putting a mustard plaster on his chest. My grandmother had been what they used to call a "practical nurse," and she was convinced that a mustard plaster, whatever that is, would help him. Even though he knew it was of no value, he was patient because it was important to his mom.

I, on the other hand, am more like my mom! My personality and nature are much more expressive, which is putting it mildly. Because of this, God has had to teach me patience. The Bible says that the way we learn patience is through tribulation (see Romans 5:3, *KJV*), and I can testify that we do learn that way. But it would be less painful to learn it an easier way!

Action Item: If you are given to a quick temper, why not begin praying that God will teach you patience? Ask Him to remind you when you need to display patience instead of exploding so that you don't have to learn the hard way.

Carole Lewis
First Place 4 Health National Director
Houston, Texas

50

paving the road with patience

A patient man has great understanding, but a quick-tempered man displays folly.

PROVERBS 14:29

I could barely see beyond my rain-splattered windshield, but with the wipers on high speed, I managed to locate my exit. Letting out a sigh of relief, I prepared for the final leg of my journey home following a long day at work—a stressful day, to put it mildly. Just as I merged onto the off ramp, another vehicle sped by, cut in front of me and headed up the ramp, only to slam on his brakes and skid to a stop before redirecting his car back onto the freeway. To make matters worse, he performed a certain unacceptable hand gesture as he raced away into the stormy night.

Shocked, and more than a little dismayed, I analyzed my choices: (1) I could tear off and follow him in a radical display of road rage; (2) I could yell not-so-nice things about him the rest of the way home; or (3) I could choose to pray and behave in a patient and kind manner regardless of the fact that no one was watching.

Honestly, I started with number two before remembering that I did indeed have an audience of one. My Savior had a front-row seat to my actions. He could hear my words. He knew my heart.

I realized right then that ranting and raving in my car at a driver already a mile down the road was just plain foolish. I could follow my Lord's example or act as ridiculous as the stranger with whom I was angry. Thankfully, I stopped my fuming and instead prayed for God to protect this person as he drove away so recklessly. In the end, I made it home in one piece, with a sense of peace that comes from exercising patience.

Patience is possible. Remember, no matter what the circumstance, practice patience and experience peace. We're foolish not to!

Action Item: Take a moment to remember the last time you lost your patience and the choice resulted in foolish actions or words on your part. What could you have done differently? Commit to choosing wisely when future opportunities arise.

Prayer: *Dear Lord, Your Word instructs me to avoid folly and instead make wise decisions in my daily life. One wise choice that will help me avoid foolishness is practicing patience. It may not be easy, but with Your help, it is possible.*

Carol Van Atta
Troutdale, Oregon

51

praiseworthy patience

A man's wisdom gives him patience; it is to his glory to overlook an offense.

PROVERBS 19:11

When I looked at this verse, I could easily understand that a wise person is a patient person. But what does it mean when it says, "It is to his glory to overlook an offense"? One of the dictionaries says that glory is a "highly praiseworthy asset." Another said that glory is "great honor and admiration won by doing something important or valuable."

God must think it is a big deal when you and I overlook offenses! How many times are we offended each day? Think about yesterday. Did someone say something rude or hurtful to you? Did someone not do something he or she promised to do? Did a friend fail to include you? Did someone cut you off in traffic? Did someone fail to thank you for a favor? All of us have opportunities every day to be offended or to overlook an offense. If we are wise, we will learn this admirable trait of overlooking offense. A wise and patient person will be a healthier person. He or she will have lower blood pressure and a lower stress level than the person who gets angry at every offense and angry at the offender.

My husband, Johnny, has had stage 4 prostate cancer since 1997, and God has used his disease to teach me patience. Some of the prescriptions he takes or has taken have caused short-term memory loss. His long-term memory is as sharp as ever, but he has a hard time remembering if he took his medicine or where he put something. Most of the time, I am patient, because I know he doesn't remember. But sometimes when I'm busy, I get that edge to my voice, which tells him I am offended by his asking. When I do this, I want to immediately take it back, but it's too late—the look or tone is already out there.

Life is too short and too precious to keep a record of offenses. When we lose patience, a quick, sincere apology will help us remember the next time. God uses our trials as heavenly sandpaper to teach us patience. Let's be wise people today!

Action Item: Practice wisdom and patience today. Jot down every time you could have been offended and give yourself a star for overlooking the offense. God will honor you because you did something important and valuable.

Carole Lewis
First Place 4 Health National Director
Houston, Texas

52

true identity

A man's wisdom gives him patience; it is to his glory to overlook an offense.

PROVERBS 19:11

It took me six hours to drive home to Elizabethtown, Pennsylvania, after attending my first Hope 4 You event in Oswego, New York. Time passed quickly as my mind was filled with anticipation of leading a First Place 4 Health program at my church. The journey went smoothly with just a few roadblocks and detours before I reached my final destination.

Soon after my safe return home, my enthusiastic momentum was stopped by a technological roadblock. Without warning, my Facebook account had become "disabled." I was not able to log in. In the profound words of Charlie Brown, "AARGH!!"

I requested an explanation. The reply from the Facebook team was: "Fake accounts are a violation of our Statement of Rights and Responsibilities. Facebook requires users to provide their real first and last names. Impersonating anyone or anything is prohibited, as is maintaining multiple profiles on the site. Unfortunately, we will not be able to reactivate this account for any reason. The decision is final."

Fake account? Imposter? I was devastated. I knew I had not done anything wrong. What could I do to defend myself? Their decision was "final." In the past, my reaction would have been anger and a desire to seek revenge for being falsely accused of an offense. How could I possibly overlook it? But the Lord is changing my heart. Instead of becoming angry, I was calm and patient. I was able to yield.

The next morning, the Facebook team sent another message to my inbox: "We apologize for the inconvenience you have experienced. Your account was disabled in error. Your account has been reactivated and you will now be able to log in."

Some say, "It's not over until the fat lady sings." Thanks to First Place 4 Health, this lady is singing God's praises, and she isn't as fat as she once was! My true identity is that I am a child of the King of kings. No fake. No imposter. That decision is final.

Action Point: Think of a time in the past when you were offended and your response was less than patient. How would you respond to that same offense if it happened to you today? Would it bring God glory?

Diane Marie Kanode
Elizabethtown, Pennsylvania

53

take out the trash!

A man's wisdom gives him patience; it is to his glory to overlook an offense.

PROVERBS 19:11

What an experience to be a landlord! We just evicted renters for the first time. They left the house in a huge mess! Trash was piled in each room, including the garage. Unwanted furniture littered the rooms, and the carpets were incredibly dirty. The filth on the floors, cabinets, and counters took many cleanings. The tenants even removed and ruined the garage door to get their belongings out. The job seemed to be more than my husband and I could manage on our own. A sense of hopelessness overwhelmed us.

But as I started to work, I began to feel hopeful, knowing that the hard work would be rewarded with a clean, livable house once again. It would not happen on this day, or even after two or three days of hard work, but it would happen eventually if we worked steadily and consistently.

As I was hauling out what felt like the hundredth bag of trash, the Lord quietly reminded me that this is what hope deferred feels like. We allow a deceiver to take up residence in our lives and begin to trash the temple of the Holy Spirit. Whether through overeating, eating unhealthy foods, laziness in spiritual and physical disciplines or mental laziness, we begin to pile up garbage everywhere. We then feel hopeless and despondent, just like I felt when I first looked at the trashed house.

It is here that we have a choice. We can continue to live in trashed houses, with piles of garbage, making us feel hopeless and discouraged. Or we can begin the process of fulfilling that longing within for a right relationship with our Lord that is characterized by balance in all four areas of personhood. We can choose to evict that deceitful tenant who has encouraged us to believe the lies and live the bad habits. This will not be an easy task, or happen quickly. But if we are consistent, we can reclaim our house, clean up the garbage left by that tenant and live a life that pleases our Father. With God's wisdom, we can make that choice that not only glorifies Him, but brings joy into our lives.

Action Item: What bags of garbage do you need to eliminate from your life to restore the hope the Father wants you to experience? Pray over this, give it considerable thought, then do not delay! Get the trash out!

Kathlee Coleman
Santa Clarita, California

the wisdom in patience

A man's wisdom gives him patience; it is to his glory to overlook an offense.
PROVERBS 19:11

I am so grateful for the Bible, the Lord's instruction manual. It is vital to our spiritual growth and journey toward health. Our heavenly Father knows that as we read and meditate on His Word, it will increase our closeness to Him and strengthen the faith of those around us. His Word gives us wisdom and patience to endure the trials of illness or loss. Indeed, we have a sure and powerful hope, even in the darkest circumstances.

Patience during affliction is what allows us to endure intense struggles here on earth. As a Jewish believer and the child of a Holocaust survivor, I have a profound understanding of the need for patience. The ability to remain joyful, patient and faithful in prayer is life sustaining. It positively impacts our physical immune system, as well as our mental and emotional state.

These days, I share my testimony of faith in Christ as a Christian comedian and speaker. I met Carole Lewis in 2008 when we both spoke at a women's conference. This encounter was a divine appointment. I weighed 230 pounds, and Carole offered to help me, through First Place 4 Health. I threw myself into the program and lost 40 pounds. With the Lord's help, I will lose 50 more pounds and reach my goal this year.

I remain faithful in prayer to uplift others in the hope we all share. The sweetness of hope in Christ lifts me up, His wisdom sustains me and faithfulness in prayer steadies my rocky path.

Prayer: *Heavenly Father, how I praise and thank You that You brought me into Your kingdom. Thank You for Your wisdom that has allowed me to be faithful and patient through my journey to wellness.*

Martha Marks
Houston, Texas

forgiveness feels so good!

A man's wisdom gives him patience; it is to his glory to overlook an offense.
PROVERBS 19:11

Forgiveness feels so good. Rather, it feels so good to be forgiven! I am usually in the habit of asking for forgiveness more than I'm the one doing the forgiving! Such was the case with my friend Kharon. We had been friends for years. We served on committees together, fixed meals and ate together, and our families even vacationed together.

We were working with a team to give a wedding shower for a friend. We were all to meet at the church at an appointed time to prepare the food and decorations. I arrived early and started working on the centerpieces. A few others arrived—all but Kharon. Someone commented on her absence. I then commented, "I've worked with Kharon on a ton of projects and she is great to work with, but she is habitually late." The words were just out of my mouth when I looked up and noticed Kharon standing in the doorway.

It was obvious that my words so wounded her. Not only did I humiliate her, but I was someone she respected more than any of her other friends. After all, I was the pastor's wife. She quickly came into the room and just pretended she had never heard my comment. You can only imagine my mortification.

We pulled off the shower and not a word was spoken about my comment. I got home late that evening, and as I was walking through the door, the phone was ringing. It was my precious friend telling me she had already forgiven me for the comment and that she loved me. Forgiveness never felt so good!

That day, she was quick to glorify our Father in heaven by overlooking my offense. I was humbled, but also made much wiser. I am not so quick to speak carelessly now. God has tempered my tongue. I hope I am also not so quick to forget how good it feels to be forgiven. I am thankful for my precious friend's patience with me and for her willingness to overlook my carelessness.

Prayer: *Dear God, grant me a patient and generous heart that is quick to overlook an offense toward me so that You will receive the glory. Amen.*

Vicki Heath
First Place 4 Health Associate Director
Houston, Texas

56

a long view of disaster

The end of a matter is better than its beginning, and patience is better than pride.
ECCLESIASTES 7:8

Looking back at my life so far, I can see the truth of this verse played out in the little and the big things in our family life experiences. Our first family calamity happened when we had a fire on Labor Day weekend in the 1970s. The entire family was doing fall housecleaning. The girls were working in each of our bathrooms and Johnny and John were outside working in the yard. Johnny decided to burn limbs in our fireplace; but a defect in the fireplace caught our attic on fire. I returned from renting a carpet shampoo machine to find fire trucks in front of our house.

Because the fire was in our attic, the firemen had to poke holes in every ceiling in our house to put out the fire. Consequently, every room had ruined carpet, drapes and furniture because of the water and smoke. We weren't able to get any help until Tuesday after the fire on Saturday, because of the Labor Day holiday.

The day of the fire, our neighbors and friends rallied around, and when my mom and dad arrived that evening from their home at the bay, we were all sitting around on the patio laughing and talking. My mom took one look at the disaster and burst into tears, saying, "How can you laugh at a time like this?"

We moved to a townhouse for three months while the house was being repaired, but what a blessing that we had insurance that paid the rent on the townhouse. Our insurance also paid a restoration company to wash every item we wanted to take to the townhouse and store the rest until we moved home.

When we moved back in on Thanksgiving weekend, we had a brand-new home. We were able to do some things we didn't have the money to do when we bought the house two years before, and everything we owned was clean, all at the same time. This was the first big trial for our family, but it helped us learn the truth of this verse. God was so gracious and faithful to us during that time and that laid a foundation of trust in Him when future trials came.

Prayer: *Dear Lord, thank You for the trials we have gone through in this life; they have taught us that You care and that You will get us through to the other side. Your faithfulness and love are the reason that the "end is better than its beginning."*

Carole Lewis
First Place 4 Health National Director
Houston, Texas

daily blessings

The end of a matter is better than its beginning, and patience is better than pride.
ECCLESIASTES 7:8

I am drinking from my "saucer" because my cup has overflowed, and I want to share with you what has caused this joy in my whole being.

About eight years ago, I was at a point that I wanted to make a change in my spiritual life. A co-worker told me about a program called First Place 4 Health, so I checked online, researched the program and showed up at the next meeting. The ladies in the class were so welcoming and kind to me from the very beginning. They had no idea of the baggage I had lugged in with me, as I was dealing with marital and family issues at that time.

I got settled into this Bible study, which helped to open my eyes to God's grace and mercy through these dear women. The ladies in my class have prayed me through various situations, and from their prayers, God has given me peace within my heart and in my family. I have learned each day to ask God's blessings upon me and to hold me in the palm of His hand.

At times the blessings have been overwhelming, so I give glory to His name for them. I have become stronger in my faith because of First Place 4 Health, and through the studies, His word has given me wisdom to make better decisions for myself and for my family. Along this spiritual journey, I have worked hard to be aware of situations and stresses, and take them as they come, seeing them for what they are and deciding just what the Lord wants me to learn from them.

I know now that I am a precious child of God. He has forgiven me and He loves me, no matter what baggage I am carrying, so I have learned to let Him carry that load. The end is so much better than the beginning. "For my yoke is easy and my burden is light" (Matthew 11:30).

Prayer: *Lord, help me to look for Your plan in the difficult situations, on a daily basis.*

Kay Jarrell
Odessa, Texas

full circle

The end of a matter is better than its beginning, and patience is better than pride.

ECCLESIASTES 7:8

I tried to stop age 50 from coming. I really did. But it came, just the same. God, however, has managed to turn my mourning into dancing in a few different areas, but especially in my relationship with my only child, my adult daughter, Krista.

She came out of the womb with her opinions firmly intact and ready for a debate team. Unfortunately, it wasn't the one I was on. I always doubted myself when disciplining her because she made so much sense. (I had promised myself I would never use my mother's favorite line, "Because I said so," but sometimes that was the only thing I could think of!) I waved goodbye to our last common thread when she was too old to "skip like Dorothy" across the parking lot with me. I resigned myself to the fact that we would never see eye to eye, mostly because neither of us was willing to give in. I know it was my pride that made it difficult to quit the debate team—we both wanted to be right.

Something amazing has been happening this last year—God has provided several brand-new areas for us to share together. She signed up for an earth science course—I love earth science! She is writing English papers—I love English papers! She is working at a preschool—I work at a preschool! She found a church she loves and even emails me some of the sermon notes. I love the sermon notes! But this is the one that took my breath away: Recently, I had written in my prayer journal that she would start spending time in the Word during the week. She emailed me that same day and shared about her quiet time!

It has taken 28 years, but now, on the flip side of 50, it's not so bad after all.

Action Item: In what areas do you need to have patience instead of pride? Thank God today for the areas in your life that have ended better than they began!

Prayer: *Lord, thank You for not letting me give up on a close relationship with my daughter. Your timing is perfect. You do work all things together for the good of those who love You, and patience is better than pride! I love You so much! Amen.*

Jeanne Deveau Gregory
Chatham, Virginia

percolating patience

The end of a matter is better than its beginning, and patience is better than pride.
ECCLESIASTES 7:8

The First Place 4 Health Leadership Summit in 2008 was the beginning of the end. After two days, I left declaring, "Why don't we lose just one pound a week and meet back here next year? How hard could that be?" It sounded doable at the time, but I didn't seem to hear pride speaking! With a revised First Place 4 Health program and Bible studies, plus my prayer partner, I had unknowingly signed up for a two-year study in God's university of patience and humility.

First year: a new vocabulary and mindset—developing *mindfulness*; eating foods *often, occasionally* or *seldom*; watching *quality, quantity* and *frequency* of choices; living in *moderation, balance* and *freedom*. Any food can have a place in a healthy diet; but not all foods should have a prominent place. Change . . . choose . . . use. It takes six months for tastes to change—that's not deprivation for the rest of your life, it's simply dedication for six months. Something is better than nothing; more is better than less. Slowly, each new concept was poured into my new wineskin.

Second year: obedience, even in food-related issues, brings spiritual breakthrough and blessings. My life-long problem was named: out-of-control eating, instant gratification, self-indulgence, gluttony. These words found in God's Word are called SIN and it forced me to face how I used food. Willful sin hinders prayer and God's blessing. Every choice is my responsibility to obey or disobey (sin). The choice I make today doesn't have to reflect my past, but it will definitely determine my future, my faith. Scripture passages bringing new life from ancient words became real to me: James 4:17, Philippians 3:17-21, Philippians 4:4-5.

The pride passing my lips in 2008 turned into God's percolating patience in more than 100 meetings with First Place 4 Health members. "The end of the matter" was that His great patience with me brought me to both my weight-loss goal and pride reduction. These last two years have truly been better than my first 11 years in First Place. And by God's grace, His lessons in patience will continue to override my pride in years to come.

Action Item: What new vocabulary word and mindset do you need to implement today? Choose it and use it for the rest of the week.

Judy Marshall
Gilmer, Texas

60

all things work together

The end of a matter is better than its beginning, and patience is better than pride.

ECCLESIASTES 7:8

"Your car is totaled," the insurance person spoke through my cell phone. "We will only pay two more days on your rental car." Those words presented a problem because it would be a couple of weeks before I could purchase another car.

I had driven 500 miles from Houston, Texas, to a small town in Arkansas and arrived safely. However, while on my way to Walmart, I had a serious accident. My insurance company said they would pay for 30 days on a rental car. Now, I suddenly discovered I would only have the rental car two more days. "The end of this matter" was not looking good, and my patience was wearing thin.

The next morning, in my quiet time, I was complaining to God about my troubles and began to read my daily devotional from *My Utmost for His Highest* by Oswald Chambers. The words jumped off the page into my heart:

> Seeking to do the will of the Father was the one dominating concern throughout our Lord's life. And whatever He encountered along the way, whether joy or sorrow, success or failure, He was never deterred from that purpose.... "He steadfastly set His face to go to Jerusalem" (Luke 9:51).[1]

I realized my circumstances were just an "encounter along the way," and I was focusing on the problem instead of the solution. God always has the solution to our problems if we will let Him solve them for us. I turned in my rental car and headed for Houston.

When I returned, my sons began to look for a car for me to purchase. My insurance paid much more for my totaled car than they expected, and it wasn't long before I had a much newer model car in my garage than my old one, plus fewer miles on the odometer. The end of my matter was much better than the beginning, because God always "works all things for our good" if we just keep our eyes steadfastly on Him and His purpose for our lives.

Prayer: *Thank You, Lord, that You are the great problem-solver. Let me remember to always keep my face turned toward You in times of joy and sorrow, success and failure.*

Pat Lewis
First Place 4 Health Assistant to the National Director
Houston, Texas

61

His Word is truth

Be joyful in hope, patient in affliction, faithful in prayer.
ROMANS 12:12

My friend Nancy Taylor has a ministry of Scripture memory called "Prove The Word." This is a great name for Nancy's ministry because most of us have learned that we only treasure a verse after it has been proven true in our own life.

Nancy gave me a wonderful verse after our daughter Shari was killed by a drunk driver in 2001. The verse was Psalm 27:13: "I would have despaired unless I had believed that I would see the goodness of the LORD in the land of the living" (*NASB*). I memorized that verse, and God has proved it to be true in my life over the years since Shari's death.

Shari's husband, Jeff, married a beautiful, godly woman named Kathryn on September 29, 2007. Kathryn loves Jeff's girls, Cara, Christen and Amanda, and Cara's husband, Michael, and their two little ones, Luke and Kate. Kathryn has no biological children, but God has given her a built-in family to love.

Kathryn and Jeff are going through their own battle with breast cancer right now, and Kathryn is beginning the last half of her chemo treatments today. All of our family are praying and believing that Psalm 27:13 will prove itself true in their lives as they go through this time of trial.

God gave me another verse after Hurricane Ike hit in 2008, destroying our home on Galveston Bay and taking everything we owned out to sea. That verse is Romans 15:13: "May the God of hope fill you with all joy and peace as you trust in him, so that you may overflow with hope by the power of the Holy Spirit." This verse has also proved itself true in our lives since the day of that awful hurricane.

Nancy taught me to memorize Scripture and hide God's Word in my heart so that when the trials come, He can bring them to mind and help me walk through them with His strength and peace.

Action Item: Write about a trial you have gone through where God proved His Word to be true in your life. If you can't think of a verse, then write about a trial you are going through right now and find a verse that will help you. Memorize the verse and say it when you begin feeling like you will never make it to the other side.

Carole Lewis
First Place 4 Health National Director
Houston, Texas

62

just shut up and pray

Be joyful in hope, patient in affliction, faithful in prayer.
ROMANS 12:12

My friend and I have a slogan we jokingly say to each other when one of us starts to stress out about things that are happening in our lives: "You know what you need to do: just shut up and pray!" It's a reminder that we can't fix a thing by dwelling on our problems. It also reminds us that we need to run to God, because He is our joy and our hope when the world seems to be falling apart around us. Our little slogan brings much-needed laughter into our sometimes very stressful lives. I'm thankful I have friends who remind me that my hope is in God when things seem to be spiraling out of control.

We don't need to be experts on anything to reach out and offer encouraging words to others. Often a simple reminder to keep going and keep looking to God are all that is needed. I can't begin to count the times my First Place 4 Health group members inspired me to not give up. They have encouraged me to keep my focus on the hope that comes through my relationship with Christ, to be patient, even on my less than perfect days, and to pray faithfully.

Never underestimate the power of friendship, and remember that just a few short words of encouragement may be exactly what one of your friends needs to hear today to keep her going on the journey to better health.

Action Item: What can you do today to reach out and encourage a friend? Is God placing a specific person in your thoughts? Write this person's name in your journal along with a way you can encourage her this week and then follow through with your plan.

Prayer: *Heavenly Father, when life seems overwhelming and hopeless, remind me to go through with Your plan.*

Joni Shaffer
Mercersburg, Pennsylvania

wait on the Lord— He loves to bless us

Be joyful in hope, patient in affliction, faithful in prayer.
ROMANS 12:12

I joined First Place 4 Health 18 months ago and have lost around 150 pounds in that time. God is so good. I didn't really think I would lose weight. But you know how the Lord is when His timing is right. You just enjoy the ride.

It wasn't all easy, like when I hit my first plateau, which is where I usually give up. The girls reminded me to take one day and one choice at a time and trust God for the strength to make good choices—to look to God for encouragement instead of using food to comfort myself. Wonderful ladies! So I took one day at a time and enjoyed God encouraging me with His promises, like Colossians 1:29: "I can do it only because Christ's mighty energy is at work within me" (*TLB*).

God has given me a whole new life that I'm enjoying to the fullest. I can't believe how well I can move and bend. I gardened for the first time in more than 20 years. I can paint my own toenails now. I even went parasailing at my fiftieth class reunion last month. What fun! I never would have gone a year and a half ago.

My husband and I are really enjoying this new life together. We are quite active now, whereas I was pretty sedentary before. Our grown sons are so happy that I have lost weight. I didn't realize how worried they all were about my health. My husband calls me his "incredible shrinking wife."

Prayer: *Dear Lord, thank You for the joyful hope You give. Help me choose to trust You to give me patience in affliction and see Your grace and blessings and the new life You have planned for me.*

Priscilla L. Works
Medford, Oregon

a time of affliction

Be joyful in hope, patient in affliction, faithful in prayer.
ROMANS 12:12

Webster's Dictionary defines "patient" as "tolerating delay, provocation, annoyance . . . without complaint or anger; persevering or diligent," while "patience" is "the quality or capacity of being patient."

It is interesting to me that in Romans 12:12, "patient in affliction" is surrounded by "joyful in hope" and "faithful in prayer." I took the time to look up the meaning of these words and thought about them a great deal throughout this week. I'm learning what it is to be joyful in hope and faithful in prayer—to be able to be patient in affliction. Learning how to live a life that includes these principles has been a very difficult challenge. This is a verse that I have had the opportunity to live out this past year, but I'm sorry to say that I didn't do a very good job.

Over the past 18 months, I was given a physical trial that affected every area of my life. I had to set aside leading my First Place 4 Health group and took a leave of absence from my position as a networking leader for First Place 4 Health. I stopped fellowshipping with other believers, reading my Bible, praying, walking and eating real food. Facing chronic pain, nausea and vomiting on a daily basis, my mental and emotional state became unstable. All I had learned about having a balanced lifestyle took a vacation. I just wanted to be well and stop hurting.

My First Place 4 Health friends, my family and my church family watched me go downhill and didn't know what to do to help, but they diligently prayed for me. Without their prayers and encouragement, I know I wouldn't be doing as well as I am now. About a month ago, something changed; I'm not sure whether it was a new antidepressant kicking in or the Lord's hand in clearing my mind, but I choose to believe the latter of the two. My mind is able to think more clearly now and I'm up and around more than before. I'm living my life learning how to "be joyful in hope, *patient* in affliction, faithful in prayer" (emphasis added).

Prayer: *Dear Lord, thank You for providing many friends who will lift us up in prayer, even when we don't know how to pray. Help us take time to implant Your words deep in our hearts that we would live lives that please You, even in our times of affliction.*

Jean Wall
First Place 4 Health Networking Leader
Bremerton, Washington

a second recovery

Be joyful in hope, patient in affliction, faithful in prayer.
ROMANS 12:12

I had been in First Place 4 Health about seven years when my cancer returned. My mother, her sister and her mother had all died of cancer. To me, its return became a death sentence. I didn't want to go through it again. Fear and anxiety filled my heart and soul. At first, I kept the news just between my husband and myself. I didn't want our sons or friends to know it had come back, and then I remembered how others in our First Place 4 Health group had shared their problems and how we all prayed for each other.

When I did begin telling others, I had prayer support from all sides. My despair turned to joy in hope as I presented my prayers to God with a thankful heart for the love of my friends. On the morning of surgery, I had the most remarkable peace. The peace of God, which transcends all understanding, stood guard over my heart and mind. The faithful prayers of my friends and family were flying to heaven, and I couldn't be anything but joyful.

Patience is not a virtue I possess, but after the surgery, I did what I was instructed to do, deciding that I would be patient and see what transpired with treatment. Much to my amazement and that of my surgeon, my recovery went smoothly and quickly. He credited my attitude and the healthy condition of my body as contributing factors for the recovery. When he told me that it was not in the lymph nodes and they'd removed all of the tumors, my heart overflowed with joy.

It's been more than 11 years since that second surgery, and I'm still cancer free. My First Place 4 Health family gave me support; the verses I memorized gave me hope; and God rewarded all of our faithfulness.

Action Item: How has God blessed you in recent years? Think back over the times your life was in turmoil and write down how God brought you through it.

Martha Rogers
Christian Author
Houston, Texas

progress, not perfection

My story is about a never-ending hunger, a need that I had for more than 40 years prior to finding the First Place 4 Health program in early 2010. I am a workaholic, a control freak, a perfectionist and a food lover. Is there anyone reading this who can relate?

I can remember my first embarrassing weigh-in experience. I was about 12 years old, and we had to weigh in at school. Our weights were announced, as we got on the scale, for all to hear. I was 5' 2" and weighed 120 pounds, while the other girls were all less than 100 pounds. Shortly after that, my first diet was grapefruit, boiled egg and black coffee for two weeks. I lost 10 pounds, but then I gained 15 pounds over the next month. The vicious cycle of the next 40 years had begun.

I tried Atkins, diet pills, shots, Medifast, South Beach—you name it, I tried it. My willpower would only last so long—a week, a month and even more than a year. I could lose weight, but once I got off the "diet," I would go back to my old ways and gain more than I had weighed before the diet. I have lost 50, 100 and 145

BEFORE AFTER

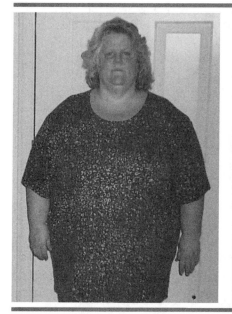

MONTH 3 : PATIENCE   89

pounds at various times in my adult life. There was always this hunger—an emptiness that could never be satisfied until I found the First Place 4 Health program.

In early 2010, I had been on Weight Watchers for over one year and had lost about 110 pounds, but I found that I was struggling with balance in my life. I was looking for a church home and went to a Sunday morning service at the First Baptist Church of Granbury, Texas, in January 2010. The church program minister shared that a First Place 4 Health 12-week session was beginning that afternoon and encouraged members to sign up and attend. I was not familiar with First Place 4 Health, but I liked the focus on balance and health, not just weight loss. I went to the meeting that Sunday afternoon and realized that my journey could be God-powered. I now know that what had been missing in my previous weight-loss attempts was the spiritual need I had for Christ to be my GPS (God-Powered System). My hopelessness was replaced with hope.

Since joining First Place 4 Health that day, I have lost an additional 100 pounds and achieved my goal weight. I learned that gluttony is a sin against God. I am God's temple, and the devil wants me to fail. Before joining the First Place 4 Health program, I would tell myself that I was not breaking any laws or hurting anyone. Isn't denial a funny thing? I had been killing myself for 40 years with unhealthy foods and lifestyle choices. How could I really expect to perform at my best if I ate excessively and put junk food into my body all the time? I am still trying to forgive myself. I now accept responsibility for my choices and know that God gave me free will; it is up to me to make healthy choices.

For me it's about progress, not perfection. My GPS is about the *Ps*: Program, Priority, Participation, Planning, Prayer, Preparation, Patience, Praise and Practice. My continued journey with my GPS will have bumps, detours and wrong turns. I know that when I listen to my GPS, He will reposition me and keep me on the road to live a balanced healthy life.

I am truly blessed through the First Place 4 Health program. You can be too.

Rossanne Day
Granbury, Texas

Note
1. Oswald Chambers, *My Utmost for His Highest* (Grand Rapids, MI: Discovery House, 1992), August 3.

MONTH 4

FELLOWSHIP

66

wisdom follow-through

*Let the word of Christ dwell in you richly as you teach and admonish
one another with all wisdom, and as you sing psalms, hymns and
spiritual songs with gratitude in your hearts to God.*

COLOSSIANS 3:16

It requires wisdom to be able to teach and admonish one another in a positive way. We want to let our friends know that we care and at the same time spur them on to good deeds.

I have a dear friend in First Place 4 Health who calls the scale "The Law," because it shows where we are but has no power to help us change. When she wants to know how I'm doing weight-wise, she says, "What did 'The Law' say this morning?"

Last week, we had the Victory Celebration for our two Tuesday noon classes. We ordered box lunches from a local deli and ordered fruit instead of the cookie that usually comes in the box. Lisa Lewis made Snicker pies for both of our classes to have for dessert so that we were assured of having a healthy treat after lunch. As the ladies in my class opened their boxes, I saw that the cookie had been placed in each box instead of fruit. What should I do? After some deliberation, I asked for the cookies and sent them home with Lisa for her teenagers.

I told my ladies that I didn't want to be responsible for sending them home with a 300-calorie cookie that might cause them to stumble. I know myself well enough to know that even if I didn't eat the cookie in class, I would probably eat it if it went home with me, and that big cookie could easily start me on the downhill slide.

In First Place 4 Health, God calls us to teach and admonish each other with wisdom. It isn't easy, but we must always set the example so that we are never responsible for another's failure to succeed.

Prayer: *Dear Lord, give me wisdom today and help me learn how to teach and admonish in a winsome way so that my class might have great success. Bless all of our First Place 4 Health leaders today, wherever they are.*

Carole Lewis
First Place 4 Health National Director
Houston, Texas

67

a recipe for gratefulness

*Let the word of Christ dwell in you richly as you teach and admonish
one another with all wisdom, and as you sing psalms, hymns and
spiritual songs with gratitude in your hearts to God.*

COLOSSIANS 3:16

Which comes first, the gratitude or the actions that turn our heart toward gratitude? Does it matter? If you are feeling grateful, run to God's Word so that it can dwell in you even more richly; share the wisdom you learn with others, then burst into song as you praise God with a heart that is already full of gratitude.

That's the easy part. But on those days when you are struggling to feel grateful, do the same thing, even though it is harder—cling to God's Word and praise Him anyway. It is amazing how gratefulness rises in your heart when you take your eyes off yourself and put them on God.

I had one of those days recently. I had just been through a time of stress, meeting some big deadlines in my ministry, all in the midst of losing a beloved mother-in-law. I was weary in well-doing and struggling to feel grateful. But I knew what to do. I put on my headphones and went for a long walk with the Lord along the beach. I listened to music that quoted the truths of His Word and it began to "dwell in me richly." Then I began to weep and sing along at the top of my lungs. Fortunately, the ocean roar covered the sound of my voice, so only God and I could hear it! An amazing thing began to happen, and my heart began to change from a weary heart to a heart of gratitude. I poured out the weariness with my tears, and I was able to breathe in the gratitude as I sang praise to my God.

The next time you are struggling to feel grateful, try the antidote expressed in this verse. And as you feel the gratefulness rise again in your heart, share your experience with a friend. Pass around this recipe for gratefulness and you will all be singing spiritual songs of gratitude together!

Action Item: Pray for opportunities to share this recipe for gratefulness with friends. Guide them through it step by step and help them get started. That's what fellowship is all about!

Jeannie Blocher
President, Body & Soul Fitness

68

and can it be?

Let the word of Christ dwell in you richly as you teach and admonish one another with all wisdom, and as you sing psalms, hymns and spiritual songs with gratitude in your hearts to God.

COLOSSIANS 3:16

Have you ever had a song stuck in your brain? I have—a hymn written by Charles Wesley. Charles was born in 1707. He and his brother were so bent on trying to live the Christian life so perfectly and so "methodically" that they were called "Methodists."[1] Charles tried hard to get it right. He and John went to the American colony of Georgia to be missionaries. Utter failure. Charles was demanding and autocratic in nature. They went back to England discouraged. Their "striving" had not brought them connection with God.

Finally, after hearing the teachings of a Christian named Peter Boehler, they got it. On May 21, 1738, Charles wrote, "I now found myself at peace with God, and rejoiced in hope of loving Christ. I saw that by faith I stood."

Such was the case for me, trying so hard to do things right. Trying so hard to please my parents, to be accepted by God and everybody else. Trying to "do" the right things will not bring you into right relationship with God.

Occasionally, I find myself going back to that old way. I wake up thinking, *Today I am going to get it exactly right . . . today is going to be a perfect day. I will start with my quiet time, exercise, choose only quality foods in small portions and write down every single bite . . . blah, blah, blah.* Then I mess up! I cannot get it all right. Jesus does not expect that. Life is a journey and we can either march our way through or we can dance in the light of His love! I choose this day to dance to a hymn Charles Wesley penned:

Long my imprisoned spirit lay, fast bound in sin and nature's night;
Thine eye diffused a quickening ray—I woke, the dungeon flamed with light;
My chains fell off, my heart was free. I rose, went forth, and followed Thee.

Action Item: Sing a favorite hymn to the Lord as a part of your quiet time today. You will both enjoy it!

Vicki Heath
First Place 4 Health Associate Director
Edisto Beach, South Carolina

69

building faith together

Let the word of Christ dwell in you richly as you teach and admonish
one another with all wisdom, and as you sing psalms, hymns and
spiritual songs with gratitude in your hearts to God.

COLOSSIANS 3:16

It was Christmas time, and I found myself with no parties to attend. Johnny and I were in California for his doctor's appointment when our church choir presented our annual musical celebration, and I was just a little bit bummed hearing second-hand how wonderful it was. I wasn't able to attend any of our six First Place 4 Health holiday sessions because I was working on a book deadline.

God was really sweet to open up invitations from out of the blue. In a one-week period, our daughter invited me to her Sunday School class dinner, I was able to have breakfast with some of my favorite women staff members at my church, and our First Place 4 Health ladies celebrated Pat's birthday with lunch! The Sunday before Christmas, I was able to attend two Sunday Bible studies, with the worship service sandwiched in between. I topped off the morning by having lunch with some of my dearest friends and prayer partners from my own Bible study class.

That night, when I climbed into bed, I was "full up" with the Christmas spirit and thanked our Lord for providing me with opportunities to worship and enjoy so many Christian friends.

I believe that we all need the fellowship of other believers. It is really hard for me to do life on my own, and it builds my faith when I am able to study and sing praises to God with fellow Christians. I need community, and this is a big reason why I continue to lead a First Place 4 Health group. I absolutely love the ladies in my class and can't wait to see them from week to week.

Action Item: What needs to happen for the verse above to come alive for you? Is the Lord calling you to lead a First Place 4 Health group or sing in your church choir? We truly are better together, so ask the Lord what community He wants you to join.

Carole Lewis
First Place 4 Health National Director
Houston, Texas

70

oh say, can you sing?

*Let the word of Christ dwell in you richly as you teach and admonish
one another with all wisdom, and as you sing psalms, hymns and
spiritual songs with gratitude in your hearts to God.*

COLOSSIANS 3:16

I love First Place 4 Health for many reasons, but one of the things that buoys me up is when the Holy Spirit calls to mind one of the many Scriptures I have memorized through the program, especially the Scripture put to music! The tips and skills I have learned and the encouragement I have received as we "admonish one another" in friendly Scripture memory competition, and as we sing psalms, hymns and Scripture verses, have been invaluable. I think the key word in Colossians 3:16 is "richly," as this is the secret to growing true, authentic gratitude in our hearts, which can't help but burst out in song (in my case, at least!).

I love being a "dorm mom" at our Christian summer camp, Camp Pitt. The girls always ask me what dorm I'll be in, for two opposing reasons. Either they're not "morning people" and want to avoid me at all costs, or they get a kick out of being roused out of their slumber by my obnoxious rendition of "Rise and Shine" and other favorites. There's really no escaping it, however. If I miss them at wake-up, I always embarrass, uh, I mean *catch* them in the breakfast line. "Everybody SING! Ri-ise, and shi-ine, and *give God the GLORY, GLORY . . . children of the Lord!!*"

I have to steal my husband's famous line when people ask him if he can sing. "Oh, sure I can sing. Not many people like the way I *do* it, but I can sing!" I know God's ways are not our ways, and I sure hope that includes His hearing. I like to think He smiles when we sing to Him, no matter how it sounds to sleepy campers or other mere earthlings.

Action Item: Be willing to explore new ways of using music and Scripture together in your quiet time and in worship experiences. Write in your journal how different types of music make you feel as you try to express yourself to God.

Prayer: *Father, thank You for the gift of song and for Your Word, which make a dynamic combination. Thank You for the musicians that bring Your words to life in ways that reach into our hearts and allow them to dwell there richly. May You be pleased with our praises. Amen.*

Jeanne Deveau Gregory
Chatham, Virginia

our power source of hope

I myself am convinced, my brothers, that you yourselves are full of goodness,
complete in knowledge and competent to instruct one another.

ROMANS 15:14

Most of us don't believe that we are good enough or have enough knowledge to instruct another person. The apostle Paul had confidence in us because of what he said in the verse previous to our verse today. In Romans 15:13, one of my favorite verses, Paul tells us that our God is the God of hope and that He will fill us with all joy and peace as we trust in Him so that we may overflow with hope by the power of the Holy Spirit.

When we are full of joy and peace and overflowing with hope, we are going to be competent to instruct others. The key is realizing that the power doesn't come from us, but from the Holy Spirit.

The last two weekends, I spoke at two First Place 4 Health events called Hope 4 You. Both weekends I met women who came with no hope but left the event full of hope. Hope is the key to success in every area of life. We must believe that there is hope for us to lose weight or that our marriage is salvageable. Without hope it is impossible to do the hard work that assures success. This is why in First Place 4 Health, we encourage you to give God a year to help you make the necessary changes to succeed.

As we experience success, we can confidently instruct others with the knowledge of how God helped us succeed as we trusted in Him. The core of the First Place 4 Health program is learning how to give Christ first place in our life. When He has first place, He can work miracles in and through us.

Action Item: What do you need hope for today? Ask our God of hope to fill you with joy and peace as you trust in Him so that you may overflow with hope by the power of the Holy Spirit.

Carole Lewis
First Place 4 Health National Director
Houston, Texas

72

court testimony

I myself am convinced, my brothers, that you yourselves are full of goodness,
complete in knowledge and competent to instruct one another.

ROMANS 15:14

I tested the First Place 4 Health program with my Sunday School class. We were committed to lose the extra pounds we were carrying—and it worked!

When I first approached the pastor about the class, he said he didn't think I was overweight. I told him the idea was to help those in our church that I knew had high blood pressure and bad knees from carrying those extra pounds. But I had to prove to myself that the program worked before I could confidently teach it to others. I also wanted the support from the group as I tried to lose my 20 extra pounds. At the end of three months, my class was successful, and so was I.

I was now wearing a size 8 instead of a 12. The girls on the tennis court noticed me and asked me all about the program. "I am starting a new session in a week," I said, and invited them to join. I had proved the program worked and was ready to teach others.

In the next class, five of my tennis friends attended. They lost the extra pounds they had put on, learned about balanced nutrition and were moved by the Bible study and prayer time. The girls stayed with the class through two sessions and were enthused. They took the program back to their churches and started a group. My daughter began a class in her church several states away. That was 10 years ago.

Through the program, I realized my biggest problem was portion control. (When I liked something, I really liked it!) I was able to discipline myself and maintain my proper weight. Many classes have come and gone since I first began teaching the program. My testimony was not what I said to the women on the tennis team, but how I looked on the courts. This is what made them curious, and they wanted what I had found.

Action Item: What is your testimony? You are the living way for people to see Christ in what you do and say and how you treat the temple He has given you.

Prayer: *Dear Lord, let me be a good example of Your love and mercy. Let my walk here on this earth draw others to You. Help me be a good testimony of Your love and power.*

Beverly LaHote Schwind
Fairfield Glade, Tennessee

73

sisters in Christ

I myself am convinced, my brothers, that you yourselves are full of goodness,
complete in knowledge and competent to instruct one another.

ROMANS 15:14

When I found myself sitting on my couch watching television, not answering the phone and wondering what I could eat next, I realized that step by step, I had become isolated, disconnected and overweight. Every once in a while, I would remember that there is a better way to live, and I would seek weight loss but ultimately fail.

First Place 4 Health was just my next weight-loss choice. Carole Lewis was in my first meeting, and she said that the good thing about First Place 4 Health was that if you didn't quit, you would succeed, because success is in the process. When the going gets tough, I still remember those words, and they encourage me.

Somehow, I became a First Place 4 Health leader. I began to watch the reality of others' successes and grew close to the ladies in my group. One by one they inspired me to be better and to do more. One member began to exercise. She started walking in a church program and soon was walking 11 miles and accomplished a half-marathon. I thought, *Wow! If she can do that, I can start somewhere.* Another member showed me what faithfulness looks like. She volunteered to lead accountability for the group and has been there every session. I saw compassion demonstrated when another member hugged someone who needed a hug. Others have taken time to pray together privately. We were all encouraged when someone sent each of us an anonymous letter reminding us how much God loves us.

Each member has special gifts and they volunteer to share them—music, bringing food, remembering birthdays, leading Bible studies, memorizing Scripture; hospitality, conversations, smiles, laughter, taking pictures, preparing wellness topics and sharing from the heart. Each week I am encouraged by their efforts, successes and fellowship. I have come to realize these sisters in Christ are valuable, and I treasure them. I am still in the race for balance, and as I take each step, I am thankful that because of my involvement with First Place 4 Health, I am no longer disconnected and I am seeing much less of my couch!

Action Item: Write a note of encouragement to someone. List in your prayer journal why you are thankful for her, and then tell her the next time you see her!

Claudia Korff
Houston, Texas

74

share your knowledge

I myself am convinced, my brothers, that you yourselves are full of goodness,
complete in knowledge and competent to instruct one another.

ROMANS 15:14

I had been in the First Place program for three years when my 17-year-old son told me he wanted to join the United States Air Force. He talked to a recruiter, who told him he would have to lose 15 pounds and get in shape.

On the way home, he said to me, "Mom, will you help me? I don't want to be too fat for my dreams." I told him if he was serious about this, and if I had his full cooperation and commitment, I knew exactly what he had to do. Immediately, I was thanking and praising God for providing me the tools and knowledge through First Place 4 Health to help my son get healthier and reach his goals.

As soon as we got home, I started teaching him the food plan. I shared Scriptures and the daily Bible studies with him at breakfast each morning as we planned out his meals for the day, recording everything on his Live-It Tracker. He began running regularly and following the food plan. It took him about six weeks to lose the required 15 pounds, and he was able to continue the recruitment process.

Our time together has brought us closer together. The Lord has opened my eyes to him as a young man of God. We are communicating better because of our discussions about fitness, First Place 4 Health and Jesus. We have bonded again! I see now that my participation in First Place 4 Health has not been just for my benefit. This is a ministry with which the Lord has equipped me to bring honor and glory to Him. I can make an impact on my family, friends and co-workers. I want to be available to instruct others about the blessings in store for them.

I encourage you not to miss the opportunities that God gives to use the knowledge He has given you to instruct others. You will be blessed beyond your wildest expectations.

Prayer: *Lord, Your Word tells us to "prepare our minds for action." Thank You that through First Place 4 Health, my mind was prepared and competent to instruct my son in the principles of healthy living. You are worthy to be praised.*

Krista Taylor
McKenzie, Tennessee

75

qualified by God

*I myself am convinced, my brothers, that you yourselves are full of goodness,
complete in knowledge and competent to instruct one another.*

ROMANS 15:14

Several years ago, a friend asked me to consider taking over as leader of the First Place 4 Health class at our church. Since I had been in the class for more than six years, I felt that the Holy Spirit had been preparing me for this role. But I was reluctant to agree as I didn't feel that I was qualified.

You see, for so many years I had felt insecure and self-conscious about myself. I was embarrassed about my weight and how I looked. I was hesitant to voice my ideas for fear of rejection or ridicule, and didn't even want to speak in our First Place 4 Health class in case I didn't have the "right" answer. And there was no way I could get enough courage to pray out loud in front of others.

Through First Place 4 Health, God made me aware that He was interested in me and my relationship with Him, not in what others thought about me. By reading and studying the Bible through daily quiet time, God helped me grow in my knowledge of Him. I was less worried about having the right answers and allowed Him to speak to me through His Word. My confidence grew by encouraging other class members as they also encouraged me on our journey to health and wellness.

Shortly after being asked to lead the First Place 4 Health class, I passed by a church with a sign in front that read, "God does not call the qualified. He qualifies the called." God was letting me know that if I was willing to answer His call, He was there to qualify me.

It has been more than five years since I answered God's call, and what an awesome opportunity and blessing it has been as a First Place 4 Health leader to encourage others to not only lose weight, but also to grow in their relationship with Him!

Action Item: What is God calling you to do today? Whatever it is, remember that He will qualify you to do it.

Prayer: *O Lord, how I praise You for calling me Your own. Help me to continue to grow daily in my knowledge of You.*

Sandy Miller
Houston, Texas

changed from the inside out

Speak to one another with psalms, hymns and spiritual songs.
Sing and make music in your heart to the Lord.

E P H E S I A N S   5 : 1 9

I meet many women and men who have lost a lot of weight on the First Place 4 Health program. When I ask them how much weight they have lost, I get the same answer close to 100 percent of the time. The person will say, "I have lost weight, but that's not the most important thing that has happened to me. The spiritual impact has changed my life." Another statement I frequently hear is, "God has changed me from the inside out."

Even though most people join the First Place 4 Health program to lose weight, they find that the weight is a secondary problem that can only be addressed after the spiritual components are learned. When I joined the program in 1981, I had never set aside a daily time of Bible reading, Bible study or prayer. I memorized many Scripture verses as a child, but without a Bible concordance, I could not locate them.

Because the program is made up of bite-sized pieces of what it looks like to become a mature believer, we find that as we do these things on a daily basis the Lord truly changes us from the inside out.

I have learned that the more I saturate my mind with the Word of God and Christian music, the more God can use me to encourage others. The other night it was almost midnight when my plane landed in Houston, coming home from a First Place 4 Health event. I prayed as I walked to my car that God would keep me safe and protect me. As soon as I got into my car, I turned the radio to a Christian radio station and sang with the radio the entire hour's drive home. Before I knew it, I was home and totally at peace in Him.

Action Item: Just for today, spend time with the Lord in prayer and Bible study. Eat only healthy foods and make time to exercise. Call or email a friend with encouragement. At the end of the day, you will have had a successful First Place 4 Health day. Do the same thing for an entire week and you will have success when you step on the scale to weigh.

Carole Lewis
First Place 4 Health National Director
Houston, Texas

when we walk together

Speak to one another with psalms, hymns and spiritual songs.
Sing and make music in your heart to the Lord.

EPHESIANS 5:19

Being with others in a First Place 4 Health group is fun! I remember the time when my friend Wilma and I went to the group meetings together on Tuesdays. Granted, we were often mumbling our memory verse to each other, and wondering if the late supper the night before was going to show an upward trend in our weigh-in! Sometimes we discussed family, how some healthy dish had gone over, and if our family was cooperating in eating the healthier food we were trying to make for all of us.

Reciting the memory verse while being weighed could be distracting at times. But the funniest of all weigh-ins was that of a precious lady who came in and kicked off her shoes, stripped off her pants and her blouse (wearing only her undies and aerobic tights) and then stepped on the scale. When someone would ask her, "Did you lose any weight this week?" she would invariably mutter, "Permanently plump," while continuing to get dressed. We could not resist laughing. She never said anything else about her weight.

After our meeting, Wilma and I would leave feeling good about ourselves and go to The Charcoal Chicken for lunch. They served a great big hamburger! We would order one, split it, split a dessert and have our drinks while discussing the meeting. We had such fun together!

Through the Bible study and our time together, we found ourselves growing closer to each other, to the other members of the group and, more importantly, to God.

Prayer: *Abba Father, thank You for Your good gift of laughter. It is music to our ears and food for our souls! Thank You for knitting us together in our First Place 4 Health groups and orchestrating life-giving encouragement to one another's hearts. Amen.*

Betha Jean McGee
Wall, Texas

7 8

my heart sings

Speak to one another with psalms, hymns and spiritual songs.
Sing and make music in your heart to the Lord.

EPHESIANS 5:19

Hearts touching hearts . . . what a sweet exchange! It is music to God's ears. From Him, we receive the gift of His Word, His Son and eternal life. From Him all blessings flow. Music is a powerful gift as well and speaks to our hearts on a core emotional level more than anything I know. It is uplifting, comforting, soothing. And when God's Word is put to music, it goes straight to the heart and overflows into the depths of the spirit.

The hymns I sang in church while growing up bring back sweet memories. Music has a way of sticking to our minds like glue. I remember my dad's beautiful voice as he sang his favorite hymns. When my mother was on her deathbed, I played special CDs of hymns and songs and read Scripture that she loved. I know that the Lord used the music and His Word to minister to her.

When we speak to one another with Scripture and song, it is as if the Lord is singing over us. Zephaniah 3:17 says, "He will take great delight in you, he will quiet you with his love, he will rejoice over you with singing."

When we need to be reminded of who God is and what He has done, the psalms are full of praise of Him and speak encouragement and healing to us. The sweetest instrument we can play to the Lord is the sincere praise offering of our hearts. And when we speak to one another with God's words, allowing His spirit to overflow from our hearts, angels' voices couldn't sound any sweeter to Him than those of His children.

Prayer: *Thank You, Lord, for the gift of music and for touching my heart with Your sweet Holy Spirit. May the words of my mouth and the meditation of my heart be sweet to Your ears.*

Connie Welch
First Place 4 Health Network Leader
Keller, Texas

we see Your glory, God!

Speak to one another with psalms, hymns and spiritual songs.
Sing and make music in your heart to the Lord.

EPHESIANS 5:19

While standing on the balcony of our cruise ship to Alaska, my sister Diane and I could not help but speak to one another in psalms, hymns and spiritual songs. As we watched the unbelievably blue ocean and saw the giant whale as it spouted off and then seconds later rose up out of the water with such grace, it was breathtaking, and we broke into squeals and songs of praise to our God.

We had prayed that we would get to see what He knew was in that vast ocean. He knew where every whale and walrus was, and we asked to see every creature in that water. When God showed us His marvelous creatures, we sang with everything in us: "You are awesome in this place, Mighty God. . . . You are worthy of all praise." (You're singing it now, aren't you?) Oh, the greatness of God in His creation that we saw so mightily that day!

Since then, Diane and I, and my other sister and her daughter, have also enjoyed times of speaking to one another with spiritual songs and Scriptures, declaring God's glory. It wasn't always as pleasant a surrounding as on a cruise ship to Alaska. Now, during Diane's journey through lymphoma, we also see God's greatness and sing her theme song, "How Great Is Our God," as we journey together through each chemo treatment.

The same God we praised while on vacation is the same great God with us every step of the way through the trials of life. Every time we are together and we experience God's faithfulness, feel His strength and see His glory, we can't help but sing and share about His greatness together. It's so much richer to share this journey with our Lord, whether in the good times or in the trials of life. No doubt about it that we are better together!

Prayer: *Lord, thank You that no matter what circumstances we find ourselves in, You are still God, You are still on Your throne, You are still awesome. Lord, Your creation declares Your glory. Thank You for those people You put in our lives to share this journey with us. Please hear my songs of praise that are only for You! Amen.*

Karen Ferguson
Houston, Texas

His love wherever you are

Speak to one another with psalms, hymns and spiritual songs.
Sing and make music in your heart to the Lord.

EPHESIANS 5:19

When life is hard, and we're going through a difficult situation, praise doesn't come as easily. It gets difficult to sing and make music in our hearts to the Lord.

Several years ago, my husband, Rex, suffered a heart attack while we were out of town to attend Baylor University's homecoming. On Saturday morning, instead of watching the parade, we sat in the emergency room of the hospital in Waco. When the doctor decided to admit Rex to the intensive care unit, I began thinking of all the things I needed to do.

After the game on Saturday afternoon, we were supposed to go to Dallas and finish cleaning out my dad's apartment, since he now lived in an assisted living facility. We were then to go see my dad and take care of some legal business with him. None of that could happen now.

Our son, who lives in Waco, went home to make calls to his two brothers and several of our friends. When I went up to the waiting room in the intensive care unit, I found two of our close friends from Houston already there. In town for the same reason we were, they had heard about Rex at their motel as our son called around trying to locate his younger brother who was scheduled to be in town also. As we talked, several other friends from Houston arrived. I couldn't believe my eyes. More than a hundred miles from home I had a support group there surrounding me in prayer. How could I do less than praise God and thank Him for His great love and mercy? He knows our needs and prepares in advance to meet them.

Instead of crying because all of our plans were ruined, I thanked Him for Christian friends and circumstances that allowed friends to be where they were needed at the right time. Their words of prayer and encouragement were indeed spiritual songs to bring us through a difficult time. Our prayers were the music of our hearts unto God.

Action Item: Is there someone who could use your songs of praise over them at this time? Write a note or several notes of encouragement to your friends or even a family member. Words sent in love will never return void.

Martha Rogers
Houston, Texas

the next right thing

But if we walk in the light, as he is in the light, we have fellowship with one another, and the blood of Jesus, his Son, purifies us from all sin.

1 JOHN 1:7

When we moved to Galveston Bay in 1997, I began driving more than 100 miles to and from work each day. Most mornings during my drive into Houston, I listened to Elizabeth Elliott at 5:00 A.M. on our local Christian radio station. I heard a phrase from Elizabeth one morning that I will always remember, "Do the next right thing."

Walking in the light is always the way to do the next right thing. The next right thing for you might be to put on your workout clothes and exercise. It might be to order something healthy from the menu at a restaurant. It might be to say an encouraging word to a family member or co-worker. Or it might be to do something you have been dreading, like clean the oven or the garage.

We have a First Place 4 Health magnet that says, "Do The Next Right Thing." I love it because it helps me remember that I don't have to worry about everything I have to do today, I only decide what the next right thing is and then do it. If I keep doing the next right thing, I am assured of having a purposeful, victorious day.

I have been practicing what I preach this morning by getting up early to write. My first four hours have been very productive, including my time with the Lord, writing, and eating a great healthy breakfast. Even though I have a busy week ahead, right now I only need to do the next right thing.

Action Item: What is your "next right thing" to do? Do it right now! You won't be sorry.

Carole Lewis
First Place 4 Health National Director
Houston, Texas

moment of truth

But if we walk in the light, as he is in the light, we have fellowship
with one another, and the blood of Jesus, his Son, purifies us from all sin.

1 JOHN 1:7

Have you noticed how easy it is to lie to yourself? I think of myself as an honest person, yet for many years, I lied to myself on an almost daily basis about the choices I made related to food and healthy living. I had fallen into the trap of "I can do it myself." Certainly, there were short periods of time when I would successfully lose 20 to 30 pounds, but those victories were short-lived and my weight continued to creep up. When introduced to First Place 4 Health's Live It Food Plan, I remember thinking, "This sounds like a great program, but why do I need to show up to a meeting every week? That's silly! I can do this on my own." I was lying to myself.

Just before Christmas of 2004, I was standing in a dressing room at Dillard's when God made me realize that I was not being truthful to myself. The reflection in the mirror was proof that I could not make the changes I needed to make on my own. I joined a First Place 4 Health group at my local church the following month. At first, my focus was on the tactical aspects of tracking what I ate, doing the Bible study consistently and memorizing the Bible verse each week. But soon I came to appreciate the value of the fellowship I found within my group. With our common bond as believers in Jesus Christ, I found that I could both offer and receive encouragement and enjoy camaraderie with the people in my First Place 4 Health groups.

Looking back over the past five years, I have a hard time envisioning my life without them, because God used those group members to help me develop new priorities and new habits related to living a healthy lifestyle. My First Place 4 Health friends have laughed with me, cried with me, prayed with me and celebrated with me. And knowing that I'll see them at the next meeting has helped me to be genuine and truthful with everyone, including myself!

Action Item: Are you basking in the light and warmth that God offers through fellowship with like-minded believers? Or is the pride of "I can do it myself" keeping you "out in the cold"? Talk to God about it and ask Him to show you areas where you need His help to change how you think about being honest with yourself.

Sandy Matthews
Houston, Texas

83

blood sisters

But if we walk in the light, as he is in the light, we have fellowship
with one another, and the blood of Jesus, his Son, purifies us from all sin.

1 JOHN 1:7

At first glance, I thought she was slightly intimidating—cool, aloof and tightly in-sulated by walls of protection. Unapproachable, or so I thought . . . until that day in the church kitchen when she said, "I always wanted a sister," and I, a displaced Yankee in Virginia, far from my two sisters in Massachusetts, spontaneously re-plied, "I'll be your sister!" During that moment of mutual vulnerability, God be-gan something wonderful.

Jo Ann was the first person I told about plans to start First Place 4 Health at our church. We still didn't know each other very well, and I was afraid she would think I thought she was fat. My fears were unfounded, because God had already been preparing her heart and, like me, she had been praying for a solution to her weight problems.

First Place became the opportunity for our sisterhood to grow and flourish. Little by little, as our individual paths toward the light began merging, we have en-couraged, challenged, motivated, bolstered, taught, cheered and strengthened each other—listened to, confided in and shared tears of joy and sorrow with each other.

Once, I said, "I wish we were blood sisters." Her wise reply? "We are Arkansas blood sisters—we are covered by HIS blood!" Chills ran up my spine at that thought, and they still do even now. A natural offshoot of walking in the light is having the privilege of the fellowship of those He handpicks to accompany us on the journey.

We were an odd couple, to say the least, a Southern Belle and a Yankee. "Sisters" separated at birth? You might say that—our earthly births were definitely separate (by about seven years and 600 miles), but we have been reunited in our family of God. I never would have believed it if I *had* seen it with my own eyes—so I needed His.

We are not alone, plentiful sisterhoods await us. Pray that He gives you His eyes to see them.

Action Item: Are you squeamish about "confessing your sins to one another"? Ask God to show you who you can trust with your burdens—look for those He has clearly placed beside you on your pathway of light.

Jeanne Deveau Gregory
Chatham, Virginia

the light of fellowship

But if we walk in the light, as he is in the light, we have fellowship
with one another, and the blood of Jesus, his Son, purifies us from all sin.

1 JOHN 1:7

Today is a beautiful day in West Texas. The temperature is pleasant, the humidity low and, of course, the wind is blowing. It's a great time for calling the folks in my First Place 4 Health group!

As we visited, I asked each one what they enjoyed about being a part of First Place 4 Health. Somewhere in the list everyone said "fellowship," whether it was during the Bible study, discussion of the lesson or having a celebration at the end of the session. I remember that's when leader Barbara Clark spoiled us with atmosphere! At the end of the fall sessions, she would have us over to her home where we found a beautifully set table, comfortable chairs set around the fireplace, a fire burning brightly and all healthy foods to eat!

The fall would be the time to reveal our secret pals. We found this to be a great way to bring us closer together. A secret pal not only surprised you on occasion with some gift, but she was also a faithful prayer warrior for you during the session.

As the evening came to an end, Barbara would often remind us that eating healthy during the holidays was just as important as during our First Place 4 Health session. Recipes were available for the foods that were served. In fact, we were encouraged to bring new healthy foods and their recipes to share.

Finally, we would gather in a circle, hold hands and go around the group in prayer, with Barbara closing. You could not help but leave there feeling the light of Jesus and love from Him and from the group members.

Prayer: *Abba Father, thank You for the warmth of Your light as we fellowship with our Christian friends in First Place 4 Health.*

Betha Jean McGee
Wall, Texas

over the lips, look out hips!

*But if we walk in the light, as he is in the light, we have fellowship
with one another, and the blood of Jesus, his Son, purifies us from all sin.*

1 JOHN 1:7

Sugar has always been a trigger food for me. In First Place 4 Health, I learned to pray Scripture in defense against temptation. One Sunday morning, before Bible study, someone brought a box of freshly baked, sugar-glazed donuts and set them down in front of me. My mouth began to water; my desire was strong, and I badly wanted a donut. But it wouldn't have been just about eating that one donut. It would have set me on a downward spiral of bad choices. I was feeling weak, ready to give in to temptation, when I prayed Psalm 119:37: "Turn my eyes away from worthless things; preserve my life according to your word." I prayed, *Lord, please help me to see these donuts in a different way—change my desire.*

I walked away to mark attendance records, and when I returned to where the donut box was, someone closed the door and a puff of wind came through the doorway right over that donut box. Standing there, the strangest sensation came over my tongue. Even though I had not eaten the donut, instead of the light, warm, sweet and delicious taste I had been fantasizing about, I had the sensation of thick, greasy film coating my tongue. I looked down at the donut box and saw the saturated grease residue on the bottom of the carton where donuts had sat. Suddenly, I felt close to nausea, and the thought *cellulite infested* popped into my mind. After that, all I could picture in my mind when I saw a donut was cellulite-infested hips and thighs. I heard a funny song in my head, *"Over the lips, through the gums, look out hips, here it comes!"*

Thank You, Lord, for answered prayer. Not only did You rescue me from my temptation, but You also delivered me from craving it to this day. I had a total shift in my mind and a super lesson in staying alert and praying in the Spirit on all occasions.

Prayer: *Thank You, Father, that no need is too small for You and that You care about everything that concerns me. Thank You for the power of Your Holy Word and Your Spirit who comes to my rescue.*

Connie Welch
First Place 4 Health Network Leader
Keller, Texas

lifting each other up

Let us not give up meeting together, as some are in the habit of doing, but let us encourage one another—and all the more as you see the Day approaching.
HEBREWS 10:25

Our First Place 4 Health meetings are more important than any of us can imagine when we first join the program. I have heard some amazing stories about the importance of meeting together.

For instance, Martha's group ministered to her after her daughter and son-in-law were killed by a drunk driver. Diane's group took her food and to physical therapy after two shoulder surgeries. The First Place 4 Health prayer warrior team prays for our staff when we travel and for many needs among our First Place 4 Health members and leaders. And one lady told me that she has gotten a call or a card at the exact time she needed it most.

I've also heard many sad stories from those who quit meeting together: Most people gain weight after they quit going to class; some have moved away and fail to find or start a new group, which is a sure-fire way to make new friends quickly; and the pressures of work cause many to stop going to their First Place 4 Health classes, greatly increasing their mental and emotional stress levels.

If you are a First Place 4 Health leader, it is important that you use the talents of the people in your class. By doing this, the class will run just fine if you need to be absent. You also are developing new leaders by allowing them to present the Wellness Spotlight or lead Bible study. If you are a First Place 4 Health member, it is important that you tell your leader what you would be willing to do to help your leader and encourage your classmates.

I remember a time at our church when Becky Turner led a First Place 4 Health class alone on Monday evening. Claudia, one of the members, volunteered to help her weigh the members and listen to them say memory verses. When Becky moved to another day and time, Claudia took over the leadership role and has led for several years now.

Action Item: In your journal, write about a way your First Place 4 Health class has been an encouragement to you, and share it with the group at your next meeting.

Carole Lewis
First Place 4 Health National Director
Houston, Texas

87

my church family

Let us not give up meeting together, as some are in the habit of doing, but let us encourage one another—and all the more as you see the Day approaching.

HEBREWS 10:25

When our church fell apart, we found ourselves heartbroken, discouraged, feeling like failures, and looking for a new church to replace the one my husband and I, along with 20 other people, helped start 15 years earlier. What was once a healthy, active, soul-winning and ministering church became very sick, problem ridden and financially devastated, and eventually closed its doors.

I thank God for First Place 4 Health at this very discouraging time in my life. All of the ladies of my First Place 4 Health class ministered to me in one way or another throughout this very painful time. Through their attendance in class, cards of encouragement, weekly prayers, a listening ear, and godly counsel, they helped me in more ways than I can express. First Place 4 Health became "my church family," while my husband and I sought God's direction for a church where we could become members and serve Him.

"Let us not give up meeting together . . . but let us encourage one another" through the difficulties of life. Better together? Oh, yes! Next time you get the thought that you don't make a difference in your First Place 4 Health class, or that it won't matter if you miss today, think of me and remember that your attendance alone might be the very thing that ministers to someone else in your class. Your very presence might be the encouragement someone else needs that day to make them realize they are not alone in the battle.

Prayer: *Lord, help me to minister to others as I have been ministered to. Help me to make the time to encourage others and to reach out.*

Karen Ferguson
Houston, Texas

88

always welcome

Let us not give up meeting together, as some are in the habit of doing, but let us encourage one another—and all the more as you see the Day approaching.

HEBREWS 10:25

I've been teaching First Place 4 Health for the past two years. I love the focus on Christ, the Bible studies, the wellness messages and the class members. The Christian fellowship that grows out of the time we share has exceeded my expectations. I look forward to class every week with the wonderful people God has put together.

Before each 12-week session, I tell the class that they are *always* welcome. It doesn't matter if they have missed one week or five, the door is always open and a warm welcome will always await them. If they must miss a class, I ask that they let me know in advance. It's important not only to me, but also to other members to know how they are doing so that we can effectively pray for them.

I've noticed that often midway through the 12 weeks, some individuals stop coming or start attending sporadically. Often their reason is that they have gotten "off track" and feel uncomfortable returning to the group. This is when the encouragement of the class is so important in providing them with the same love, acceptance and grace that Jesus provides us when we have wandered or strayed from Him individually. The class prays, sends emails, calls and reassures these "wanderers" that they are missed and that we desire to have them with us. When they return, they are welcomed with open arms and loving acceptance.

Action Item: Are there individuals in your sphere of influence who need encouragement to keep attending their fellowship group of believers? Guide them back so they may be encouraged and also encourage others.

Prayer: *Lord, thank You for the community of fellow believers who, by Your example, have encouraged me and helped me to be a source of encouragement to them and others, to honor and serve You.*

Deb Stark
San Antonio, Texas

89

spirituallywarm

Let us not give up meeting together, as some are in the habit of doing, but let us encourage one another—and all the more as you see the Day approaching.

HEBREWS 10:25

I was out on my two-mile run on a brisk October morning, dressed in layers and using Dick Eastman's prayer prompt as I ran. I spend three to four minutes on each of these topics: praise, waiting, confession, Scripture praying, watching, intercession, petition, thanksgiving, singing, meditation, listening, and praise again.

As I was on the "watching" portion, I saw a small group of birds flying through our neighborhood. I sensed that I should extend my watching, when off in the distance the small group of birds joined with a larger flock to fly in a migratory pattern. How amazing to see a large group of birds flying as one flock, swooping and swaying together in the quiet of the morning. God reminded me that when we meet in First Place 4 Health groups we are preparing ourselves to become part of the larger flock. And when we come together in celebration at our weekend worship times, conferences and leadership summits we are the larger flock, singing His praises and honoring Him as the Body of Christ.

As I entered the "listening" section of my prayer run, I realized that my fingers were getting cold. Even though I had gloves on, my fingers were starting to ache. So I pulled my fingers and thumbs into the center part of my glove, and as I wiggled them together inside my glove, they started to get warm again. As Christians, we are like fingers in a glove. Inside the glove, God provides protection, yet we still get cold and start to ache if we are standing out alone for extended periods. When we come together, rub against each other and even create friction at times, we warm up. Hebrews 10:25 reminds us that we need to meet together and encourage one another. We need to rub up against each other. When we keep each other accountable, we might even create some healthy friction. Our coming together is God's way of keeping us spiritually warm.

Action Item: Are you trying to go it alone with God? Are you feeling the chill and ache of isolation from other people? Join with others so that you can encourage one another. We are better together.

Helen Baratta
First Place 4 Health Networking Leader
Oakdale, Pennsylvania

90

obedience school

Let us not give up meeting together, as some are in the habit of doing, but let us encourage one another—and all the more as you see the Day approaching.

HEBREWS 10:25

My pug puppy Stella Rose is doing great in puppy obedience school. She's my fifth pug, but the first I've had to take to school. My wild child has learned how to behave and even shine around other dogs and the teacher/trainer. We've both had fun getting to know people "owned" by a varied mix of breeds.

Stella Rose and I watched the tiny, shy poodle finally come out of her shell. We were thrilled when the boxer mix eventually developed control of his incessant bark. Everyone was proud and relieved when the huge Irish wolfhound stopped jumping up on people. All the dogs had "issues," and we will never know why or how they developed them. What we saw was how they learned to overcome them by sitting under the teaching of a masterful dog trainer (we nicknamed her the Dog Whisperette). I remembered thinking the first night that everyone looked like they wanted to exclaim, "I know my dog's not bad; he just needs a little help." And they all got it.

We humans are the same. It is so much more fun and effective to gather together in Bible study to learn from the Master. He allows us to help each other to grow when we meet in His name. We come with unique and individual struggles that are sometimes irritating to outsiders. But not to seasoned classmates—they know that with time and effort, God teaches us how to overcome, and we blossom into humble, grateful, appreciated "oaks of righteousness."

We watch, assist and celebrate classmates' victories and usually (probably always) glean understanding for ourselves. Everyone is different, but we all have the same compassionate, patient Trainer/Teacher. How much better to sit at His feet with other precious students than to struggle alone! "They will be called oaks of righteousness, a planting of the LORD for the display of his splendor" (Isaiah 61:3).

Action Item: Think of a time when the growth of a fellow classmate ministered to you. Pray for preservation of that victory.

Prayer: *O God, You are the Teacher. Thank You for all my precious classmates. Help us to learn what You need us to know.*

Beth Serpas
Houston, Texas

INSPIRATIONAL STORY

God is still at work

I started First Place 4 Health in January 2008. I weighed 255 pounds and was desperate for change. I had been using food in place of relationships with people and God. Food was my friend, or so I thought. But I knew that if I did not change my lifestyle, I would never experience God working in my life. I was embarrassed about my size and I hated to go anywhere for fear of the looks and pity I would see in others' faces. My fear was really about my own opinion of myself; I felt disgusting. I was on medications for depression, anxiety and sleep, but nothing was working. Nothing was filling the void I had inside.

I had to make that first right choice to join a group where God was front and center in order to start my incredible journey. Once I joined, I told God I would give my all, and I did. That first year, week after week, I cried all the way to the scale. I thought that eating real food would make me gain weight, and I was terrified of failing. But God did not leave me to do it alone. He was there the

BEFORE

AFTER

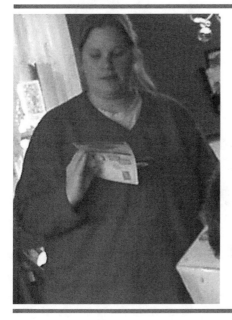 

whole way. I lost 60 pounds that first year. The next two years were a struggle for me, but God worked with me, and I lost another 28.5 pounds—a total of 88.5 pounds.

I thought that losing weight would be the end of my transformation, but God wants me to change other things too. He has changed me inside and out, but He is far from done. I am no longer on any medications, and I can honestly say that the only way to break free from food addiction or any addiction is through my Lord and Savior, Jesus Christ. He did this, not me.

Colleen Hammond
Kingsley, Pennsylvania

Note

1. Robert J. Morgan, *Then Sings My Soul: 150 of the World's Greatest Hymn Stories* (Nashville, TN: Thomas Nelson, 2003).

MONTH 5

COMPASSION

tell it to Jesus

This is what the LORD Almighty says: "Administer true justice;
show mercy and compassion to one another."

ZECHARIAH 7:9

My mom used to say, "At the end of your life you can count your true friends on one hand and have fingers left over." I know who these people are in my life, and I'm sure you know who the people are in your life as well. They are there for you at any time of the day or night. Let me tell you about one of these people in my life.

Joy Stephens and I have been dear friends for more than 40 years. Joy was the wife of our pastor and was my Sunday School teacher when I was in my twenties with three young children. I learned so much from Joy's teaching that I still use today. Three of the "joyisms" I learned were: (1) Being comes before doing; (2) mercy triumphs over judgment (see James 2:13); and (3) tell God on them.

Being a pastor's wife, Joy knew that she didn't have many people she could talk with when she was going through a tough time. She knew that our God is the Righteous Judge, so her philosophy was to "tell God on them" when someone hurt her or made her angry.

If we used these four words "tell God on them" more often, it would save us from so much pain and grief. I believe that God desires for each of us to take the high road with others. He will administer "true justice" in response to our prayers. Our job is to "show mercy and compassion to one another."

When we are in ministry, and every believer is, our job is to talk to God about any concerns we might have with another person and leave justice to Him. Then we are to show mercy and compassion to that person, the same kind of mercy and compassion God has shown to us. When we do this we are "turning the other cheek," as Jesus taught His disciples in Matthew 5:39.

Action Item: Write in your journal about a person who has hurt you in some way. Ask God to work in this person's life so that true justice is served. Ask God to be your mercy and compassion and to administer these qualities to this person through you.

Carole Lewis
First Place 4 Health National Director
Houston, Texas

92

be willing

*This is what the LORD Almighty says: "Administer true justice;
show mercy and compassion to one another."*

ZECHARIAH 7:9

Some situations we walk through in life are completely for someone else as God uses them in our life to have an influence on others. God has used people and His Word to teach me a thing or two in the last two years.

I was really struggling with being single. I didn't understand why God would give me the desire to be married but not lead me to the right person. Friends would say, "Oh, it will happen," or "all in His timing." The worst thing I ever heard was, "I just don't know why a girl like you isn't married!" *Yeah, well, neither do I.* I now realize that God had been preparing me my entire life for what he was bringing into my life.

I recently heard a speaker tell her story of marrying a man with children. My mom and I talked on the way home and she said, "You should always be willing to hear someone's story," meaning, "Don't judge before you know." God began to change my view about second marriages, divorce and even people who have "bonus" children.

In a perfect world, there would be no divorce or unfaithfulness, and broken homes would never exist. But we live in a fallen world where we need God's mercy and compassion. God not only changed my view, but He also softened my heart. He has shown me that He is totally trustworthy. He wants me to be a light to people with whom I come in contact daily.

Zechariah 7:9 speaks to God's purpose for doing life together: administering true justice and showing mercy and compassion to one another. I have a new friend in my life. He has precious children. I am a blessing to them as they are to me. God has shown through this situation that it's not what I get, but what I give.

Be willing to listen with kindness and compassion to Him and to others, and God will bless.

Prayer: *Thank You, Lord, for Your love and compassion for Your children. You have a wonderful plan for our lives—a plan to give us hope and a future as we trust in You to show us Your will and Your way.*

Megan Heath
Charleston, South Carolina

crowned with compassion

This is what the LORD Almighty says: "Administer true justice;
show mercy and compassion to one another."

ZECHARIAH 7:9

After a week of erratic sleep in a very hard recliner while my mother was in the hospital, I was definitely in need of compassion. My niece Cindy began to show mercy and compassion during the week by bringing snacks to the hospital and relieving me for a few hours to run to Mom's house to shower and change clothes. She sat with me, ran errands and we had lunch together each day.

After it became obvious that I would need to bring my mother back to Houston to live with me, my family began to pour out their mercy and compassion on our situation. My son Terry came from Houston with computer equipment so that I could continue my work at First Place 4 Health while preparing for the move. My niece Sandra came from Waco, Texas, and helped me sort and pack all of my mother's belongings and also provided our lunch each day. My nephew Josh and his wife, Gin, disposed of all that we were unable to bring with us.

When we were ready to return to Houston, my son Tim and son-in-law Bobby came with a U-Haul and drove my mother and me back to Houston. When we arrived, my daughter Tamara and daughter-in-law Audra had cleaned my house and filled my refrigerator and pantry with food. They were waiting, along with my grandchildren, to welcome us home.

Matthew 9:36 says that Jesus had compassion on the helpless. My family joined together with mercy and compassion, each doing their own part to help us in a time when both my mother and I felt quite helpless. As the psalmist wrote in Psalm 103:4, we were crowned "with love and compassion" by our wonderful family, who continued to show their love to us while we settled my mother into my home. God shows His mercy and compassion to us through His children as we reach out to those who are hurting or in helpless situations. Once you have been a recipient of that kind of love, you are eager and willing to give a helping hand to others in need.

Action Item: Be watchful for those who are in need of God's mercy and compassion by speaking a kind word, doing a good deed or praying for them.

Pat Lewis
First Place 4 Health Assistant to National Director
Houston, Texas

94

vengeance is not the answer

This is what the LORD Almighty says: "Administer true justice;
show mercy and compassion to one another."

ZECHARIAH 7:9

If left to my own devices, I would have killed him. Someone I loved had horribly hurt someone I loved and for whom I was responsible. It fell on me to make the next move. Somehow, I had enough sense to know that that was exactly what I *shouldn't* do—move. If I did, I feared I would not be able to stop the rage from spilling out into a maelstrom.

I went back and forth between the overwhelming desire to take justice into my own hands and the haunting echo in my mind, "Vengeance is mine . . . says the Lord" (Romans 12:19, *NASB*). Frozen and numb, alone in the dark, but safe in my car in an empty parking lot, I finally turned my life over to God. I told Him what He already knew—that I couldn't face this person without killing him. *He* would have to do it. *He* would have to drive the car and make my feet move. *He* would have to speak for me. *He* would have to hold me back. And He did.

That was a very long time ago. People still ask me why I didn't kill him. All I can say is that God took my rage, replaced it with a calm sense of peace and showed me that that person was also a beloved child of His—sick and in need of help, yes—but His just the same. It wasn't my place to exact vengeance. Sometimes their facial expressions in light of my answer make me question my actions. But then I remember that what they thought of me really didn't matter. It was not them I needed to please. God and I did this together, and it is the most in step with Him I have ever felt. So far, it is the one thing I can say I did right.

Action Item: In what areas are you trying to take matters into your own hands when the only One who can handle it is God? How can you use mercy and compassion to turn a situation around, with God's help?

Prayer: *Lord, I wish this life didn't have to hurt so much, but I know Your salve of mercy and compassion is as healing as the wounds are painful, and somehow You make it right in the end. We can never understand Your ways, but I'd rather be with You than without You.*

Jeanne Deveau Gregory
Chatham, Virginia

95

what we all need

This is what the LORD Almighty says: "Administer true justice;
show mercy and compassion to one another."

ZECHARIAH 7:9

Some people just seem to be natural encouragers! I knew of Cathy several years before I had the privilege of meeting her. She is now one of my biggest encouragers and a wonderful friend!

Cathy encouraged me long before she knew me. Several years ago, my husband and I went through a very difficult period with one of our sons, and it was Cathy and her husband who encouraged him. He mentioned numerous times how kind, compassionate and encouraging they were, and I'm sure he would have preferred them as his parents during that time! I never got a chance to meet Cathy then, but I definitely remembered her impact in my son's life.

Fast-forward several years. One of Cathy's daughters unexpectedly passed away in her sleep, leaving behind a young husband and toddler. By this time, I knew Cathy, but we had not developed a close bond of friendship. I prayed for her and her family and sent her a card, but beyond that, I didn't know what to do to encourage her.

Cathy has now joined our First Place 4 Health group, and I am so blessed! She continues to do what she has been doing all along—encouraging others. Cathy is sensitive to everyone in the group and somehow seems to know what to say at just the right time. She comes up with ideas to help others and is constantly encouraging others to keep going. When a member's spouse had a health crisis, she was quick to organize sending a fruit basket. When I've been at my most discouraged moments as a leader and felt like quitting, she has sent notes that have encouraged me. She has administered true justice and compassion by her consistent example of building others up, regardless of her circumstances.

Action Item: Write a note of encouragement to someone today. Your kind act may be the only hope from human hands that person receives today.

Prayer: *Dear heavenly Father, thank You for sending people into my life who have encouraged me. I pray that You would show me ways to be an encourager to those I encounter today.*

Mary Chin
St. Charles, Illinois

96

a friend in deed

Therefore, as God's chosen people, holy and dearly loved, clothe yourselves
with compassion, kindness, humility, gentleness and patience.

COLOSSIANS 3:12

Pat Lewis, my assistant at First Place 4 Health, and I have been best friends for more than four decades. We met shortly after Pat and her husband, Bill, moved to Houston from Arkansas. Pat and Bill had three young children, like Johnny and I, and we were in the same Sunday School class.

Pat and I have gone through many momentous occasions over the years of our friendship. We went through the time when Pat's son, Tim, broke his neck playing football. We were also together during happy times like our children's weddings and the birth of grandchildren. We wept together when Pat's husband, Bill, went to heaven in 2000.

Pat has been there for me when my dad, mom and daughter Shari were called home. She has been there for me during the happy times to celebrate and the sad times to commiserate.

When I look at the qualities mentioned in today's verse, I see those qualities in my friend Pat's life. Because of this, Pat has earned the right to speak into my life. Like E. F. Hutton, when Pat speaks, I listen. Pat has kept me from doing and saying a lot of stupid things because of her kindness and compassion. She has gently spoken into my life when I needed to hear from God, and she has been patient with me beyond belief.

I never send an email when I am upset without letting Pat look at it first. She almost always says to wait a little while before sending it. After a while, I usually don't send it at all.

We all need a friend like Pat in our life, and I am one blessed woman indeed! Better still, we need to pray that we will be a "Pat" in someone else's life, always clothed in compassion, kindness, humility, gentleness and patience.

Action Item: Write in your journal about a friend who has the qualities mentioned in this verse. Make it a point to call or write today and tell your friend how much her (his) friendship means in your life.

Carole Lewis
First Place 4 Health National Director
Houston, Texas

they just get it

Therefore, as God's chosen people, holy and dearly loved, clothe yourselves with compassion, kindness, humility, gentleness and patience.

COLOSSIANS 3:12

I joined First Place 4 Health after many years of attempting to lose weight using almost every method/program available. I grew desperately tired of failing. I knew that I must employ a different avenue with a clear goal to finally change my life so that I could become and stay healthy. This need coincided with my growing desire to serve God.

So, before I knew about First Place 4 Health, I decided to ask God to help me—to be my diet counselor. The basis of my program with God was to eat only three times a day and to ask Him during grace to let it satisfy me until the next meal. I will never forget that first meal. I sat down and immediately burned the roof of my mouth on the first bite! I had not prayed! I quickly began to pray with a piece of ice in my mouth, which made me sound funny, and my little dog went crazy thinking a stranger was in the house. I was shocked I could not get it right for even one day.

Thus, I discovered that I was not going to be able to do it alone. I attended a First Place 4 Health class in a neighboring church and then started a group in my church. I told the ladies at orientation that on the "burnt mouth" day, I wanted to tell someone of my misadventure—someone who would laugh with me, not at me. I needed someone who would understand my desire to please God, and appreciate my frustration at my shortcomings, someone who could empathize because they had been there themselves.

My First Place 4 Health classmates fill the bill beautifully. It is truly wonderful to be with a precious set of women who understand each other's defeats and victories week after week. Our stories are vastly individual, but we share a common theme. In our Bible study groups, we are among kindred spirits. It's a gift from God.

Action Item: Think of those who have ministered to you in your First Place 4 Health group. Send a thank-you note with a return display of encouragement.

Prayer: *God, thank You for the compassionate encouragers in my class. Reward them with personal success, and hear their prayers, even as I humbly acknowledge they are praying for me.*

Beth Serpas
Houston, Texas

Jesus with skin on

Therefore, as God's chosen people, holy and dearly loved, clothe yourselves with compassion, kindness, humility, gentleness and patience.

COLOSSIANS 3:12

My father was in a severe automobile accident three weeks after my mother passed away, and he was put in the trauma intensive care unit. This was a very difficult time for our family. We were still grieving Mother's death, and seeing my father suffer was very difficult. We were only allowed to see him for a short time every other hour.

He had a special nurse named Katie. I will never forget her as long as I live. Katie worked with a humble spirit and a passionate heart that was full of great skill, compassion, kindness, gentleness and patience. I remember watching her and appreciating her attentiveness to my dad. Katie was a ministering angel sent from the Lord. In an early morning hour on the fourth day after Daddy's accident, Katie called and said Daddy was passing away and I needed to get to the hospital quick. When we arrived, Katie was by his side, attending him. An hour later, surrounded by his family, Jesus came to take Daddy home.

In the following weeks, my grief was so heavy that I didn't think I could bear it. I prayed and begged God to let me see Him at work. I will never forget this moment as long as I live, for it was as if a video was played in my mind. What I saw was Katie leaning over my dad with a damp washcloth, wiping his forehead and talking so softly and kindly to him. I saw Katie holding a cup of water with a straw for him to drink. I saw Katie give him medicine when he needed it. What I saw was Jesus with skin on, and her name was Katie.

You never know when someone is watching and how your actions will minister to their lives, but Jesus does. I am so thankful for that ministering angel God used to bless our lives, and for her willingness to be Jesus with skin on.

Action Item: Thank the Lord for the people in your life who have been Jesus with skin on. Ask Him to help you minister to someone this week in a special way.

Prayer: *Dear Father, Your compassion is great and Your mercies never fail. Use me as Your instrument to show compassion to others so that Your Son may be honored. Amen.*

Connie Welch
First Place 4 Health Network Leader
Keller, Texas

when we cannot help ourselves

Therefore, as God's chosen people, holy and dearly loved, clothe yourselves with compassion, kindness, humility, gentleness and patience.

COLOSSIANS 3:12

Many years ago, my First Place 4 Health class demonstrated to me their kindness and compassion. I had been experiencing multiple health issues when I severely injured my left rotator cuff. As a single mom with two children in high school, I was completely overwhelmed and totally unprepared for recovery needs. I took the surgeon's advice and scheduled immediate surgery.

When I awoke from surgery and eventually arrived home, I was in unimaginable pain. Several days later, I realized that driving to physical therapy was the least of my problems; I wasn't even able to dress myself.

I had enrolled in the fall session of First Place 4 Health and attended one class. Carole Lewis made an announcement and inquired if anyone was available to drive me to physical therapy. Two women I didn't know stepped forward and volunteered. I was so embarrassed when they phoned and I had to tell them I needed them to come in and help me dress first. The first day arrived and the volunteer walked right in. She wasn't shocked by the state of my house or my unwashed hair. She calmly and kindly assisted me with my clothes and drove me to my appointment. These two kind and compassionate members continued to drive me for several months.

Eight years later, I finally went to the doctor to see about my right torn rotator cuff. The new surgeon suggested that I have surgery immediately before I lost the use of my arm. This time, members from three classes came forward. They helped me wash and dress, fed me, drove me, shopped, chopped and cooked for me.

These women are truly living proof and witnesses to Christ's work in the world by their actions, not just during a season, but every day.

Action Item: Look at the needs of others around you every day. Do the strangers you meet experience your kindness and compassion?

Prayer: *Dear Lord, help me to be a daily witness to Your incredible love for all of us. I pray that I will have such compassion that I would take action rather than just listen.*

Diane Hawkins
Houston, Texas

check your clothing

Therefore, as God's chosen people, holy and dearly loved, clothe yourselves with compassion, kindness, humility, gentleness and patience.

COLOSSIANS 3:12

When I think of people who are compassionate, my friend Amy comes to mind. Amy is the youngest member in our First Place 4 Health group and she has been such a blessing to the rest of us.

Amy has not been able to have any biological children, but she and her husband adopted a dear little boy for whom they provide a loving home. She has such genuine love and compassion for children and orphans that she went to China last summer to volunteer her time in an orphanage to just love on those children. Recently, God opened the door for her to adopt a child with special needs, and it has been very exciting to watch this process unfold. We group members feel like we are going through the adoption process with her, and each week we wait with eager anticipation to hear the latest developments. When she goes back to China to bring her next child home, we know that child will have the opportunity to grow up in a home where compassion, kindness, humility, gentleness and patience are lived out daily.

Our heavenly Father is the ultimate example of compassion, and we are His children who are so dearly loved. The more that we are aware of and understand God's compassion toward us, the more compassionate we will become. When we clothe ourselves with these qualities, others will see Jesus in us. Every week in our group, I hear of someone showing compassion to another by encouraging words, prayers or actions as we all serve God and one another. I am amazed at the compassion shown to me by my heavenly Father and also by the members of my group. I pray that I will always remember the comfort and compassion I have been shown and that I will show the same to others.

Action Item: Using Jesus as your example, go out of your way to show someone an act of compassion today.

Prayer: *Father, I pray that You will help me to be mindful of Your compassion and show me ways that I can show compassion to others I meet today.*

Mary Chin
St. Charles, Illinois

101

right living

Learn to do right! Seek justice, encourage the oppressed.
Defend the cause of the fatherless, plead the case of the widow.

ISAIAH 1:17

I was at a friend's home once whose kitchen stove had a ceramic stovetop. The burner was on, but because it wasn't red, I touched it to see if it was hot. Was it ever! I spent the next few hours with four of my fingers immersed in ice to alleviate the pain.

Most of us learn to do right by many instances of doing wrong. In the early years of my walk with Christ, I learned to do right by running into a brick wall over and over again. When the pain became great enough, I finally thought about what I might be doing wrong. This applied to finances, marriage, raising children and relationships.

Doing life wrong is a great teacher if we learn from our mistakes. How can you and I learn to do right? The absolute best teacher for right living is the Word of God. Everything we need to know about doing right is in the Bible. There are many Scriptures to help us grow as Christians.

We all need to learn to do right when it comes to taking care of our bodies, but what about other things? Are our finances a mess? What about our marriage? Kids messed up? Having trouble loving someone? Is forgiveness hard to offer? Every answer we will ever need in this life is found in our Bible.

When I am having a problem of "doing right" in a particular area, I look in the concordance in the back of my Bible for verses that speak to the problem. Then I look up those verses and begin meditating on what the Bible tells me to do. As I pray and ask God for direction, He gently guides me into what is right.

Action Item: Look up some verses that speak to a particular area where you need to "learn to do right." Write those verses in your journal and begin reading, meditating and praying about your situation until God gives you the answer.

Carole Lewis
First Place 4 Health National Director
Houston, Texas

102

God cares

Learn to do right! Seek justice, encourage the oppressed.
Defend the cause of the fatherless, plead the case of the widow.

ISAIAH 1:17

The old hymn "God Will Take Care of You" played on my car radio, and I sang along as I made my way home from work on a busy freeway in Houston. "When dangers fierce your path assail, God will take care of you." I last heard that song the day before my oldest son left for college. I was singing in the church choir at the time, and we sang the song as our closing hymn. It was an emotional time for me, as I was very apprehensive about my first child leaving home. God assured me with a great peace that He would take care of my son.

As I reminisced, I looked down at my gas gauge and realized I needed to stop on the way home for a fill-up. I pulled up to the gas pump at my neighborhood Kroger store and began pumping gas into my nearly empty tank. As I stood waiting for it to fill, a thought came into my mind to check my tires.

I am a widow, so there is no one else at home to check my tires, yet I never think to look at them. However, the thought was so strong in my mind that I walked around my car, looking at the tires, and sure enough, my right front tire was dangerously low. I immediately drove to a nearby tire store where they showed me that all the tread was worn off the inside of the tire. I made plans for a new set of tires and thanked the Lord profusely for "watching my path for danger."

God is a mighty and holy God, yet He stoops to whisper in our ear when we are in trouble. He put an old song in my mouth many years later to remind me once again that He cares for me and guards my path as we walk together through this life.

Prayer: *Thank You, Lord, that I am most definitely better together with You. I can't imagine living a moment without Your presence. Thank You that You go before me and that You are my rearguard. You keep me totally in Your loving care. Amen.*

Pat Lewis
First Place 4 Health Assistant to the Director
Houston, Texas

103

making a difference

Learn to do right! Seek justice, encourage the oppressed.
Defend the cause of the fatherless, plead the case of the widow.

ISAIAH 1:17

The first time I ran in the Komen Race for the Cure was in 1995. It was held in downtown Charleston, South Carolina, and my friend Vicki Curry and I ran together. I remember not being overly impressed with the crowd, maybe about 1,000. On Saturday, October 16, 2010, I ran again. As I walked toward the starting line, I was astounded at the number of people who showed up. The announcement came over the loud speaker that at least 9,000 had registered so far! My first thought was, *What would motivate this many people to get up early on a cold October morning, drive down here and run this race?* I soon had my answer.

I arrived early for the 5K and decided to walk the one-mile family fun run as a warm-up. It wasn't long before I realized that I was walking on holy ground. There were children running for their moms, husbands running for their wives and mothers, and on and on. As I passed one family with a dad and three children (a toddler on his shoulders and two little girls), they were singing the lyrics from that infamous Queen song, "We will . . . we will . . . rock you!" As I got closer, I realized they were singing, "We will . . . we will . . . find a cure!" I was moved beyond words, and I finished the race sobbing all the way!

All the crazy pink-clad people around me were running for one reason—love. It is the strongest force in heaven and on earth to get people moving. I know people in my life who would move heaven and earth for me, and I for them.

The race reminded me that the greatest demonstration of love I have ever known was when God sent His Son, Jesus, as the sacrifice for our sins, for one simple reason—He loves us! John 3:16 is so familiar yet still so powerful: "For God so loved the world that He gave His only begotten Son, that whoever believes in Him should not perish but have everlasting life" (*NKJV*). God did move heaven and earth for me and you.

Action Item: How about you? Get up and exercise today and let *love* sustain you for the journey. You will lead others to do the same, and it will make a difference.

Vicki Heath
First Place 4 Health Associate Director
Edisto Beach, South Carolina

104

escape from temptation

Learn to do right! Seek justice, encourage the oppressed.
Defend the cause of the fatherless, plead the case of the widow.

ISAIAH 1:17

When I worked as a school nurse, my office was next door to where the snacks were kept for children to buy each afternoon. One particular day, I noticed the principal restocking the candy shelves with a box of Almond Joys. I could smell them when he walked by my door, so I decided to have one. I got out my 50 cents and was about to walk out my door when a little boy came running from the playground telling me to come quickly because his friend "fell and broke his leg!" I ran to the playground and found the child on the ground, but without a broken leg. By the time I helped him back to my office and patched up his scratched knees, the end-of-recess bell was ringing.

I started to go to the snack cart but hadn't taken two steps before my phone rang. I had a phone call from a concerned mom who asked me to go check on her son who hadn't felt well that morning but she'd made him come to school anyway. I ran back to the playground and found her son running and playing like nothing was wrong. He said he felt fine, so I called his mom and reported that he was okay.

Then I saw my money still lying on my desk, so I started for the snack cart for the third time. And then I heard God say to me—almost audibly, "I got you away from that Almond Joy twice; don't you go back in there again." God promised to help us "do right" by providing us a way out of temptation, but it's up to us to see it and take it. To this day I never see an Almond Joy without remembering the lesson I learned that day.

Action Item: Temptation is never so obvious as when we're really trying to stick to our food plan and do First Place 4 Health "right." Describe in your journal a time when you know God was providing a way of escape and you took it.

Donna Odum
Heber Springs, Arkansas

a big heart

Learn to do right! Seek justice, encourage the oppressed.
Defend the cause of the fatherless, plead the case of the widow.

ISAIAH 1:17

I have a friend, Scotty, who is the director of one of our church's missions. At the mission, we have a food pantry, a clothes closet, a preschool and a parole board office. There is also a bread ministry, an after-school apartment ministry and a women's job corps program. I am sure there are many other programs that Scotty directs, but these are the ones that immediately come to mind.

Recently, I was having breakfast with some of the women staff members at my church. This was especially sweet because I had been on staff at the church for 25 years and hadn't seen them much since First Place 4 Health became an independent ministry and we moved our offices. Scotty was supposed to attend the breakfast, but she had an emergency and needed to help a family. When I heard this, I said, "When we get to heaven, I won't even live in the same neighborhood as Scotty!"

The most amazing part of Scotty's story is that she was married to a professional golfer for many years. She lived in a beautiful home with all the trappings of success. Yet Scotty always had a heart for the underprivileged, and she even took a 12-year-old boy into her home who lived in one of the apartments where she ministered.

After Scotty's divorce, she moved into one of the apartment buildings where she ministered and became a real part of the community. She has a big heart, but she is not a pushover. Sometimes she says, "They will need to hit bottom."

I am always amazed to read in our church report that the mission center has anywhere from 30 to 60 people each month who become believers. Scotty is directing an eternal ministry that will have eternal ramifications.

Action Item: How are you doing in living out Isaiah 1:17? Why not call a local mission and offer your help?

Carole Lewis
First Place 4 Health National Director
Houston, Texas

106

a mercy-filled life

Be merciful, just as your Father is merciful.

LUKE 6:36

One of the reasons we are "better together" is that we are strengthened when we see another person model mercy. Jesus is speaking in Luke 6:36, and He is saying that any of us can be merciful when someone is treating us right; but Christlike behavior is to show mercy to someone who is treating us wrong.

I have a dear friend who is married to a woman who is bipolar. This woman has good periods when she takes her meds and bad periods when she doesn't. I have watched this man for many years exhibit Christlike behavior to his wife. They are separated, but my friend supports her financially, not because a court has mandated it but because it is the right thing to do. I marveled when this woman sold all of my friend's antiques from his parents and grandparents in a garage sale. Instead of feeling anger toward his wife, my friend felt sorrow and pity for her.

If you and I want mercy shown to us, then we must learn to be merciful. Mercy is treating another with kindness when they don't deserve it. I cannot remember one instance when my earthly father did not show me mercy. When I hit the gas pedal instead of the brake and drove through the garage and into my parents' kitchen, my dad said, "I can fix that." When I trenched a neighbor's yard and went home crying, my dad went to the neighbor's house with me and our neighbor showed me mercy when he said, "My son can fill up the trenches."

You and I have people in our life who need for us to be merciful toward them, if for no other reason than the fact that our God is merciful. Being merciful is not a suggestion; it is a command from the Lord Jesus.

Action Item: Determine to show mercy to everyone you encounter today. Tonight, write in your journal about your experiences today. God will bless you for being merciful.

Carole Lewis
First Place 4 Health National Director
Houston, Texas

it takes a little time sometimes

Be merciful, just as your Father is merciful.

LUKE 6:36

I wish I could say that I have followed the First Place 4 Health program perfectly, but that would not be the truth. The truth of the matter is that I have been on this journey for several years. The most important part of the journey is that I have never given up on myself, and neither has God.

There have been times when I have stalled and could not move forward; and there have been times when I have even gone backward. I see these times as a big waste, but God sees them as times to pour out His mercy and grace on me.

At one point on this journey, it felt as if I could not get turned around. I knew the direction I needed to go, but I was having a tremendously hard time getting turned around. God, in His mercy, brought to my mind words to a song by Amy Grant. The words were: "It takes a little time sometimes, to get the Titanic turned back around."

I realized that my eating issues were much larger than just the physical aspect. There were emotional, mental and spiritual issues involved as well. God is not worried about the amount of time it takes to get me completely turned around, and I should not be worried either. His mercies are new every morning, and each day is an opportunity for me to receive that mercy and find grace in my time of need.

The Titanic was a huge ship that went down; but God has assured me that even though my eating issues might be huge, I am not going down, because His mercy is much larger than my issues. Remember, it takes a little time sometimes to get the Titanic turned back around, but God has an abundance of mercy to get you back on course. Receive God's mercy and be merciful to yourself as well.

Action Item: Stop being so hard on yourself in your First Place 4 Health journey. Rest in the fact that God is not going to let you go down. His mercy and grace will get you back on course no matter how long it takes.

Prayer: *Merciful Father, thank You for Your wonderful and much-needed mercy. Help me to receive it each day and never give up on myself or on You. Help me also to be merciful to others. In Jesus' name, amen.*

Debbie Norred
Lynn Haven, Florida

backseat driver to God

Be merciful, just as your Father is merciful.

LUKE 6:36

When my husband and I are going somewhere in the car, we joke with each other about a special button in the glove compartment that when pushed produces a steering wheel and brakes on the passenger side of the vehicle. We laugh, but the point is, don't be a backseat driver.

I often think that I do this very thing to God. I begin my day with Him behind the wheel, in control and taking me down the road of life. I start with feeling compelled to assist Him by advising Him which road is better to take. When to speed up or slow down, or turn this way—no, that way. You get the picture. It's a control issue.

The Lord is very merciful. He is a gentleman who calmly allows me to eventually take the driver's seat while putting Him in the backseat. I continue on my way, but as usual, I turn the wrong way on one-way roads, come across detours and get lost. Regret and remorse inevitably set in. Oh, how I should have listened and obeyed Him from the start!

When I cry out to Him in my distress, He is so merciful to me and takes the wheel once again. When will I ever learn to keep my mouth shut and my ears open? I am so thankful that I have a loving and merciful Father who loves me in spite of myself. He reminds me that I in turn need to be merciful to others, just as He is merciful with me.

Action Item: Get a mental picture of you being a backseat driver with God the next time you feel compelled to take control or not show mercy to someone else. It's a real eye-opener.

Prayer: *Lord, please forgive me when I backseat-drive You and go my own way instead of trusting that You know best. Thank You that You are merciful and patient with me. Help me to remember to treat others with that same mercy. Amen.*

Connie Welch
First Place 4 Health Network Leader
Keller, Texas

109

all the difference in the world

Be merciful, just as your Father is merciful.

LUKE 6:36

My dad died in 2006 from an abdominal aortic aneurysm. His death was sudden and unexpected. He was a pretty healthy guy. He watched what he ate and was always ready to get into a discussion with me about the latest news on health and nutrition. We were a lot alike. We even looked alike. If you put our baby pictures next to each other, the resemblance was amazing. I was a daddy's girl and did whatever he did down to eating pickled pigs feet when I was a girl. He liked them, so I liked them. Can you imagine? An eight-year-old girl eating pigs feet? I think about it now and shudder.

I was heartbroken when he died. I missed him like crazy. In the following days and weeks, I received cards and phone calls from many of my First Place 4 Health friends. Losing my father was like a weight pressing me down. But with each call or note, I was lifted up. With each prayer for me and my family, I was carried along. For those days after he died, my First Place 4 Health family showered me with grace and mercy, and I was made better. They banded together to plan and prepare a reception for my family.

All the details that were impossible for me to focus on during that awful time were taken care of. I'm very good at hiding my feelings. But one time, several weeks later, when I was feeling bruised and beat up inside from missing him, I arrived at my First Place 4 Health class, and Diana came up and asked me how I was doing. She spoke from her own experience of losing a parent and reassured me that it was okay to have those feelings, and I would for a long time. How thoughtful of her to think of how I might still be feeling and to take the time to show how much she cared by coming up to me. That's what First Place 4 Health friends are all about—noticing and caring and making time to let each know that we do. It takes time and effort to reach out, but it's lifegiving to those you touch.

Action Item: Is there someone you know who might need an encouraging word from you? Take the time right now to write out a card or give him or her a call. It can make all the difference in the world to him or her right now.

Lisa Lewis
First Place 4 Health Director of Events
Houston, Texas

110

mercy after mercy

Be merciful, just as your Father is merciful.

LUKE 6:36

"Lord, I need mercy." I had clothes in my washer and clothes in my dryer when the lights went out. The dryer had tripped the breaker. An appliance repairman had told me I needed a new dryer, but I thought I could make it through the holidays. I reset it and plugged in my vacuum cleaner in another plug, and it tripped the breaker. Obviously, I had some serious electrical problems. Did I mention it was Thanksgiving weekend—no repairmen available?

I called my son-in-law, who is always available to help me. However, he is not an electrician, so he called his good friend and neighbor, Scott, who was also my former neighbor. Although Scott had a house full of company, he said he would come on Monday. After checking my breaker box, he bought and installed a new breaker. I purchased a new dryer that was delivered on Sunday (yes, Sunday), and we were in business. Scott had mercy on me and only charged me the cost of the breaker.

I was catching up on my laundry well into the evening hours when I smelled something burning. It was my new dryer! "Help, Scott!" He came as soon as possible and installed a new dryer plug, a new plug in my bathroom and one in my kitchen. His only charge was the cost of the dryer plug. I begged to pay him a service charge or labor, but he told me, "I just can't." Scott was the personification of our Scripture verse by showing mercy to me just as our Father is merciful.

God's greatest gift of mercy was that of sending His only Son, Jesus, to redeem us from this sinful world. He was to be called Emmanuel, which means "God with us." God is always "with us" no matter the circumstance. What comfort and peace that brings to my heart.

O give thanks unto the LORD, for he is good: for his mercy endureth forever (Psalm 136:1, *KJV*).

Prayer: *Merciful Father, how can we not show mercy to others when You have so wonderfully demonstrated mercy to us? Let my eyes ever be watchful for those who are in need of Your mercy.*

Pat Lewis
First Place 4 Health Assistant to the National Director
Houston, Texas

on-track health

For years I had joined and participated in every First Place 4 Health class available, along with many other weight-loss programs offered in my community. At the completion of each session, the result was the same. I weighed more at the end than when I began. In the final analysis, any pounds I lost were soon regained, plus a few extra. What I was doing to my body was starting to take a physical toll.

The visits to my physician were more frequent and two serious problems emerged. My blood pressure and cholesterol were consistently high. For the first time in my life, I was taking prescription drugs on a regular basis. It did not take long for me to realize that being overweight was contributing to my health problems. Eating too much was no longer a matter of lack of self-esteem or of self-confidence; it was a matter of whether I wanted to enjoy good health.

The break in the chain of failure occurred when I observed my precious daughter-in-law losing weight and maintaining her loss. I knew she was practicing all of the principles she learned through the First Place 4 Health program.

BEFORE

AFTER

Knowing that I needed to do something, I reluctantly decided to join First Place 4 Health for what seemed to be the hundredth time. The real difference this go-around was a strong desire to succeed and the confidence to stay on track.

As the weeks went by, I started to develop more confidence that I could reach my goal. I firmly believed that God was intervening on my behalf. I faithfully attended each session. My determination increased with the help of close friendships, prayer partners and God's Word.

Gradually, the weight began to come off, and after 18 months, I had lost 90 pounds. With the weight loss and regular exercise, I was feeling my best. Visits to the doctor were less frequent, and finally, the physician indicated that prescription drugs for high blood pressure and cholesterol were no longer necessary. I had truly reached my goal.

With some healthy nutritional habits established and daily exercise, I had no problem maintaining my weight, but I noticed my midriff and abdomen were not showing results or toning from the physical exercise like the rest of my body. During one session, I felt a pain as though a muscle had been strained in my abdominal region. The pain lingered for several weeks and would not go away.

A CT Scan revealed a 10-inch tumor, so surgery was scheduled the following week, with the expectation that the tumor was a fibrous growth and I shouldn't be concerned. After the surgery, I was told the tumor was malignant and I had ovarian cancer.

Had I not lost the weight, I am convinced the tumor would not have been discovered early. I never thought nutrition was so important. Today my focus and attention is clearly on the Scriptures as I cling to God's promises. My loving family and friends are constantly praying and fasting in expectation of a miracle. A prayer web page has been established and more than 400 people have signed on, most of them names I do not recognize.

In my current circumstance, God is teaching me to submit and trust Him, whether it pertains to my eating habits or to other areas of my life. No matter what this journey yields, I will praise and glorify God.

Now I share with everyone who hears my story the importance of taking charge of your health. When you have your annual physical exam, insist on the blood test that can screen for ovarian cancer.

People in the medical profession are gifts from God, but remember that our hope is in the Lord Jesus Christ.

Ruth Alderman
Rock Hill, South Carolina

MONTH 6

ENCOURAGEMENT

way to go

Encourage one another and build each other up, just as in fact you are doing.
1 THESSALONIANS 5:11

My own personal definition of the word "encouragement" is to catch someone doing something right and to tell him or her. When we encourage someone, the words we say need to be true. Encouragement can transform another person and give them hope for a brighter future.

Encouragement is an important part of the First Place 4 Health program. In our classes, we are assigned one person each week to pray for and encourage. I have never been disappointed when I take the time to call my prayer partner on the phone. I learn things about this person that I would never learn in class, and then I know how to encourage her or him even more. Getting to know another person is the key to being an encourager in a person's life.

I have seen God work miracles through the simple act of encouragement. When a woman in a miserable marriage begins to encourage her husband when she catches him doing something right, God uses her encouragement to begin the healing of her marriage. A mom or dad begins encouraging their rebellious teenager when they catch him/her doing something right, and before long, God begins to soften the child's hard heart.

Encouragement is like a soothing balm put on a bad burn; it takes away the pain. Life is hard, and all of us need those "atta girl" or "atta guy" encouragements from people in our life. I always try to remember that it takes a lot of encouragement to counteract criticism.

Criticism, rather than inducing good behavior, causes us to put up a wall. Encouragement, on the other hand, takes down those walls one brick at a time.

Action Item: Do you know someone who needs a word of encouragement from you today? Try giving encouragement instead of criticism. You won't be sorry.

Carole Lewis
First Place 4 Health National Director
Houston, Texas

112

a friend stands with you

Encourage one another and build each other up, just as in fact you are doing.
1 THESSALONIANS 5:11

The First Place 4 Health Wellness Retreat in Round Top, Texas, begins with a health assessment that includes a blood pressure check and blood draw. In previous years, I have approached this portion of the retreat with apprehension. My blood pressure always rises temporarily at the prospect of dealing with a needle. This year was no exception. Two friends attended the week with me and were aware of my nervousness. We three waited together, and when my turn came, Annie and Debbie prayed that I would be calm and trust God.

Even though my blood pressure reading was elevated, I felt calm . . . until I went to the station to have blood drawn. Annie mentioned to the nurse that I usually requested a smaller (butterfly) needle, so the nurse prepared one. Suddenly, I became aware that Debbie was lightly massaging my neck and shoulders, and I immediately began to relax. My mind wandered from the job at hand, and because of these two precious friends, I began focusing on God. I knew I was surrounded with love as I heard Annie praying quietly, while Debbie's touch on my shoulders spoke of her compassion. Before I knew it, the procedure was over! It was so much better with friends supporting and encouraging me through a challenging time.

Action Item: Are you facing a difficult challenge? Perhaps you can confide in one or two praying friends. It is better when you come together with those who care and love you through difficult times. God gave us friends to encourage and build us up and to point our thoughts to Him. When you allow friends to share your burden, the task is less painful.

Prayer: *Father, thank You for friends who are willing to stand with me, encouraging me to trust You, building me up through their love and friendship. Help me to be that kind of friend to others.*

June Chapko
First Place 4 Health Networking Leader
San Antonio, Texas

everyday encouragement

Encourage one another and build each other up, just as in fact you are doing.
1 THESSALONIANS 5:11

My neighbor Marcia lives just a few houses down from us. What a blessing she is to me as we walk together six days a week early each morning, starting out in the dark, but ending in sunrise, and thanking God for it!

One morning this week, it was apparently too early for me. I put on two shirts, as it was a chilly morning (in Texas, a *cold* morning), laced up my walking shoes and was ready to go—except, I looked down and noticed that I was still in my "glow in the dark" pajama bottoms. I quickly changed, but Marcia is such a good friend that she would have gone with me in those pj's, and we would have started our morning walk with a good laugh.

We spend the miles sharing our lives with one another—family news, church news, First Place 4 Health news, weather, sports, news-news, and always prayer requests. We build each other up, encouraging one another as the Scriptures instruct us to do, and finding the sweet fellowship our Lord wants for us. Proverbs 17:17 says, "A friend loves at all times." The Lord has blessed me with Marcia, who is that kind of friend!

Our First Place 4 Health group is also filled with encouragers! We take that part of First Place 4 Health seriously and joyfully. It is an added blessing if our friends and family outside of First Place 4 Health are encouragers too. We benefit if the people we see at home, in our neighborhood, and at our work notice our progress and support us in our efforts to live the balanced life before them and before our Lord and Savior. Encouraging one another gives us a witness to others as well. "But you will receive power when the Holy Spirit comes on you; and you will be my witnesses" (Acts 1:8).

Action Item: Looking at yourself through the eyes of another person, are you someone she would be drawn to as a friend?

Susan Ray
Houston, Texas

114

better than sleep

Encourage one another and build each other up, just as in fact you are doing.
1 THESSALONIANS 5:11

I am so thankful for the encouragement I receive from friends every day. There was a time when it was hard for me to exercise consistently. I knew that it was important to build daily exercise into my life, but other things—often, good things—came up and gave me an excuse to put it off. I finally begged God to show me how to be obedient in this area of my life.

One day, one of my neighbors invited me to walk with her and three other ladies in the morning before they went to work. That sounded great to me, but when she said that I should be out in front of my house at 5:00 A.M., I wished I had kept quiet about wanting to walk with them! As I set my alarm clock for 4:40 A.M., I thought to myself that I would try it one morning and then make some kind of excuse to avoid having to continue to get up that early.

The next morning, there were five of us walking together. They were all women who wanted to be healthy. It was particularly interesting to me that there was no neighborhood gossip, just friendly kidding around or, sometimes, sleepy silence. That was more than 10 years ago, and we have exercised every weekday since then. We walked together for several years, and then we began riding our bikes.

I am blessed with such wonderful neighbors. These days, my neighbor from across the street and I ride together every morning. I must admit that there are some mornings when I would pay lots of money to stay in bed. However, when I wake up and realize that she is dressed and waiting for me, I have no choice but to get up and get going. I am so thankful that my friend encourages me every morning. I probably would have given up long ago if it were not for her, and she, if it were not for me. We depend on one another to do this beneficial activity.

God never sleeps or slumbers (see Psalm 121:3-4). So be careful how you pray, because God may answer your prayer when you would rather be in bed!

Prayer: *Father, thank You for providing a way for me to be obedient to You. I am so grateful that You have blessed me with friends who encourage me and help me to do what I know I need to do. Thank You that I feel so much better for doing it. I love You so much.*

Dee Matthews
First Place 4 Health Networking Leader
Sugar Land, Texas

115

connecting with people

Encourage one another and build each other up, just as in fact you are doing.

1 THESSALONIANS 5:11

I was a cheerleader in high school. It was a natural fit for me, because I had lots of friends in school, and I loved to spread positive school spirit. I loved inspiring my friends on the various teams to do their best, and I loved inspiring the crowd to cheer them on. Later in life, I became a cheerleader sponsor for my daughter's cheerleading squad, where it became my role to "cheer on the cheerleaders," encouraging them to do their best, lifting them up when they got discouraged, but most of all, sharing words of encouragement and always believing in them.

We all need cheerleaders in our life, don't we? We need people to encourage us, to build us up, just as the Scripture says. The world can beat us down, and people often speak words of discouragement, even when they don't mean it. We need to overcome that with receiving large doses of encouragement, and then opening our eyes to grow in awareness of the ways that we can honestly encourage other people on a daily basis.

We should look first to those we love—our family and friends. How can we build them up? How can we be a cheerleader for them today? And then there are the people we pass every day. We might notice a stranger wearing a cute scarf and tell her that we like it. And there are people in our church who are seeking connection—those who serve there and those who have just walked in the door for the first time. As we look to the people we meet in our church, and when we are out and about in our world, we should speak uplifting words of kindness and connection as often as possible.

I am sure that God is pleased when we give unexpected encouragement to a stranger, and the smile we receive in return is a blessing back to us.

Action Item: Create an encouragement habit! Have the courage to encourage someone today. If you pray for opportunities, the Lord will provide them.

Jeannie Blocher
President, Body & Soul Fitness

116

reach out today

But encourage one another daily, as long as it is called Today,
so that none of you may be hardened by sin's deceitfulness.

HEBREWS 3:13

All of us have the need to be loved and to love in return. This basic human need can lead us down many wrong paths. Some people have chosen to walk in addiction to pornography, illicit sex, overspending or overeating. One lady told me, "Food is my lover."

I believe that we are sometimes hardened by sin's deceitfulness because another human being has not taken the time to reach out in love and encouragement to us. As Christians, God is calling us to love people unconditionally. We don't love their sin, but we love them. Love has the power to radically snatch someone from the grip of sin.

I have a friend whose son is involved in a homosexual relationship. This has been a painful transition for both my friend and her husband, but God is using their pain and calling them to work with families going through the same kind of pain.

My friends Carol and Gene Kent have a ministry to parents of children in prison. Their only child, J.P., murdered the ex-husband of his wife, and he is in prison in Florida for life, without the possibility of parole. God has used their pain in a positive way to encourage others who are experiencing the same kind of pain.

Johnny and I have experienced the pain of losing our daughter Shari after she was struck and killed by a drunk driver. God has used our pain to encourage others who are going through the same experience. Just recently, I spoke to a group of women who had each lost a child. All of these women have different stories, but every story has a common thread—their child is gone.

In 1 Peter 4:8, we are told, "Above all, love each other deeply, because love covers over a multitude of sins."

Action Item: How does God want to use your pain for good? Ask Him to bring people to you who need your encouragement so that they will not be hardened by sin's deceitfulness.

Carole Lewis
First Place 4 Health National Director
Houston, Texas

117

sincere hearts

But encourage one another daily, as long as it is called Today,
so that none of you may be hardened by sin's deceitfulness.

HEBREWS 3:13

One of the aspects I enjoy the most about a First Place 4 Health Wellness Week is being secluded and shielded from the world for seven days. The absence of electronic devices and newspapers, having freedom to enjoy or decline programmed activities, and seeing the openness of attendees and the authenticity of the staff all combine to encourage me with its atmosphere of love and sincere concern.

It is in this setting, among like-minded people, that my broken heart (broken over concern for a fractured family relationship) was healed, and my spirit refreshed and my mind renewed. When I arrived at Wellness Week, I wasn't aware of the need buried deep in the crevices of my heart. But words spoken during the outdoor worship service pricked my heart, and I confided my pain to the one who spoke. She prayed passionately with me and later sent another sweet sister to counsel with me. God gave that woman words that chipped away my need to "fix" things that I could not fix and helped me realize there was nothing more I could do about the relationship. She spoke truth and brought me out of my hurtful state into a place where I could grow and be used by God in a mighty way.

These two precious sisters-in-Christ heard my heart cry and reached out to break apart the hardened layers of hurt that could have distracted me from focusing on God's love for me.

Action Item: Do you need encouragement over a broken relationship? Has your heart hardened toward God? Ask God to send someone into your life to help you find relief.

Prayer: *Father, thank You for Christian friends who have a heart for You. Bless them as they serve You through their willingness to give of themselves to help others mend. Allow me to become more like You, so that I can be used to scatter seeds of encouragement into the lives of those who are needy.*

June Chapko
First Place 4 Health Networking Leader
San Antonio, Texas

118

a simple invitation

But encourage one another daily, as long as it is called Today,
so that none of you may be hardened by sin's deceitfulness.

HEBREWS 3:13

Lillian has been my hairdresser for 15 years, so you can imagine the conversations that have transpired while I have sat in her chair. We've discussed family, world events, books and our own struggles with weight issues.

Many years ago, I invited all of her salon staff to an evangelistic Luis Palau ladies luncheon; during that event, Lillian made a personal commitment to Christ. Since then, we've talked frequently of faith and church, seeking to mutually encourage one another.

This fall, Lillian and her husband, Tom, joined my First Place 4 Health class, even though it meets an hour from their home. The second week, she announced, "At home, I always said these stairs are going to be the *death* of me! But now that I'm moving more, I realize these stairs are going to be the *life* of me!"

Today, when I opened my email, I realized that God *always* uses our efforts to encourage one another:

> Dear Cindy, we pray for you each day and thank the Lord for your encouraging words that got us to First Place 4 Health and this wonderful Bible study. We are learning so much and enjoying the prayer together each day as a couple. It has brought us even closer to each other by the miracle of His Holy Word!! Thank you so much for your personal encouragement about my weight. I have never lost so much weight with as little ease, knowing that I am restoring the "temple" that God the Father prepared for me to house the Holy Spirit. Looking at it in this different way and putting God first has made all the difference! Blessings, Lillian

Action Item: Take a bold step this week to encourage someone with a word of hope, comfort, an offer to help or an invitation to your First Place 4 Health group. Write in your journal the person's name and the action you will take, and then pray for God's guidance and timing.

Lucinda Secrest McDowell
Christian author and speaker
Wethersfield, Connecticut

positive target fixation

But encourage one another daily, as long as it is called Today,
so that none of you may be hardened by sin's deceitfulness.

HEBREWS 3:13

Losing weight and keeping it off . . . you've heard all the plans and tried lots of the diets, but nothing seems to last. So you don't think you can do it? Well, neither did I.

There's a term in motorcycle racing called *target fixation*—when a rider's eyes focus on a point in the distance—a line, or debris on the road or race track—that causes them to inadvertently steer the bike toward that area rather than the intended path. The majority of riders fall prey to this, because it's easy to target fixate on a bump or hole in the road or something you don't want to run over. This can turn into a negative thing.

I remember when I was racing, and my focus was on the rider in front of me and not on my goal. As we approached a corner near the finish line, he missed the turn, and because I was following too closely, and my attention was too much on him, I did the same thing.

Many times, it's our culture that causes target fixation. We have the best intentions, but when we are presented with a choice (like the buffet line) we cave in. In this context, target fixation is negative, and because it's negative, we often live life like that. We say, "I can't change," so we give up. We focus on the things that block our goals, like social activities during the holidays, birthday parties and potlucks.

How do we stop negative target fixation? Maybe we need to stop thinking negatively about how losing weight will never happen and consider our goal in the long term—"Where will I be a year from now?" Let's start focusing on a closer walk with God—this is positive target fixation!—and where He wants us to be. Hebrews 12:1-2 says, "Let us run with perseverance the race marked out for us. Let us fix our eyes on Jesus, the author and perfecter of our faith." Remember, this race is long-term, and so is weight loss and maintenance. We can do this by fixing our eyes on Jesus and making target fixation a positive thing.

Prayer: *Lord, help me to follow only You and not the world. Give me the discipline to stay on course, always keeping You in my sight. Amen.*

Mike Friedler
Rochester, New York

120

no excuses!

But encourage one another daily, as long as it is called Today,
so that none of you may be hardened by sin's deceitfulness.

HEBREWS 3:13

Walking is an important part of any health regime. It is also one of the hardest habits to get started. Weather is a leading excuse for not walking, isn't it! At First Baptist Church in Houston, First Place 4 Health members could not use that excuse unless a person lived too far away to drive on a regular basis to use the Christian Life Center there. It was protected from the elements, and the folks who were there were warm and friendly. Besides providing a safe environment to walk, there is an exercise room totally equipped to give you a complete workout.

While I was living in Houston, my friend Wilma and I would often go to the Christian Life Center to walk. We found that going around the track was more fun when we were together. In fact, we often walked farther than we thought we could, because we were not concentrating on the laps but rather on having a good time. After a brisk walk, we would go down to the Garden of Eating to have a cup of coffee or a glass of iced tea.

The other day, when Wilma and I were visiting over the phone, she brought this memory up. We did have fun! We did our walking, which counted on our records as exercise, and we spent precious time building good memories. We both reside in other places now, miles from Houston and each other, but we both have been a part of First Place 4 Health groups in the area where we now live.

While living in Houston, we did not give in to the alternative of staying home and not exercising, because we found that it was just better together!

Prayer: *Dear Lord, help me encourage someone today, and give me a soft heart that is never hardened by the deceitfulness of sin.*

Betha Jean McGee
Wall, Texas

for others' benefit

Let us consider how we may spur one another on toward love and good deeds.

HEBREWS 10:24

I have seen the First Place 4 Health program used by God as a vehicle to spur others on to love and good deeds.

My friend Kay said that when she first joined the program and needed to lose more than 100 pounds, her group members were happier about her weight loss each week than they were about their own. Kay said that when she could barely walk, a neighbor invited her to walk with her every morning. When Kay tried to explain that she walked very slowly, the neighbor said, "If you have to crawl back, I'll crawl with you."

My friend Diane came into the program hating to cook. Little by little, Diane started cooking, but she really blossomed after Linda, a lady in Diane's class, offered to help her. Diane went over to Linda's house, and they shopped for groceries and cooked together. Today, Diane enjoys cooking and is becoming a great chef.

My friend Cheri has severe cerebral palsy. Cheri was suicidal and full of fear when she came into the program. The love of our group spurred Cheri on to lose more than 70 pounds, and Cheri spurred us on to exercise more each time she came into class soaking wet after walking a mile on the track with her walker.

My friend Martha has a degree in home economics. She didn't use her degree all the years that she taught high school English, but God is using her mightily in the First Place 4 Health program to spur us on to a healthier lifestyle. Martha shares so many great tips to make healthy eating fun and enjoyable.

Perhaps you have the gift of photography, scrapbooking, sewing, cooking, organizing, encouragement or teaching. God has gifted us all, and He desires for us to use our gifts to spur one another on toward love and good deeds

Action Item: Is there someone you know who needs spurring on? Use your gift to help that person today.

Carole Lewis
First Place 4 Health National Director
Houston, Texas

three types of people

Let us consider how we may spur one another on toward love and good deeds.

HEBREWS 10:24

When I was in high school, I remember our youth pastor teaching us that we need three types of people involved in our lives. We need a Paul, someone who is more spiritually mature and who can teach and encourage us. We also need a Barnabas, someone who will walk along with us and be that "son of encouragement" that we all need. And we need a Timothy, someone who is younger spiritually that we can help grow in their spiritual walk. Throughout my years in First Place 4 Health, I've enjoyed having all of these relationships.

Joann was a sweetheart of a lady who was in my group for a few sessions. She was older than I am, but younger in her faith. She and I had some great discussions regarding spiritual growth and worship, and God gave me the privilege of helping her develop a closer relationship with Him. I enjoyed those talks with Joann and seeing her grow in her faith as Timothy did.

Jennifer was a great friend before we began attending our First Place 4 Health group. Our participation together in First Place 4 Health drew us closer, showing me what a "Barnabas" I have in her. Jennifer encouraged me and spurred me on to be a better leader and friend to my group members. I knew she was there each week with a supportive attitude that gave me the strength to endure.

Two ladies have been my "Pauls" in First Place 4 Health—Diann and Susan. Susan was the first leader who pushed me to overcome my issues with food through her spiritual perspectives that helped me turn around my thinking. Diann has been a continual encouragement to me in many ways. She makes me think about things differently. I can tell her anything and know that she'll share her godly wisdom freely.

As I look over the people I've been blessed to serve with over the years, I see how God has put them in my life to grow me and to show me His love through others.

Action Item: Think through your life. Do you have a Paul? A Barnabas? A Timothy? List them out. Write them an encouraging note today to tell them how influential they have been in your life.

Kathlee Coleman
First Place 4 Health Networking Leader
Santa Clarita, California

123

yee-haw!

Let us consider how we may spur one another on toward love and good deeds.

HEBREWS 10:24

Today's Bible verse took on a whole new meaning when my middle son purchased a pair of spurs. That might seem to be an unusual thing for a young man to invest his money in, but for *this* young man, it made perfect sense.

Aaron was born with a love of horses. I have a picture of him at two, sound asleep under the dining room table with several plastic horses at his side. He used to like to play there because he imagined that the braces for the legs of the table were a corral.

From an early age, he asked for a horse. That is something many children do, but most parents have a legitimate reason to refuse—no facilities to house a horse. For us, that was not a problem. We live on a farm, so boarding a horse was not the issue. Instead, the question was if Aaron would take responsibility for a horse.

Finally, we determined that getting a horse was a good decision, so Aaron became the proud caretaker of Lady. It was sometime after Lady arrived that Aaron bought the spurs. He had no intention of using these sharp spikes to encourage Lady to move. He simply thought a good horseman should own a pair.

The Lord is not calling us to literally "spur" one another. Instead we are to encourage and prompt our fellow believers to action. We are called to urge others to make an even greater impact in the world, an even greater effort to exhibit love and good deeds.

No need to invest your hard-earned money in a set of spurs (unless you, too, are a horseman and see them as an essential part of your gear). Instead, invest in encouragement!

Action Item: Encouraging others is many times a gentle act. Take a moment and think of how you can encourage others to live out their love of Christ through good deeds.

Kendra Smiley
Christian author and speaker
East Lynn, Illinois

124

choice friends

Let us consider how we may spur one another on toward love and good deeds.

HEBREWS 10:24

I grew up on a farm, so when I see the word "spur," I know that means to push forward with a little bit of pain until you are running in your potential. That is what my First Place 4 Health friends have done for me.

My family DNA has given me the potential to die early of a heart attack, but I do not believe that my "sisters" will allow this to happen. I run an organization called Seasoned Sisters, where the word "sister" is a building term, which means to hammer two-by-fours together. My First Place 4 Health friends and my Seasoned Sisters "spur" me forward by nailing their lives to mine. They hold me accountable for making better life choices by making them *with* me.

Maria walks the 5K race by my side. Debbie and I kayak. Gail and I cycle to wellness. Kendra orders a salad when we have lunch together, instead of the dessert we both love. Carole, Gwen, Georgia and I get up early to walk city streets at sunrise. Robin, my personal assistant, prayer walks with me on "Tennis shoe Tuesdays" in my "joy zone" office. Catherine sent me a towel that reads "jubilee" to remind me to take good care of myself as I take good care of others. Penny emails me a simple *w?*, which is her way of asking if I have lifted weights that day. Carol and Gene go on active double dates with my husband and me. Vickie, who also has some harsh family DNA, prays for me as we dance away the blues with aerobics.

The Bible doesn't have the word "accountability" in it, but it has two powerful words that describe how to "spur" a friend on to wise life choices. "Exhortation" means "called alongside to bring out the best in another." "Admonish" is "to put in mind" and carries the idea of putting the right thoughts into the minds of others. So, who does God want you to "spur" on today?

Prayer: *Dear Lord, today help me spur others on by "sistering" with positive words and actions to bring out his or her best.*

Pam Farrel
Author of *Woman of Confidence: Step into God's Adventure for Your Life*
El Cajon, California

125

persistence, not perfection

Let us consider how we may spur one another on toward love and good deeds.

HEBREWS 10:24

Years ago, in my first session of First Place 4 Health, my leader, Joy Huber, spoke a word of encouragement to our group that has ministered to me ever since.

She told us that our First Place 4 Health journey was about "persistence, not perfection." She would continue to speak that encouragement over us that entire session. My heart's desire was to learn everything I could about the program and follow it without fail. But in my struggles along the way, Joy's encouraging words echoed in my mind—it's persistence, not perfection.

I am so thankful to the Lord for using Joy in such a practical way that continues to minister to me as well as to our First Place 4 Health group. Temptation will rise, faulty thinking can make us feel entrapped, discouragement can trip us up; but we need to remember that the journey we are on is indeed a journey. Sometimes I think about this journey being a race, with all of our First Place 4 Health family together on the course.

There are times when we might trip and fall. That's not the tragedy. It's when we choose not to get up and get back in the race. I think about our members cheering each other on and how that fuels our passion and gives us strength to carry on. When I am on the ground after a tumble, I see the hand of Jesus extended to me. He is speaking to me, "It's about persistence, not perfection; lean on me, and carry on."

The burden of failing to live up to perfection is too heavy. But encouragement to be persistent is vital to our health and wellness. It is fuel for our hope and passion to live in the freedom of Christ.

Action Item: In what ways can you spur others on with encouragement toward love and good deeds? You may never know how the impact of your encouragement may be the hand of Christ reaching out to help someone up.

Prayer: *Dear Lord, may You use me as Your instrument to spur others on so that You can make a difference in their lives.*

Connie Welch
First Place 4 Health Network Leader
Keller, Texas

126

the back of the tapestry

You hear, O LORD, the desire of the afflicted;
you encourage them, and you listen to their cry.

PSALM 10:17

I have a long history of walking with God, and I can testify to the truth of this verse.

- God heard me when, as a 12-year-old girl, I asked Jesus into my heart.
- God heard me when, as a 42-year-old woman, I cried out for Him to make me willing to be willing.
- God heard us when my husband, Johnny, was diagnosed with stage 4 prostate cancer in 1997, with only a two-year life expectancy.
- God heard us when our middle child, Shari, was killed by a drunk driver on Thanksgiving night in 2001.
- God heard us when our home was destroyed by Hurricane Ike in 2008.

In every single instance, God not only heard our cry, but He also encouraged us because He listened to us. How did He encourage us? The most important method God used was His Word and the truth found in its pages.

God has also used all the Scripture I have committed to memory to encourage me. Scripture memory is one of the greatest parts of the First Place 4 Health program. As we memorize the verses in our First Place 4 Health Bible studies, God continues to bring those verses to remembrance whenever we cry out to Him.

I have heard it said that our life is but a weaving of various threads—a tapestry of which we see only the back side. God, on the other hand, sees the front of the tapestry and has a plan to weave every affliction of our life into a beautiful picture that shows how He used it for our good and for His glory.

Do I understand this truth at all? No, but I have experienced it, so I believe it. God has not only encouraged us in our afflictions, but He has used them to encourage others who are also going through a time of pain.

Action Item: Write in your journal about a time of affliction you have gone through or are going through right now. Cry out to Him and ask Him to encourage your heart. He will hear and answer you.

Carole Lewis
First Place 4 Health National Director
Houston, Texas

stand strong!

You hear, O Lord, the desire of the afflicted;
you encourage them, and you listen to their cry.

PSALM 10:17

My childhood was marked by traumatic events that produced a lifestyle of emotional pain. As an adult, I became caretaker for both of my parents. Food became an addiction and resulted in major health problems. I wanted to die. Daily I asked, "God, why did You wake me up?" Now I ask, "Lord, what are we doing today?" That transformation began to take place through knowledge of God's Word, the work of the Holy Spirit and encouragement from First Place 4 Health friends.

Sometimes our journey takes an unexpected turn. On March 26, 2005, I was almost killed in an auto accident. In the ER, although my body showed no visible signs of injury or pain, further diagnosis revealed the true picture of my life-threatening injuries. My family was told that I would not live. When I did live, I was told that I might never walk again. But I did learn to walk again!

My nephew contacted Beverly Henson, a First Place 4 Health friend, informing her of the accident. Within 24 hours, prayers and encouragement from First Placers (some I had never met) began to pour in! Their outpouring of love was so incredible that hospital staff came to see and ask who I was. The day before I went home, a hospital volunteer delivered more gifts and cards and asked, "Are you someone special?" My answer was, "Yes, I am a child of the King." She asked, "What country?" I said, "All of them!" Through her tears, she responded, "I am too!"

I stand amazed in the presence of a loving, powerful and holy God! The physical therapist told me that before I could walk again, I must learn to stand. Standing is more than a physical position; it also is a mental, emotional and spiritual position. We are able to stand strong through the promises and instruction contained in God's Word, and the support of prayers and encouragement from God's people. God hears the cries of His children and leaves evidence of His presence in every situation!

Prayer: *Lord, give me the strength to stand strong mentally, physically and spiritually. Help me to see who needs a card or helping hand today.*

Stephanie Rhodes
First Place 4 Health Networking Leader
Arlington, Tennessee

128

fill 'er up!

You hear, O LORD, the desire of the afflicted;
you encourage them, and you listen to their cry.

PSALM 10:17

I have a gauge on my car that tells me how many miles 'til empty. So many times, I let that number get really low. I have actually let it get all the way to zero and kept going! How foolish is that! My husband calls it driving on fumes and a prayer. The simple thing would be to take the time to stop and fuel up my car. But as I am driving, I make excuses like, "I'll get gas on the way back when I have more time."

How many of us do life based on that same concept? Many of us give so much of ourselves that we may be on the brink of exhaustion and running on empty. In order to be the best we can be for the Lord, we need to take care of ourselves in every area—physically, mentally, emotionally and spiritually. We need to intentionally keep our tanks full.

Right now I am experiencing a deep weariness in my soul from the death of my mother. She had a yearlong bout with lung cancer. As you can imagine, the traveling, the phone calls and a constant concern for her wellbeing have taken a toll. So I am very intentional about doing my quiet time with the Lord, eating well and making sure that I am exercising regularly. But what has really kept me going is encouragement. Knowing that my First Place 4 Health family is crying out to the Lord on my behalf has filled my tank and my heart!

I know that God has heard the desire of the afflicted as we have walked through this illness with my mother, and it has made all the difference.

Prayer: *Oh Lord, use me today to fill someone's tank. I ask You to encourage those who are afflicted. Thank You for hearing their cry.*

Vicki Heath
First Place 4 Health Associate Director
Edisto Beach, South Carolina

129

side by side

You hear, O LORD, the desire of the afflicted;
you encourage them, and you listen to their cry.

PSALM 10:17

I arrived at the First Place 4 Health Wellness Retreat in Round Top, Texas, on October 7, 2010, and had no idea what to expect. My group leader, Monique Johnson, who encouraged me to attend, said, "It will be an adventure like no other." Well, that was putting it mildly! As I stepped off the bus, I knew something great was in store for me. The love, concern and encouragement the staff gave to all of us were such a blessing.

"God, how I have cried to You for help with my back pain and to give me strength to walk without pain, if it is Your will." God must have a large binder to contain all my tears and pleas for His help. I came to the Wellness Retreat with a back brace and a cane, but God walked by my side, and for the last five days and a total of 22 miles, I did not once have to use the brace or the cane—not once.

I received so much encouragement by just being in that beautiful and godly environment. "God, I gladly get on my knees and thank You."

Prayer: *Father in heaven, You are the great physician. Thank You for hearing my cry and providing such a wonderful place to bring healing to my body and soul.*

Janet McCluskey
Attleboro, Massachusetts

130

waiting for rescue

You hear, O LORD, the desire of the afflicted;
you encourage them, and you listen to their cry.

PSALM 10:17

When I was a new Christian, the story of Moses and God's rescue of the Israelites took on a very personal meaning in my life, a message that was reinforced when I joined First Place 4 Health. The Israelites, God's chosen people, had been crying out for deliverance; and God, in His perfect wisdom, sent an unlikely deliverer in the form of Moses—a murderer. With God's power and direction, Moses helped free the afflicted from their slavery. God had indeed heard their cries for help, and He responded with an awe-inspiring rescue, ultimately featuring a parting of the sea and their enemies being destroyed.

For years, like the Israelites, I'd been crying out to the Lord for a new life, for Him to save me from slavery. I was not held captive by a dominating nation, but I was captive to my own sinful desires that left me feeling empty and alone, afraid and hopeless. Even as God's child, I wondered at times if He truly heard my call. I questioned why He didn't respond faster to my suffering. *Where was my Moses?*

I suspect the Israelites wondered the very same things before Moses' long-anticipated return and rescue. In Psalm 10:17, many, many years following the historic escape from Egypt, David penned a promise that affords us great encouragement today: God hears. He encourages. He listens to our cries. He can rescue us from our own personal "Egypt."

For me, First Place 4 Health was a major part of that rescue process. Just as God provided daily manna from heaven for the weary Israelites traveling across the desert, the First Place 4 Health program has provided the tools and support I needed to find freedom and hope from years of unhealthy behaviors, giving me and so many others reason to celebrate. Even now, God hasn't forgotten us. He still hears our cries and will encourage us in our times of need. We can expect His best.

Action Item: Make a list of the ways in which God encourages you. Has He delivered you from captivity? Take time to share with someone how He rescued you from your personal Egypt. Your story not only serves to encourage you, but it also encourages others who are waiting for God's rescue.

Carol VanAtta
Troutdale, Oregon

INSPIRATIONAL STORY
a God-blessed health diagnosis

People at my church always asked, "How are you?" Should I be honest? Should I just say the typical answer: "Fine"? I wondered this for six months as I was plagued by physical ailments I could not explain. Nothing made me sick enough to stay down; yet, I was not feeling well. I did numerous Internet searches, trying to diagnose myself. At last I came to this conclusion: I was diabetic.

It was a Sunday night when I realized that I must be a Type 2 diabetic. I knew immediately that I wanted this kept secret. The doctor had warned me years earlier that if I didn't change my behavior, watch what I ate and get more exercise, I eventually would become a diabetic. I was angry and embarrassed with myself for not following his advice.

After a call to my doctor and a subsequent 12-hour fasting blood test, it proved that I was indeed a Type 2 diabetic. I was sent to the emergency room

BEFORE   AFTER

for a dangerously high blood count reading. This also made me angry, because I wanted my diabetes kept secret, and now everyone would know. As I lay in the ER, I let God hear my complaints. His reply came gently, "This is not about you; this is about others." I immediately understood what God was telling me. My anger disappeared with my next heartbeat.

I understood why God had spoken these words, because nine months before this, I had been asked to lead a women's weight-loss Bible study. I did my research and found First Place 4 Health study guides in our local Christian bookstore. I began to lead these discussions every week. We were in our third book at the time I was diagnosed with diabetes.

No one in the group was being very successful at losing weight, yet I kept encouraging each one to do the lesson. I kept promising the girls that this Bible study was not about weight loss; it was about being obedient to God. I also knew that given enough time, and by constantly staying in a close relationship with God through prayer, Bible study and being unified with other Christian women doing the same, eventually the weight would start to slide off. We even had a name for our study—we called it "Side-effect: Weight loss."

This has proven to be true. At the time I started leading our First Place 4 Health study, I weighed 283 pounds; and when I was diagnosed nine months later, I weighed the same. I may not have lost weight during this time, but my relationship with God had grown. When God spoke to me in the ER, I was ready to hear His voice.

I no longer am angry for being a Type 2 diabetic. I have given God any fear of this disease. In return, God has helped me shed more than 100 pounds and regain physical strength.

The encouragement I received from church elders and friends, the girls of the First Place 4 Health study, my family and other friends, has been a powerful, positive force in my life. I joined a gym and have gained new friends there who shower me with encouragement. My doctor monitors my progress closely. I look to prayer, exercise, diet and relationships with these people to help me lose more weight.

I do not know what my future holds, but I do know who holds my future. The verses we memorize in First Place 4 Health have been a great help. My favorite verse is Galatians 6:9: "Let us not become weary in doing good, for at the proper time we will reap a harvest if we do not give up." God never gave up on me, and I will not give up either.

Margaret Keaton
Montague, Michigan

MONTH 7

HARMONY

131

living in harmony (part one)

Live in harmony with one another; be sympathetic,
love as brothers, be compassionate and humble.

1 PETER 3:8

The verse above could be used as a tried-and-true recipe for a successful career as a boss, employee, friend or marriage partner. This verse commands us to live in harmony with one another and then tells us how to do it. Living in harmony means we don't fly off the handle when things don't go our way. We live out the true meaning of love as spoken so eloquently in 1 Corinthians 13:4: "Love is patient, love is kind. It does not envy, it does not boast, it is not proud." Let's look at the first two characteristics it takes to live in harmony: sympathy and brotherly love.

Sympathy. I love it when someone understands me and loves me when I am going through a rough time. Being sympathetic means that we love another person enough to stand by him or her until that person reaches the other side. Recently, a lady in one of our classes had serious shoulder surgery, and it was beautiful to see how our members rallied around her to shop, cook and take her to physical therapy until she was able to function again on her own.

Brotherly love. Living in love also means to love as brothers and sisters in the Lord. Many years ago, our son, John, was up on the roof of our home. A bully down the street was in our yard and started pushing his sister Shari around. John never even gave a thought to the danger of jumping off our roof, because he saw that his sister was in danger. He jumped off the roof in a flash to stand up for his sister. I have some Christian friends, and I imagine you do too, who are closer to me than an actual blood relative. This is what it means to love as brothers. We stand up for our friends and protect them when they can't protect themselves.

To be continued tomorrow . . .

Prayer: *Dear Lord, I want to live in harmony with everyone. Help me to be sympathetic and loving to others today, in every situation. Use me as a vessel of peace in my world.*

Carole Lewis
First Place 4 Health National Director
Houston, Texas

132

living in harmony (part two)

*Live in harmony with one another; be sympathetic,
love as brothers, be compassionate and humble.*

1 PETER 3:8

I wrote about this verse yesterday, but there is so much richness in it that I just had to take another day to do it justice. I believe that one of the hardest things we do in this life is to live in harmony with one another. Today, let's look at the last two characteristics it takes to live in love: compassion and humility.

Compassion. To be compassionate means to put yourself in another person's place. Compassionate people feel our pain and make every effort to help in any way they can. When our daughter Shari was killed by a drunk driver in 2001, the daughter of a dear friend recruited a friend of hers, and the two of them drove from Yorktown, Texas, to our home in Galveston Bay and stayed for several days in our home, cooking and cleaning for our family. I used to have a plaque in our home that said, "One kind deed is worth many kind thoughts." These two ladies personified the meaning of the words on that plaque.

Humilty. True humility is a character trait that is beautiful to behold. A truly humble person does nice things for others and doesn't care if he or she gets credit. Recently, we were in Oswego, New York, for a First Place 4 Health Hope 4 You event. We mentioned that we would love to purchase some New York apples to take home with us. At the end of the conference, the pastor of the church where we had the event had gone out and purchased four huge sacks of different kinds of apples for us to be able to take home with us. This act told me a lot about the humility of this man of God. True humility seeks to bless others without a thought of self-promotion.

Action Item: Is there someone who is struggling with their circumstances and needs compassion from you today? Is there an area where you could practice humility . . . like doing a chore that isn't yours to do but would help someone else?

Carole Lewis
First Place 4 Health National Director
Houston, Texas

133

helpful confession

Live in harmony with one another; be sympathetic,
love as brothers, be compassionate and humble.

1 PETER 3:8

Scripture memory is so important in First Place 4 Health, but for some, it is a difficult thing to put into practice. In my class one day, one of the ladies blurted, "I'm embarrassed to admit it, but I don't know where all the books in the Bible are located!" Several others said, "Me, too!" I could see the relief on some of their faces.

So often, we think we are the only one who didn't lose weight this week; the only one who can't eat just one bite of dessert; the only one who doesn't know how to write down lunch on her (his) First Place 4 Health tracker. So, we sit there silently and feel like we're not as good as the others, or that we've failed.

On another day, someone in the class shared that she had eaten three pounds of candy over the past week. She had excuses for why she did it—this bad thing had happened that week, and so on, but it led others to admit that sometimes they rebel like that too! When you admit something like that in class, it lifts a weight off others who might also be struggling in that same area, and the confession begins an important discussion. Many times, group members will mention things that helped them. It frees everyone to talk about things they might have been embarrassed to share. Just saying something out loud and getting it out of the dark and into the light can start someone on the path to success in that area.

If you think that you shouldn't go to class because you had a bad week, or that you shouldn't speak up because you're embarrassed, keep in mind that sometimes you're going to class or sharing your struggles to help someone else, as well as yourself.

Prayer: *Lord, give me the strength to humble myself and share my struggles, to seek the support of my friends and classmates and to trust them with my concerns.*

Lisa Lewis
First Place 4 Health Director of Events
Houston, Texas

134

going out of your way

Live in harmony with one another; be sympathetic,
love as brothers, be compassionate and humble.

1 PETER 3:8

Debbie drives a long way to our First Place 4 Health class and sometimes uses the extra time between work and class to get a bit of shopping done. Last night, she was leaving Target when she happened upon a woman sitting on the curb with lots and lots of packages but no transportation in sight. Our Bible study lesson for the week had been on reaching out to others with compassion, so Debbie was prompted in her spirit not to simply ignore the situation right in front of her. "Are you waiting for someone to pick you up?" Debbie inquired, tentatively.

"Yup, but it doesn't look like he's gonna show . . . how will I ever get all these bags back to my place in Hartford tonight?" the woman replied.

As Debbie consulted both her watch and her will, she knew what "seeking God first" would mean in this situation. "I'll be happy to drive you home," she said.

When they arrived at the high-rise apartments where the woman lived, there was only a moment's concern about toting everything up many flights to the woman's apartment. Why? Because as soon as Deb had parked, a young man from the neighborhood came up to the car and offered his help. Just as God had provided Deb for this woman, He had also provided the man for Deb so she could get to class on time after her detour.

I must admit that as Deb shared this story with our small group, I wondered if I would have done the same thing in her place. In the Bible, Peter reminds us to love as brothers by being "compassionate and humble." Seeing a need and stepping in to fill it is exactly what brothers, sisters and the whole family of God *do*!

Living in harmony doesn't mean just getting along with those we know and like and enjoy. It also means reaching out as a bridge to those in the wider community, perhaps even to those who are quite different from us. If we make the effort, God will meet us there and honor our compassion.

Prayer: *Lord, help me to seek You first in every situation and to be compassionate and humble to those I encounter each day. Help me to reach out as a bridge to those in my community.*

Lucinda Secrest McDowell
Christian author and speaker
Wethersfield, Connecticut

135

couples' weight loss

Live in harmony with one another; be sympathetic,
love as brothers, be compassionate and humble.

1 PETER 3:8

My first husband, Ray, joined a different group than I did in First Place 4 Health. He could not attend on Tuesday mornings, and I was busy on Sunday nights in the preschool department. We were both doing the same Bible study, so we tried to work on it together in the evening if he was home. We had some lively discussions. Ray was a perfectionist with everything he did. I had problems doing the Bible study as quickly as he did, because my mind has a tendency to wander or to want to look up something else that might add to what I am studying.

I would write the memory verse on the bathroom mirror so that we could both learn it more easily and quickly. We both carried paper with the verse written on it to review as we went through the day.

When things got difficult was when Ray started losing weight at a much faster rate than I did! Of course, it seems like that is the nature of things. I was working as hard as he was, but the scale did not show it! When Ray realized how difficult it was for me to see the weight fall off him while my weight seemed to cling like a screaming child, he became sympathetic and compassionate—encouraging me that if I kept up the work, I would reach my goal as well.

Fortunately, in San Angelo, when there was a couple attending a First Place 4 Health group, Barbara Clark was quick to tell the wife to be patient. She could meet her goal but shouldn't expect to lose pound for pound with her husband since his greater muscle mass meant faster weight loss.

Ray has gone home to be with the Lord. Now, if I can just convince my present husband, Harold, that things go better together when we are in a First Place 4 Health class . . .

Action Item: If you are in a coed class, show compassion to those who are not losing weight as quickly as others.

Betha Jean McGee
Wall, Texas

1 3 6

living easy

How good and pleasant it is when brothers live together in unity!

PSALM 133:1

In 1963, Johnny and I had three little ones under the age of four. It was a busy but happy time of life for us. Our children were so close in age that we had three preschoolers at the same time, three in elementary school and then, horror of horrors, three teenagers!

The saddest part of having our children so close together was that they were all gone from home in a little over a year's time. Lisa and Kent married in September 1980, Shari and Jeff married in February 1981, and John started to college in August 1982.

From the time our children were old enough to quarrel, I quoted a saying to them that I have no recollection of its source: *Little birds in their nest agree.* The idea behind this saying is that little birds that fight in their nest will fall from the nest before they are old enough to survive on their own.

I believe the saying has value for adults, too, because life is so much more pleasant when we live together in unity. Living is easier when we don't have to live it alone. God gives us family to love, even during the times when our family members might not be very lovable.

There were times when our children were angry and said hurtful things. Johnny and I tried to never take it personally but to understand that home was a safe place to unload their anger and frustration. They knew that their parents would forgive them unconditionally.

How much better it is for us to pour out our frustration to God, our heavenly Father, instead of the people we are living life with every day! God hears, cares and heals our every hurt, and He will teach us how to live together in unity.

Action Item: Is there a member of your earthly family who needs a loving word or touch from you today? Why not pick up the phone and call or send a card to this person?

Carole Lewis
First Place 4 Health National Director
Houston, Texas

137

paradox explained

How good and pleasant it is when brothers live together in unity!

PSALM 133:1

I felt a conflict of emotion driving away from Round Top Retreat. All week I had felt loved and absolutely accepted by the other "campers" at the First Place 4 Health Wellness Retreat. I, in turn, found myself feeling very close to women I had just met. It was beautiful.

Now, as I watched everyone scurry to their cars with their luggage, it seemed they were only concerned with getting home. *They don't really care about me,* floated from my subconscious. I knew that was crazy, because of the "care" I'd received all week. The next thought was definitely a divine counterattack from God: *It's from Jesus. He supplies the care and concern received from other Christians.*

Their care was true and genuine, and they really do like me, but God gives them the means to love me. I don't ever have to depend on anyone to make me feel loved, and all the attributes that come with that love. Only Jesus—He's all I need, and He's always available. With that, I smiled in blessed understanding that because true love comes from God, I don't always have to see it from all the people, all the time. What a wonderful, warm and fuzzy revelation!

"And so we know and rely on the love God has for us. God is love. Whoever lives in love lives in God, and God in him" (1 John 4:16).

Action Item: Do you need to release someone from the duty of always showing you the "right" amount of love? Ask God to remind you daily that He alone is the ultimate source of your happiness, even and especially when it comes from other Christians.

Prayer: *Precious Father, thank You so much for loving me through my beautiful Christian sisters. Help me always to realize that it comes from You. Love others through me—that is perfect and ever true.*

Beth Serpas
Houston, Texas

138

spa sisters

How good and pleasant it is when brothers live together in unity!

PSALM 133:1

So what happens when you put 25 high-powered authors and speakers together in a country lodge for a whole week of nutrition, exercise, soul care, laughter, worship and seeking God's face? Chaos . . . envy . . . pretense . . . competition?

Make that harmony . . . acceptance . . . support . . . authenticity. And, may I just agree with the psalmist that it is indeed "good and pleasant" to live together in this spirit of unity. So much so that I truly treasure this Wellness Retreat at the beginning of each new year with my spa sisters. First Place 4 Health invests in the spiritual, emotional, physical and mental health of those of us who spend the rest of the year ministering through conferences and books.

Here, we can be real with one another and share from our hearts all that concerns us personally and professionally. Here we can walk, bike and even dance together on our own terms, not fearing judgment or comparisons. We can ask each other the hard questions and challenge one another to dig deeper, take a risk or maybe even slow down, if that's what seems necessary at the time.

When God is at the center of our relationships, we share a bond and depth that inspires loyalty, prayer support and true friendship. We are able to rejoice when sisters rejoice and weep when they weep. Would you like this kind of fellowship in your own life? Perhaps you should consider starting a prayer support group, an affinity group or plan to attend one of the First Place 4 Health Wellness Weeks.

Harmony is indeed a beautiful thing.

Prayer: *Lord, thank You for friends and colleagues and fellow travelers on our journey of faith. May we always keep You at the center of our relationship, and may our lives honor You. Amen.*

Lucinda Secrest McDowell
Christian author and speaker
Wethersfield, Connecticut

139

unity pleases the Father

How good and pleasant it is when brothers live together in unity!

PSALM 133:1

Just yesterday, I was visiting with a father of four adult children ranging in age from 20 to 32; as I asked him about his life, he said he spends most of his time trying to get all of his kids together so that he can just sit and watch. The next day they were all going on a trip together, just the siblings, and he and his wife were going to watch their first grandchild. He was beaming!

Oh yes, it is good and pleasant for "brothers" to dwell together in unity, but how much joy it gives the Father in heaven to see His children playing well together. In the third epistle of John, God says through the apostle, "I have no greater joy than to hear that my children are walking in the truth" (3 John 1:4). John was talking about his spiritual children, but I believe that is also a word from the Father that we bring Him joy when we walk in truth.

However, this unity is not conformity. The children of God don't all look and act alike. There are different forms of worship. Different expressions of the spiritual gifts. Different styles of preaching. Different types of baptism. These differences should not divide us, but bring us closer together as we see God's unique characteristics displayed in others. If the differences are nonessentials in the faith, then instead of judging, criticizing or belittling these differences, we need to celebrate the awesomeness of God that through His Spirit we can be one, even though it seems impossible to the world. And when that happens, the brothers and sisters are rejoicing, the Father is pleased and the world is amazed! Now isn't that good?

Action Item: Ask God to reveal to you if there is any prejudice or criticism in your heart toward other brothers and sisters in Christ. If so, study the Word and ask yourself if these are essentials to the faith. If not, then ask God to soften your heart toward them and be willing to do what He calls you to do.

Becky Turner
First Place 4 Health Speaker
Houston, Texas

140

double joy

How good and pleasant it is when brothers live together in unity!

PSALM 133:1

When I arrived at the 2010 First Place 4 Health Wellness Retreat, I had a back brace and a cane due to chronic back pain. I'm usually limited in the physical activity in which I can participate. Well, the Lord did a miraculous thing while I was there. Not once did I use my back brace or my cane that whole week. I walked every day and was even able to attend First Place 4 Health Fitness Instructor Debbie Brown's Pilates class.

During her class, I was having great difficulty with my balance. I was unable to balance on one foot with my arms outstretched and eyes closed. I looked to my right and saw Betsy also struggling. I reached over and said, "Let's hold hands." We just touched our hands together and, lo and behold, we did it! With our hands locked together, we had perfect balance! What joy!

How true this is as we struggle in other areas of life. With the support of our friends, our group, our First Place 4 Health leader and, of course, our Lord, we are able to achieve balance. As God was holding Betsy's hand and my hand together, we became forever friends. Thank You, Jesus! Thank You!

Betsy also had great success during that week. She was able to ride a bike all during the week and she participated in every exercise class offered. At the end of the retreat, Betsy won the award for losing the most weight during our week together.

It has been two months since the Wellness Retreat, and I am still pain free. God performed a physical healing miracle for three women that week, and I am forever grateful to be one of them. I know He performed many other miracles that might not have been so obvious, but miracles, nonetheless.

Action Item: Who might need your helping hand to balance during an unsteady time in her (his) life?

Janet McClusky
Attleboro, Massachusetts

Betsy Dunn
Henry, Tennessee

work in love

I appeal to you, brothers, in the name of our Lord Jesus Christ,
that all of you agree with one another so that there may be no divisions among
you and that you may be perfectly united in mind and thought.

1 CORINTHIANS 1:10

I can't think of a more miserable situation than to work five days a week with people who can't agree with each other on how things need to be done. I am a blessed woman to be able to work with my dear friends Pat Lewis, Vicki Heath and Bob Matthews. I also am privileged to work with my daughter, Lisa Cramer, and my daughter-in-love, Lisa Lewis. People are amazed that we love working together so much, but they see it in action at our Wellness Retreat each October.

Working together as one unit, though many different parts, is nothing more than being allowed to work in the gifts you have been given from God. My assistant, Pat, is the "behind the scenes" person who keeps us all going in the same direction. Lisa Cramer has the gifts of administration and service, which give her the ability to handle our customer service and also plan all the meals for the Wellness Retreat. Lisa Lewis also has the gift of administration and is perfectly suited to handle every detail of the Wellness Retreats and many other events we have each year. Vicki is perfectly suited to work with our First Place 4 Health Networking Leaders and to function as the associate director of the program. Bob keeps us all on the same page with finances.

The reason we work so well together is that we all first love God and then we all love each other. We have a deep respect for each other and for the calling on each of our lives.

Action Item: Write in your journal about the problems and challenges in your work or at home. Ask God to help you to never be the person who is disagreeable or causes division at work or at home.

Carole Lewis
First Place 4 Health National Director
Houston, Texas

142

united we stand

I appeal to you, brothers, in the name of our Lord Jesus Christ,
that all of you agree with one another so that there may be no divisions among
you and that you may be perfectly united in mind and thought.

1 CORINTHIANS 1:10

Each summer, First Place 4 Health has their annual Leadership Summit in Houston, Texas. Leaders from all over the country and Canada make the trek to Houston to spend two days with other leaders. It's a wonderful time of fellowship, training, inspiration and fun. Attendance has ranged from 42 in 2003 to 309 in 2008. It's a huge undertaking that involves many details.

This event is one-of-a-kind and empowers leaders to go out and "lead loud" for Christ and First Place 4 Health. Because of that, we've learned to expect attacks from Satan every year. When crazy things start to go wrong, we just look at each other and laugh, because we should have known it was coming. But through it all, Christ's love shines through everyone.

Just when I feel like so many things are going wrong and it cannot possibly be a good event, someone will come up and tell me a heartbreaking story about all that has happened to them that year, but that this event has renewed their strength. Someone else will come up and say, "Lisa, what can I do?" Or someone else will say, "You guys are doing a great job. This is awesome!" A staff member might say, "No big deal, why don't we just do it this way?"

And after it's all over, and I look back, I'm overcome with emotion at how much First Place 4 Health people care about each other. We are part of this big family that truly is united in mind and thought. We lift each other up; we listen, we care, we encourage and we love one another, as Christ loves us—and we are made better, together.

Action Item: Is there someone who needs a call or an email of encouragement from you today? Stand with that person in her weakness. You will be amazed at what two or more can do together.

Lisa Lewis
First Place 4 Health Director of Events
Houston, Texas

143

planting seeds

I appeal to you, brothers, in the name of our Lord Jesus Christ,
that all of you agree with one another so that there may be no divisions among
you and that you may be perfectly united in mind and thought.

1 CORINTHIANS 1:10

What kind of seed is in your heart today? Is it a seed of love and obedience . . . or is it a seed of pride, selfishness and divisiveness?

God gives us talents and gifts to use in service and blessing to others. Especially as women, God designed us to nurture, love and serve. People should easily recognize each of us as a sincere, genuine, trustworthy, willing servant of the Lord. Therefore, we need to be careful how we conduct ourselves. We should never engage in gossip, slander or coarse jesting, and we should never do anything to cause disunity. If we are serving our pastor, our boss, our spouse, children, our neighbors or friends, we are ultimately serving the Most High God, and He will empower us to do what He has called us to do.

We are called to a high standard. Consider your conduct. Surround yourself with wise, godly people. Choose your words and actions wisely and carefully. The seed in your heart will be planted in others as they observe how you live your life.

Pray always for the Lord's guidance, discernment and strength to carry out His design for your life. Spend time with Him in His Word and in prayer. Ask Him to use you as the tool through which His purposes are accomplished in the lives of people you come into contact with. Be the woman in your church family that sets the standard for purity and holiness. Be united with your brothers and sisters in everything you do and say. Your behavior will influence everyone you interact with.

You are a candidate today for God's blessing, and you should desire that blessing in you to spill out onto every person whose life you touch.

Action Item: What kind of seed are you planting in others today?

Prayer: *Precious heavenly Father, please help me to be a woman with a faithful spirit that always conceals a matter and never gossips or criticizes (see Proverbs 11:13). May I be known as an encourager and Christ-follower.*

P. J. Bahr
Rapid City, South Dakota

144

keeping your balance

I appeal to you, brothers, in the name of our Lord Jesus Christ,
that all of you agree with one another so that there may be no divisions among
you and that you may be perfectly united in mind and thought.

1 CORINTHIANS 1:10

What does an orchestra sound like when all the musicians are tuning their instruments at the same time? It sounds like a lot of disconnected noise. Yet, when the maestro lifts his baton and gives the downbeat, we hear the start of a melodious harmony. Each musician is responding to the conductor, playing the designated notes for that instrument, uniting with the others to produce sounds that are beautiful and inspiring.

If a car is out of alignment, soon the tires begin to wear unevenly and the shocks don't perform their duty to absorb bumps on uneven roads. The ride will be very bumpy and noisy. Once the wheels are realigned, the car will run smoothly and quietly. Even the gas mileage will improve.

Our bodies are just like that out-of-tune orchestra or misaligned car when we are out of balance. If the lung refuses to breathe because it is angry with the heart, we will be "flat lining." If an organ is diseased and not functioning, it affects the overall response of the system of which it is a part. All organs and systems must be in tune and working together for the body to function as God designed it.

Likewise, to be all that God created us to be, all parts of our lives must be working in balance—physically, mentally, emotionally and spiritually. The orchestra conductor has a score to follow and leads the musicians through it. The mechanic has a manual to guide him in maintaining all the parts of the car. We have Christ, the Bible, prayer and the Holy Spirit to help us maintain a balanced life, united with Christ in mind and thought and living in harmony with others.

Action Item: Is any one of the four main areas of your life—body, emotions, mind, spirit—out of alignment with the other parts? If you need realignment in that area of your life, what steps will you take today to start the process?

Prayer: *Father God, keep our lives in balance so we can be united with You and use our gifts appropriately to build Your kingdom and bring You glory.*

Gigi Falstrom
Irving, Texas

145

be at peace

I appeal to you, brothers, in the name of our Lord Jesus Christ,
that all of you agree with one another so that there may be no divisions among
you and that you may be perfectly united in mind and thought.

1 CORINTHIANS 1:10

Where there is harmony, there is peace. There is nothing more precious than being perfectly united in mind and thought with others. If you are human, then you know what it feels like to be at odds with others! It is pure misery. It affects every part of your being. Tension fills the air almost as thick as fog, and you can't see anything else. Your thoughts are turbulent. It feels like the wheels of progress have slowed down to a mere crawl.

There is nothing that will take me to my knees quicker than broken fellowship. Division is the breeding ground for all kinds of grief. Many times what we cannot see is the barricade of pride standing in the way of harmony. It's the wooden plank in our eye that we overlook as we concentrate on the speck in someone else's. Before long, we begin singing the "shoulda, coulda, woulda" blues.

None of this leads to a happy place. Jesus came so that we could live in harmony and fellowship with God and with each other. The first step to restoring that fellowship is to examine our own prideful thoughts. The second step is to ask forgiveness from God and anyone with whom you are at odds. God's Word clearly tells us that we need to be on guard against any division. If we are not careful, this break in harmony can become a foothold for Satan to divide and destroy our relationships and witness for Christ.

If you have experienced a break in fellowship with someone, remember, the Lord is in the restoration business, and He can turn discord into harmony and peace once again.

Prayer: *Lord, thank You that all peace and restoration begins with You. Help me take the steps I need to take to restore harmony in my relationships with others.*

Connie Welch
First Place 4 Health Networking Leader
Keller, Texas

146

have a great day!

If it is possible, as far as it depends on you, live at peace with everyone.

ROMANS 12:18

This verse is broken into three distinct phrases. If we only look at the last phrase "live at peace with everyone," we see the verse as quite impossible to live out in daily life. Some people are just not peaceful, and they seem to always be stirring up trouble.

The keys to this verse, however, are the first two phrases: "If it is possible, as far as it depends on you." These two phrases put most of the responsibility for living a peaceful life on each of us. What would this look like? Here are some examples:

- I don't react when someone shakes his or her fist at me in traffic.
- I show kindness to the clerk when she is rude to me.
- I sincerely apologize when a neighbor is angry because our dog tipped over their trash can.

Does doing any of these things make me a wimp or a wet dishrag? No, quite the contrary. The Bible has a lot to say about keeping the peace. Proverbs 15:1 says, "A gentle answer turns away wrath." Psalm 34:14 says to "Turn from evil and do good; seek peace and pursue it."

Johnny and I have been married for more than 50 years, and we have finally learned how to live this verse. The way we do this is to realize that everyone has a bad day from time to time, but rarely do both of us have a bad day on the same day. So, when one of us is out of sorts, the other has learned not to react, but to wait awhile for the truth of what is going on to come out. Most people who are angry are not really angry at us. They have had a bad experience at some point in their day and need someone who will listen and not condemn, someone to love and not preach.

Action Item: If it is possible, and as far as it depends on you, try to live at peace with everyone today. Before you go to bed tonight, write down in your journal what happened during the day. I think it will be a great one!

Carole Lewis
First Place 4 Health National Director
Houston, Texas

147

family advance

If it is possible, as far as it depends on you, live at peace with everyone.

ROMANS 12:18

I live in Houston, and others of my family live in central Texas. I invited one of my sisters and her family to come visit me for the Fourth of July holiday. My sister said, "That is when we are having our family retreat." I'm in the "family," and I had not heard of this, nor was I invited by my sister-in-law who was hosting the retreat.

I kept waiting for the invitation. As the time approached, the rest of the family was asking if we were going. I also heard that people who were not in our family were going to our family retreat. It was a fact that my sister-in-law and I had never had any problems in our relationship. I chose not to be offended and to take every thought captive and not allow myself to be hurt or feel left out.

I kept hearing about the plans for the retreat. When the family retreat was over, I heard how great it was and how God had worked in the lives of everyone who went. I had to once again choose not to be hurt or feel left out, even though it sounded so good. Even up to December, I kept hearing details about the retreat. It was getting on my nerves. Each time I had to choose not to wonder why we had not been invited.

Looking at Christmas lights with my sister-in-law brought more stories about this retreat and how they wished we could have been there. *What?* I thought, *Lord, I've done pretty well up to now, but enough is enough!* When my sister-in-law finally explained why we had not been invited, I was glad that I had made the choice to "live at peace with everyone." You see, my sister-in-law had good reasons for her choices, and I applauded them.

It's never wrong to choose the right action that will result in peace.

Action Item: Is there anyone with whom you need to choose "to live at peace"? If so, the first step is to pray about it and ask the Holy Spirit to take away any sense of offense you have been feeling. What is your next best step?

Prayer: *Lord, please forgive me for the times I have not chosen to live at peace with everyone through my deeds or even my thoughts. Please help me to live every day at peace with everyone. In Your name I pray, amen.*

Karen Ferguson
Houston, Texas

our part in the world

If it is possible, as far as it depends on you, live at peace with everyone.

ROMANS 12:18

In most of Paul's writings he is very direct, giving instructions and admonishing us to live righteously. He was speaking to a very young Church that was just taking form, and he wanted to be very sure they understood what it meant to live in Christ and to have Christ in them.

However, in our Scripture today, he seems to understand that peace is not easy to obtain or sustain. He includes two qualifiers in this passage that make it a unique statement from this very plainspoken apostle.

First, he says, "If it is possible . . . live at peace with everyone." I think this is an indirect way of saying that there are some people and some situations that you cannot make peace with. In Paul's world, "everyone" included living at peace with those who differed with these new believers, and that was just about everyone. It included the Jews, the philosophers, the government and those who believed in other gods. In our world today, that would be our families, our neighbors and our co-workers.

Second, he says, "as far as it depends on you." Many times, in an ongoing situation, there are group dynamics involved. A group, a church, neighbors, the workplace have a contingency of individuals who are not at peace with others. Paul tells us that we can come apart and "as far as it depends on us" we should be at peace with those on the other side of the conflict. It may not cause peace in the overall conflict, but you have pulled apart and done all that you can.

Does world peace begin with one person living at peace with everyone? I am not sure about that. But I am sure that as born-again Christians, we are challenged to bring as much peace as possible in our part of the world "as far as it depends" on us.

Prayer: *Father, put into my heart a spirit of peace and help me radiate that peace wherever I go.*

Geni Hulsey
Houston, Texas

"little peacemaker"

If it is possible, as far as it depends on you, live at peace with everyone.
ROMANS 12:18

I called him "my little peacemaker" before he was even born. Just hearing the words, "Mom, I think I'm pregnant," were enough to change the mood of our whole family forever. We knew it would take every bit of nine months to prepare our hearts and minds to come together in support and unity for the sake of this child. Little did we know that we needed him more than he could ever need us. God, in His infinite wisdom, would use our first grandson to bring hope and healing to our wounded family relationships.

Having a baby in the family after 26 years brought a fresh appreciation of the genius behind the idea of the Christ *child*. I had forgotten the incomparable joy and awe, healing and peace a baby brings—any baby; but add to that the power and majesty of God, and the results are mind-blowing. There is nothing better than the sweet innocence of a newborn babe to break through the defenses of the thickest skin and the coldest heart. It is comfort and joy in its purest forms.

It is hard to believe that someone so small can have such an overwhelming ability to blanket our lives with warmth, laughter, joy, gladness and, yes, *peace*. Recently, there was an argument in our family. Arguments are few and far between these days (thank You, Jesus), but this one was a doozie. Avery, now "twoanna-HAAFF," was far removed from it, but the volume and tone filtered down to his happy spot. Rather than become fearful or even inquisitive, he unconditionally wanted to go bring comfort and peace to the argue-ees. His pure heart and total devotion to our undeserving selves were so humbling and so like Jesus. He knows he is called to be a peacemaker, and I didn't even tell him. His little "piggy toes" came out of the womb already shod with the gospel of peace.

Action Item: In what ways do I need to be more childlike in order to bring harmony to my family?

Prayer: *Dear Jesus, help us to stop trying to force children to be more like grown-ups, and help us to start being grown-ups who are more like children. Thank You for washing us clean with Your blood so that we can again be pure as babes. Help us to get it right this time.*

Jeanne Deveau Gregory
Chatham, Virginia

150

peace and daily bread

If it is possible, as far as it depends on you, live at peace with everyone.

ROMANS 12:18

Recently, Johnny and I were in Los Angeles for his oncologist appointment. After the appointment, we drove to Ventura, where the First Place 4 Health publisher is located. We were there four days for meetings and for me to speak at the annual sales conference.

On Monday, after being at Gospel Light for meetings, I stopped at a popular Italian chain restaurant and picked up some spaghetti with marinara sauce to take home for Johnny's dinner. I ordered a salad and a loaf of bread, which we planned to share.

We shared the bread and salad, and when we opened the spaghetti, it was dry beyond words. Johnny is not a perfectionist about anything but his food. He cooked for our family for years, and everything he prepared was always perfect. He likes his spaghetti with the marinara sauce on the top, but this was mixed together and had absolutely no moisture. He just closed up the box and said, "I'll take it back in the morning."

The next morning, before Johnny drove me to Gospel Light for my meetings, we stopped at the restaurant. I prayed for Johnny before he went inside that the person he spoke to would be cordial and that Johnny would stay calm. Off he went and came back to the car in just a few minutes. He told me the same lady who had waited on me was at the desk, and she remembered me. She was gracious and asked if he would be willing to take coupons good for use later. Johnny thanked her for the coupons and was on his way.

What could have been an ugly scene was diffused by prayer. We cannot always anticipate conflict, but as far as it depends on us, we must live at peace with everyone. It really helps to stop and pray over every situation.

Prayer: *Dear Lord, I want to be a person who lives at peace with everyone. Help me to be a peacemaker instead of a peace shaker today.*

Carole Lewis
First Place 4 Health National Director
Houston, Texas

great things He has done!

This morning I woke up with a melody in my heart: "This is my story, this is my song, praising my Savior all the day long . . ." Both my husband and I have had major health problems over the years. But in every problem, we can see God's blessing, healing and faithfulness.

My husband has had heart problems for years, resulting in bypasses, stints, atrial fibrillation and a pacemaker. He also had colon cancer and back surgeries. We've been hospitalized so many times that we have the hospital food menu memorized. God used Joel's heart problems to get us into cardio rehab, which includes an exercise program we can do together. I had never been on a treadmill previous to that.

My health problems stem from allergies, a brain tumor that left me deaf in my right ear and balance problems. I have fallen many times, resulting in various injuries. I also had to have my thyroid irradiated. That's when I began gaining a lot of

BEFORE   AFTER

weight, and I didn't realize the toll the weight was having on me. One of my most humbling moments came when I had to pay for two seats on a helicopter ride.

Through it all, Jesus became closer and dearer to me, showing His grace and mercy and giving both Joel and me hope for the future. "May the God of hope fill you with all joy and peace as you trust in him, so that you may overflow with hope by the power of the Holy Spirit" (Romans 15:13). God has blessed my husband and me through our many trials and has always shown His faithful love to us.

I joined First Place 4 Health a year and a half ago and didn't really think I would lose weight. It wasn't all easy. When I hit my first plateau, the point where I usually give up, the group members reminded me to take one day, one choice, at a time, trust God for the strength to make good choices and look to God for encouragement instead of using food for comfort. Wonderful ladies!

As of now, I have lost around 150 pounds and 21 inches from my waist. My cholesterol, triglycerides, and blood pressure have dropped dramatically to normal. My BMI was 49.32 in March 2009, and is now 32.19.

God has given me a whole new life and the energy to enjoy it to the fullest. I can't believe how well I can get around. I helped my husband with gardening this year for the first time in 20 years. I can even paint my toenails.

This September, my husband and I went to my fiftieth high school reunion on a Mexican cruise. I wouldn't have wanted to be seen a year and a half ago. While on the cruise, I went parasailing and swimming with dolphins. What fun!

Our grown sons are happy that I have lost weight. I didn't realize they were so worried about my health. My husband calls me his "incredible shrinking wife." Before, I was always so big that I hated shopping for myself. Now I love to shop for clothes!

God works everything together for good. We are both eating healthy foods; we are stronger and enjoy exercising regularly. We love this new life that God has given us. "Delight yourself in the LORD and he will give you the desires of your heart. Commit your way to the LORD; trust in him and he will do this" (Psalm 37:4-5).

Priscilla Works
Medford, Oregon

MONTH 8

FORGIVENESS

follow God's example

Bear with each other and forgive whatever grievances you may have against one another. Forgive as the Lord forgave you.

COLOSSIANS 3:13

God's Word is quite clear on the subject of forgiveness, given the numerous verses about the subject. Jesus asked His Father to forgive the ones who were putting Him to death. I think it is interesting that the reason Jesus gave was, "They do not know what they are doing" (Luke 23:34).

This verse helped me forgive the young girl who drove while intoxicated and killed our daughter Shari on Thanksgiving night in 2001. I knew in my heart that this girl didn't begin her day planning to kill anyone. She made some very bad choices all day long, which culminated in her choice to drive while under the influence of alcohol that night. In fact, she was so drunk (24 percent alcohol level, three hours after the accident) that I doubt she even remembers what happened, except for what she has been told.

I have heard it said that when we refuse to forgive someone, it is like a chair with that person sitting in it strapped to our back. We carry that person around until we forgive him or her. Someone else said that when we refuse to forgive, "It is like taking poison and expecting the other person to die."

Most people don't set out to say or do malicious things designed to hurt us. Knowing this makes it easier to forgive whatever grievances we have against them. Why is this? Because we know that we have said and done some things that have hurt others. And when we ask God to forgive us, He does just that.

Personally, I have never asked another person for forgiveness and had that person refuse to forgive me; but even if the person did refuse, I have done what the Bible commands me to do. We can do no less when someone asks us to forgive them.

Prayer: *Dear Lord, help me to be quick to forgive and quick to ask for forgiveness when I hurt another person.*

Carole Lewis
First Place 4 Health National Director
Houston, Texas

152

a legacy of forgiveness

*Bear with each other and forgive whatever grievances you may have
against one another. Forgive as the Lord forgave you.*

COLOSSIANS 3:13

If you have never thought of how powerful it is to live a legacy of forgiveness, think about if the Lord had not been willing to forgive us. We would be totally lost and without hope. The gift of His forgiveness lives on through us. Has someone from your past handed down the legacy of forgiveness? Perhaps his or her example of extending forgiveness has encouraged you to do the same.

Forgiveness or lack of forgiveness can change the course of our lives and affect generations to come. Holding grudges acts as a barricade that prevents us from living the life God means for us to live, and we are blinded by its oppression. But forgiveness opens the door to a new life. It has the power to transform relationships. If we truly forgive others as the Lord has forgiven us, then the past is gone. He does not throw it up into our faces, nor should we throw up the past to others.

In Psalm 103:12 we read, "As far as the east is from the west, so far has he removed our transgressions from us." In Jeremiah 31:34, the Lord says, "I will forgive their wickedness and will remember their sins no more." This is about "letting go" and letting God do something that we cannot do on our own. This is also about not allowing those grievances from the past to rule our emotions and thoughts.

Both giving and receiving forgiveness bring freedom. He gave us life so that we could live it abundantly (see John 10:10). When we hold on to grievances and unforgiveness, we are putting "handcuffs" on our children. Bitterness and hard feelings can spread down through the generations. But the power and legacy of forgiveness bring freedom for generations to come.

Action Item: Do as James 1:19 says: "Be quick to listen, slow to speak, and slow to become angry." If you have hurt someone's feelings, be quick to ask forgiveness. If you have forgiven someone, don't dwell on the past or bring it up again.

Prayer: *Father, help me to forgive others the way You have forgiven me. I desire to pass on Your rich legacy of love to my children and the generations to come.*

Connie Welch
First Place 4 Health Network Leader
Keller, Texas

153

move beyond the offense

Bear with each other and forgive whatever grievances you may have
against one another. Forgive as the Lord forgave you.

COLOSSIANS 3:13

Forgiveness is one of the hardest acts God calls us to do. As wickedness in the world increases, the levels of offense increase as well, thus making forgiveness even harder. To truly walk in forgiveness of these offenses takes much prayer and even counsel to move beyond the offense.

Many times, I focus more on the second half of this verse, "Forgive as the Lord forgave you," and the overwhelming quality of that concept almost paralyzes me. "How can I forgive that offense?" "It hurts so much." "They will just do it again." "It will not change anything." These are some of the mantras that repeat in my thoughts, and I often do nothing to move past the offense.

However, if instead of focusing on the second half of the verse, I focus on bearing with others, then walking in forgiveness isn't so overwhelming. Not because in any way it lessens the offense, but because it causes my heart to begin to soften toward others and to the things of God. (Please note that "bearing with others" may or may not apply to the offender.)

I like to think of bearing with others in terms of extending grace to them. Yes, they just did something that could cause me to be offended, but I am going to think the best of them and offer grace. And even though grieved, I am not going to seek justice in this matter, but release them from the debt I believe they owe me and trust God to deal with them. Jesus Christ, on the day He was crucified, bore the burden of our sins and offenses on His physical body. Through His Spirit, we can bear with those around us and move toward forgiveness and beyond the offense.

Action Item: When someone offends you, are you quick to seek justice for that offense, or are you quick to bear with them and extend grace? Throughout the day today, bear with others and intentionally extend grace to all those around you.

Becky Turner
First Place 4 Health Speaker
Houston, Texas

154

choose your attitude

Bear with each other and forgive whatever grievances you may have against one another. Forgive as the Lord forgave you.

COLOSSIANS 3:13

A few years ago, Carole Lewis wrote a book titled *A Thankful Heart,* and Elizabeth Crews wrote an accompanying Bible study called *Choosing Thankfulness.* In Elizabeth's study, she asked us to begin keeping a "thankfulness journal." She suggested that we purchase a really pretty journal to use as we prayed about and recorded what we were thankful for that day. We were to write five short sentences each morning and five sentences each night telling God what He had done in our lives and why we were thankful.

I bought a soft lilac velvet journal, and it wasn't long before I loved recording all the things for which I was thankful. It was easy to praise God for 10 things each day. This exercise changed my life! I learned that it is very difficult to stay angry at someone or hold a grievance inside when you are thanking God each morning and evening. My negative attitude about things changed to an attitude of gratitude. As I thought of what my Lord Jesus had done for me, and the many, many times He had forgiven me, I knew that I must forgive others as well. I needed to learn to be patient with others, just as God has been patient with me.

These days, I find that when I neglect my thankfulness journal, my day does not go nearly as well. My mood is entirely different, and I am reminded that thankfulness is a choice.

Action Item: Pray about beginning a thankfulness journal in which you list 10 things each day (five in the morning and five at night) that you are thankful for. I promise that it will change your attitude in every way.

Prayer: *Lord God, thank You for being so patient with me and for Your forgiveness. May I always remember to thank You and praise You for all that You have done and are doing in my life each day.*

Janet Kirkhart
First Place 4 Health Networking Leader
Loveland, Ohio

155

how many times?

Bear with each other and forgive whatever grievances you may have
against one another. Forgive as the Lord forgave you.

COLOSSIANS 3:13

Whenever I hear the words "bear with," I always think of "put up with," like when I had to help my mom with housework before I could go out with my friends. *Oh, all right,* I would think. *It's the only way I'll ever get to have any fun.* Reluctant acceptance with an underlying selfish motive is not really what God is looking for here.

Don't think I'm not compassionate. I was moved to pity when I read how Peter asked Jesus in Matthew 18:21, "Lord, how many times shall I forgive my brother when he sins against me? Up to seven times?" I thought that was a reasonable amount. Seven times is a generous number, in my opinion. It's a bit of a stretch for my capabilities, but I could probably handle it with a little bit of effort.

But Jesus answered, "I tell you, not seven times, but seventy-seven times" (verse 22). WHAT? Oh man, you have *got* to be kidding. This is a joke, right? I mean, I know that God has a great sense of humor, but come on. You can't really expect me to forgive that lummox . . . how many times IS that, anyway? And why should he get off the hook when I'm still paying for . . .

Oh—"Forgive as the Lord forgave you." Um, that would be *me,* right?

I think my problem is with the opening line. Instead of thinking of "put up with" when I hear "bear with," I need to picture the beaten and bloodied image of Christ, God's beloved Son, turning the other cheek and speaking not a word. I need to see Him receiving slash after cutting, flesh-tearing, slash on His tender skin, and hammer after hammer to His aching body stretched across a splintery frame of wood. I'm sure He knows exactly how much 77 times is, and it is just a drop in His bucket of blood.

Action Item: Write a prayer list of everyone who needs your full forgiveness, and then resolve to destroy any record of how many times it has been required.

Prayer: *Father, how dare I hesitate to be as gracious and merciful with others as You are with me. I do not deserve Your compassion, love and forgiveness. I pray that the Holy Spirit will remind me of Your suffering Son each time I am tempted to withhold forgiveness. Amen.*

Jeanne Deveau Gregory
Chatham, Virginia

156

getting past the loss

When you stand praying, if you hold anything against anyone, forgive him,
so that your Father in heaven may forgive you your sins.

MARK 11:25

Years ago, I was deeply hurt by another person. He was my employer. I had taken a leave of absence to help Johnny get his new forklift business up and running. During the six weeks I was away, my boss hired another person to take my place without telling me. I simply received a letter in the mail from him telling me what a great employee I had been, but that he was forced to replace me due to the length of my absence.

I have heard it said that there are only three great fears in life: loss of face, loss of place and loss of life. I experienced the first two fears during the next year. Frankly, my feelings were hurt. Why didn't my boss tell me to my face? Why did he write a letter? I kept that letter; and every couple of months I would read it again. Each time I read the letter, the hurt would well up inside me again.

Finally, after almost a year of refusing to forgive this man, I realized that I wasn't even able to pray. When I finally forgave my former boss and asked God to forgive me for nursing my hurt and waiting that long, it was like a huge burden was lifted from me, and I was free again.

I saw this man and his wife at a church luncheon a few months after I had chosen to forgive him, and I was amazed that I felt not an ounce of anger or hurt. I was able to go over and talk with them both in true Christian love.

What could I have done differently to avoid that miserable year? I could have gone to my brother, as the Bible says, and told him I was hurt by his action. I know that my boss would have apologized for not talking to me personally, and the entire incident would have been over.

Prayer: *Dear Lord, help me to be a person who deals with offense and loss by practicing forgiveness rather than nursing the hurt and damaging my relationship with You.*

Carole Lewis
First Place 4 Health National Director
Houston, Texas

the power of forgiveness

When you stand praying, if you hold anything against anyone, forgive him,
so that your Father in heaven may forgive you your sins.

MARK 11:25

How could someone be so selfish as to violate someone else and give her a life-threatening disease? I was angry, in shock, robbed of my future. When I was diagnosed with Hepatitis C, I had to come to terms with the true meaning of forgiveness.

I was reminded of what God's Word tells us about forgiveness. I also knew that forgiveness did not mean that what he did was okay, but it would make me free to not live as a victim. When unforgiveness moves in, it brings the baggage of hardness into our hearts. It affects our spirit, overshadowing our perspective, and leaves little room for anything else. It will dominate our lives. But God gave us free will. We can choose whether or not we will allow something to move in and take up residence in our hearts.

God tells us to walk in obedience, and to honor Him by forgiving others. I knew that it was important for me to forgive, but I couldn't do it on my own. I prayed, "Lord, I know that Your Word tells me to forgive. I don't feel that right now, but I am asking You to help me do what I cannot do on my own. Help me to forgive and let go of this hurt, bitterness and anger. By an act of my will, I choose to forgive and remove this stone of bitterness and anger, in Jesus' name."

The Lord and I had many conversations about what I was feeling. Through His strength, I was able to do what I could not do on my own—forgive completely. The bitterness and anger I once wrestled with are gone. That gift of mercy and forgiveness comes only from our heavenly Father through Jesus Christ, because of His grace in forgiving us.

Prayer: *Lord, I ask for You to come in and help me do what I cannot do on my own. In obedience to Your Word, I choose by an act of my will to forgive. Melt this bitterness and resentment from my heart. Help me to choose to walk in Your footsteps of forgiveness every day.*

Connie Welch
First Place 4 Health Networking Leader
Keller, Texas

158

my husband's secrets

When you stand praying, if you hold anything against anyone, forgive him,
so that your Father in heaven may forgive you your sins.

MARK 11:25

It amazes me how few things upset my husband. I recently heard something that I think is the secret to his sweet disposition. We had a conversation about forgiveness, and he discussed how we all have a choice in the amount of offense we decide to take on over something done or said by another, and we can choose to take no offense at all. I tend to jump to conclusions, blow things out of proportion and dwell on the little things more often than not; whereas, he considers what else might be going on with the other party, even things he might not know about, and in his wisdom (and having three older sisters) he has learned not to take things personally. He has also learned to pray for his potential offenders.

He is a tenderhearted man, and as a cancer survivor, he knows that life is too short to waste on petty grievances. He also knows that the not-so-petty grievances can suck the life right out of you. "It's just not worth it." His words carry much weight with me, for I know many of the horrors he has dealt with in his life. You see, I also know that he has another secret, found in Philippians 4:12-13:

> I know what it is to be in need, and I know what it is to have plenty. I have learned the secret of being content in any and every situation, whether well fed or hungry, whether living in plenty or in want. I can do everything through him who gives me strength.

Even to forgive the unforgivable.

Action Item: What petty grievances am I wasting my life on? What not-so-petty grievances do I need to turn over to God because they are just not worth it? How can I better use my time and energy to serve God?

Prayer: *Lord, I thank You for teaching us about forgiveness by example and by Your wonderful healing Word. Thank You for helping my husband forgive my many faults and for being You with skin on for me.*

Jeanne Deveau Gregory
Chatham, Virginia

lighter inside and out

When you stand praying, if you hold anything against anyone, forgive him,
so that your Father in heaven may forgive you your sins.

MARK 11:25

As a young girl, I participated on a swim team and was one of the top contenders in my age group. I was also bullied mercilessly by a group of my swimming peers. This teasing and tormenting lasted for several painful years. At one point, I was held under water for an extended period of time, leaving me gasping for air and terrified of what horror might occur next.

Unsurprisingly, these events affected me in profoundly negative ways. I became angry, and tightened a newly acquired "tough girl" belt around myself. In other words, I hardened my heart and developed an "I'll hurt you before you hurt me" attitude. No one was going to hold me under water or anything else ever again. Little did I know just how much my unforgiveness would keep me weighted down.

Years later, when God swept me into His grace-filled embrace, I had quite a laundry list of things that desperately needed washing in God's forgiving waters. I also discovered that I was required to forgive others. And it wasn't just a simple suggestion, but a clear-cut command requiring action on my part. Not to mention the not-so-fine-print stating that we were to forgive *anything* we were holding against *anyone* before our Father in heaven would hear our prayers. I knew I wanted my prayers heard, so I tackled the forgiveness challenge.

First Place 4 Health provided me with an array of practical tools. I learned that I wasn't the only one who'd suffered at the hands of others, and I certainly wasn't the only one struggling with forgiveness. Yet I could sense a certain peace in those group members who had chosen to forgive. Many believed that their release of unwanted pounds was a direct result of their willingness to surrender their anger, resentment and bitterness. I wanted more than a lighter body; I wanted a lighter heart. Forgiving those girls and every other person who hurt me has freed me to have better relationships with others and, most importantly, with God.

Action Item: Ask God to reveal anyone you need to forgive and write down the name(s). Choose to release them into God's capable hands. Don't hesitate to ask for help with this critical process.

Carol VanAtta
Troutdale, Oregon

160

the hold

When you stand praying, if you hold anything against anyone, forgive him,
so that your Father in heaven may forgive you your sins.

MARK 11:25

I have made it a part of my devotional time with the Lord to always pray Mark 11:25 and ask the Lord to reveal to me anyone from whom I may be withholding forgiveness. On many occasions, His Holy Spirit has responded, "Yes, you need to forgive yourself."

Wow! Now that's a hard one. I have learned that there is much danger in our not forgiving ourselves. Unforgiveness creates fertile ground for a stronghold to take root in our hearts. In her book *Praying God's Word*, Beth Moore describes a stronghold as "anything capturing my mind with a sense of hopelessness and causing me to accept as unchangeable something I know to be contrary to the will of God."[1]

Self-loathing, guilt and shame are contrary to the will of God and can become strongholds in our life, snuffing out the joy and fulfillment God has for us. The truth is, Jesus paid it all. If you have asked for His forgiveness, He has given it to you. Since He has forgiven us, we must do the same. Anything less would be rejection of the beautiful gift of Calvary. We were not designed to carry around a lifetime of guilt and shame; Jesus died for that very reason.

The song "I Am Free" says it this way: "You've buried my sin in the depths of the sea; carried my guilt far away. As far as the east is from the west, you've removed my transgressions from me."[2]

Action Item: Thank Him today for the beautiful gift of forgiveness, and live like you are forgiven, because it's true—you *are.*

Vicki Heath
First Place 4 Health Associate Director
Edisto Island, South Carolina

healing a wounded heart

Be kind and compassionate to one another, forgiving each other,
just as in Christ God forgave you.

EPHESIANS 4:32

I have led a First Place 4 Health class continuously since the fall of 1981. I can honestly say that it has been fascinating to see the interactions between the members of my classes over the years.

In some instances, lifelong friendships have been formed. In other instances, I have had women who instead of bringing "warm fuzzies" to the class have brought "cold pricklies" several times during each session. Usually, after whatever rude thing was said during class, another person would call me and say she was hurt by the remark.

This is always a perfect time for me to encourage the offended person to forgive her sister in the Lord and to assure her that if we forgive and continue to love this person unconditionally, God will change her heart. It has been said that "the Christian army is the only army that shoots its wounded." When we refuse to forgive, we are in essence shooting our wounded.

People come into the First Place 4 Health program with deep hurts and wounds. Some cover their hurts better than others. I believe that when a person is openly critical, negative or rude, she is screaming for someone to love her. Instead of wishing that person would move on, why not begin to pray that Christ would love her through you? I have done this and have found that a miracle takes place inside of me before the miracle takes place inside of the other person. As I start loving someone—really loving—that person feels it and begins to let down the high walls she has erected to prevent more pain.

I have seen this happen many times, and it has been beautiful to watch God heal a wounded heart with His love.

Action Item: Is there someone in your life who has hurt you, but who needs your love? Write about it in your journal, asking God to love this person through you. You will be amazed at what God does to heal your heart and the other person's heart as well.

Carole Lewis
First Place 4 Health National Director
Houston, Texas

162

walking in the Spirit

Be kind and compassionate to one another, forgiving each other,
just as in Christ God forgave you.

EPHESIANS 4:32

If you were to ask my friends, they would be quick to tell you that walking in kindness and compassion are not my strongest character traits. However, on a recent mission trip to Honduras, I learned a new way of thinking from a dear Honduran brother named Emilio. It has really helped me live out this command on a daily basis.

We were blessed to have Emilio as the in-country leader for Living Water International. As we were driving through the mountains of Honduras on the way to Saba, our home away from home for the next six days, Emilio spoke a line that I will never forget: "I am not going to let that get to my flesh." What is so impactful about this is that it begins with the thought process, which is where true change has to happen. I have been on enough trips to respond appropriately when challenges occur, at least on the outside; but I have been known to pick up an offense or respond, in my mind, judgmentally.

I distinctly remember one time when things were not going correctly (at least as I saw it), and I started to grumble and complain in my mind while I still had a fake smile on my face. (To be honest, I don't think I was fooling anyone but myself.) Immediately, Emilio's line came to my mind and I repeated it to myself. Then my pasted-on smile became a true grin as I chose to be kind and compassionate to others.

What has been so cool since returning to Houston is that the line works here as well! I can make the decision as to whether or not I will let something get to my flesh. When I choose this way, I have won the victory, and the enemy and my flesh have been defeated!

Action Item: Write the words "I am not going to let things get to my flesh" on an index card and place it on the dashboard of your car. Each time you use your turn signal, read that line out loud.

Becky Turner
First Place 4 Health Speaker
Houston, Texas

163

justice satisfied

Be kind and compassionate to one another, forgiving each other,
just as in Christ God forgave you.

EPHESIANS 4:32

Forgiveness is the willingness to relinquish the pursuit of justice in response to a wrong done to you—a willingness to free the offender of the debt he or she owes you. Our motivation to do this is because God forgave us. Because of the shed blood of Jesus, God's justice was satisfied, and He has forgiven us of the debt we owed to Him.

Even with this great motivation, forgiveness is still one of the most challenging character traits to walk out. What makes it so difficult is our inability to forget the offense. I wish that when I forgave someone, the memory of that offense could be wiped from my mind, but that is just not the case. I often want to seek justice for things that have already been forgiven and to shed "blood in peacetime as if in battle," as David said to Solomon in 1 Kings 2:5.

David's army commander, Joab, lost a brother in war at the hands of the enemy. After the war was over and the peace treaty signed, Joab killed the man who had killed his brother. He sought justice for a wartime offense after peace had been established.

Unfortunately, I can do the exact same thing—not murder, but revisiting the forgiven offense. I have extended forgiveness, the person has responded appropriately and we are fully reconciled. Then, one day, one week, one decade later, the memory comes back to me and I seek justice . . . again. I want to hear another "I'm sorry." I am seeking forgiveness in peacetime for something that has already been covered.

When the memory comes back, instead of going to the forgiven offender, I need to go to God and ask Him to heal me in that area and then walk out the forgiveness that was freely given to me.

Action Item: When we don't forgive, it is like drinking poison and expecting the offender to die. Take a few minutes and journal your thoughts on this subject. Even if you are not willing to forgive, ask God to make you willing to be willing.

Becky Turner
First Place 4 Health Speaker
Houston, Texas

164

come together

Be kind and compassionate to one another, forgiving each other,
just as in Christ God forgave you.

EPHESIANS 4:32

This year during Wellness Week at Round Top, the friends I made there truly impacted my life in more ways than one.

After a wonderful week of food, fun, fellowship, exercise, laughter and tears, I packed up to go home. I went to bed relaxed and happy that I had lost 2.8 pounds. During the night, a horrific pain hit me in the chest. I felt as though someone had slammed me with a sledgehammer. No matter how I moved or what position I was in, relief did not come. The pain was so bad that I cried and begged God for relief. Finally, at 6:00 A.M., I was able to get up and pull on jeans and a shirt. I grabbed a jacket and headed for the dining hall, thinking that a cup of hot tea would help.

The tea didn't help. Several others came in around that time. One of the women saw me and realized something was wrong. She went to find the doctor who was there and called Lisa Cramer. Nancy and Lisa insisted on taking me to the hospital. The pain had lessened, but common sense prevailed, and we went to the ER.

All the way there, Nancy prayed with one arm around my shoulders and one hand on my pulse, reassuring me every step of the way that I was okay. An ultrasound at the hospital revealed the source of my pain to be a gall bladder attack. Bob and Dee Matthews came to the hospital and told me about the prayers of all those remaining at the retreat that morning. What a blessing to have a group of people praying for one of their members. As Jesus said in Matthew 18:20, "Where two or three come together in my name, there am I with them," and prayers are answered.

I am fine now, but I will never forget the love, kindness and compassion those men and women had for a new friend.

Action Item: Is there someone in your life you need to forgive or show compassion and kindness? Let today be the day you reach out and touch that person. Perform at least one act of kindness toward someone else, even a stranger.

Prayer: *Heavenly Father, thank You for compassionate friends, and may we always be loving and kind to others, no matter the circumstances.*

Martha Rogers
Houston, Texas

165

the hard part

Be kind and compassionate to one another, forgiving each other,
just as in Christ God forgave you.

EPHESIANS 4:32

I had it easy. It was easy to honor my father and mother simply because they were honorable people. However, what is easy for one is not easy for another. In the sheltered innocence of my childhood, I thought *all* parents were honorable. Imagine my shock to learn of the horrors that some children experience at the hands of those entrusted to love and protect them. It was bad enough to read about such things, but I was at a complete loss when listening to those who turned to me for comfort or guidance.

Over the years, I've observed some amazing survivors who had the hard part of honoring a dishonorable father or mother. Four common elements constitute their success: The first is having a *desire* to be obedient. Because they have developed a close personal relationship with Jesus Christ, they do not want to hurt Him in any way, and therefore *want* to honor His commandments. The second is *grace*. They know they cannot do it in their own power, and acknowledge that they must call on the One who can provide the grace they need. Third, they must rid themselves of any hostility, hate, resentment or desire for revenge by turning it over to the Lord and seeking the ability to *forgive* those who have harmed them. Fourth, they *pray* for the redemption of their parents.

Ephesians 6:3 reveals what the promise is: "That it may go well with you and that you may enjoy long life on the earth." In this case, it *is* about us. Our loving Father in heaven knows all about the healing power of forgiveness and the destruction caused by our refusal to seek it. He knows the harm that comes to our emotional, spiritual and physical health when we don't abide by the commandments He set up for our own good. After all, He is the ultimate Father *and* Mother.

Prayer: *Oh, Lord, how my heart breaks for the children trapped in abusive homes. How I pray that they will come to know You and cling to You, the Father and Mother who will never leave them or forsake them; and I pray for the adult children of dishonorable parents, that You will lead them to a place of healing and forgiveness. Thank You, Jesus, for providing the example by honoring Your Father above all.*

Jeanne Deveau Gregory
Chatham, Virginia

166

no use hiding

*If we confess our sins, he is faithful and just and will forgive us
our sins and purify us from all unrighteousness.*

1 JOHN 1:9

I don't know about you, but it is hard for me to confess my sins. But I have no problem confessing other people's sins. I can run through the list of the sins of others as I pray for them, so why is it so hard for me to list my own sins?

One reason is that I think I can hide my sins if I don't voice them. This goes all the way back to the Garden of Eden when Adam and Eve first sinned and then ran and hid from God.

Another reason is that when I confess my sins, I am admitting that I am flawed. I know it myself, and God knows it, so why do I make it so hard on myself by putting off the act of confession?

This is especially critical in the area of overeating. I don't want to confess my sin to God or to another person. I have a friend who will ask me how I'm doing, and when I confess to her what is going on, then it is much easier to confess it to God and receive His forgiveness.

When I finally confess, it is as if a huge weight has been lifted from my back. Confession is necessary before I can get back on track and begin again. This is what I love about my First Place 4 Health class. We are all in this together and we have a safe place to confess our sins, knowing there is no condemnation in Christ Jesus.

When a person emails me and confesses a sin he or she is struggling with, I always pray for that person in my reply. Prayer is the most powerful weapon we have against the ravages of sin in our lives.

Action Item: Write in your journal every sin with which you are now struggling, and then pray and ask God's forgiveness and cleansing from each one.

Carole Lewis
First Place 4 Health National Director
Houston, Texas

167

finding self-forgiveness

If we confess our sins, he is faithful and just and will forgive us
our sins and purify us from all unrighteousness.

1 JOHN 1:9

The life I led before accepting Christ was characterized by activities of which I am not proud. Although I lead others to believe that I am transparent—an open book—the reality is that I don't share what is really affecting my life, and especially my journey to health. I am careful to not get close to anyone, and I spend my life on the outside looking in. The committee in my head churns with lies that I am "less than," "different" and "not suited for God's work." These lies have so pervaded my life that I tend to isolate myself and not make commitments. I never place myself in situations that might lead to any level of intimacy, especially with fellow believers.

Healing and understanding blessed me this past week during the First Place 4 Health Wellness Retreat. Attending the retreat was a huge step of faith for me. Although I was recovering from surgery and not cleared to drive, I took my car in case I needed an escape hatch. I planned on minimal participation and was apprehensive when I learned that I had to go to small group meetings.

I shocked myself by sharing that I felt distant from the Lord. At a later meeting, I blurted out that I had had an abortion when I was 17, a secret that I have never discussed with anyone. My shock at the outburst quickly changed to an overwhelming feeling of relief and freedom, as if a huge weight had been lifted off my shoulders.

I have confessed my sins over and over and extended forgiveness to the man who raped me and impregnated me so violently. So why was I still stumbling around in the dark? How could I believe that I was an exception to God's promise to forgive my sins? Why did I medicate these feelings with food? Clarity came through sharing and prayer with this group of warm and compassionate women. Together we learned that God's forgiveness allows self-forgiveness.

Action Item: Purchase a pretty box. Write down a negative thought, a lie, a prayer, and put it in the box. Once it is in the box, do not obsess about it; relinquish your attempt to control it and give it to the Lord. Open the box on New Year's Day (or a special day) and read what you wrote, and then destroy the paper.

Diane Hawkins
Houston, Texas

there is now no condemnation

*If we confess our sins, he is faithful and just and will forgive us
our sins and purify us from all unrighteousness.*

1 JOHN 1:9

For almost 25 years, I struggled with a decision I made when I was 21 years old to have an abortion. The reason I chose to abort an innocent baby does not matter; there is no reason to justify this decision. The consequences of my decision have resulted in years of guilt and shame and a decision to stuff down this sin and not tell anyone. I went to God many times asking for forgiveness and I am sure He forgave me immediately. But it took years of getting to know God and His character to really believe that I was forgiven and worthy of having a happy life.

Through First Place 4 Health, I continue to learn more about Christ and His amazing love for us. He does not desire us to live in bondage or condemnation. There is no sin, no addiction and no bondage from which He will not forgive or deliver us. We have to confess our sin and believe that God is a God of His word and will forgive us and make us clean again.

What Satan tried for many years to do—keep me paralyzed emotionally using food to cope and sedate me—Christ has used to bring me closer to Him and seek Him for my emotional healing. Satan also convinced me my service to God could never be effective because of my sin, but God has used my testimony of forgiveness and hope to help others who have made the same choice in the past.

It is a sad statistic, but 40 percent of women in the United States have had an abortion, and it is very possible that you or someone you know have walked through the doors of an abortion clinic.[3] If that is your story, I invite you to knock on God's door, confess your sin and receive His forgiveness.

Action Item: If someone you know is living under condemnation regarding an abortion, contact your local pregnancy care center or church for post-abortion counseling and Bible study. God wants to heal this pain and use it for His glory.

Prayer: *Lord, thank You for Your promise that if we will just confess our sin, You will forgive our sin. I don't want to waste another day of my life believing that abortion is unforgivable. Your blood covered it all. Amen.*

Vickie Martin
Stephenville, Texas

169

be quick to confess

*If we confess our sins, he is faithful and just and will forgive us
our sins and purify us from all unrighteousness.*

1 JOHN 1:9

Even though I've heard this verse used many times in leading people to salvation, it is actually written to Christians. Though we have been saved from the guilt and power of sin, we still have the presence of sin while we are in this body and in this world. Therefore, we all sin and are in need of daily renewal.

It has been said that we get to choose our sin, but we don't get to choose our consequences. I find this verse to be one of protection in my personal walk with the Lord. Every sin starts with a thought. If we do not take our thoughts captive and confess them to God, we will act them out. A time of confession before God each morning for wrong thoughts, attitudes and feelings will protect us from committing the very acts we think about.

I was instructed, as a new Christian, that God knows our every thought, so I might as well confess it and talk to Him about it. That has proven to be very beneficial to me through the years. I've seen families split, ministries ruined and testimonies destroyed all because thoughts that were not taken captive resulted in gross sin and its consequences.

Having an accountability partner can also help you through the struggles of life and is a great way to keep yourself pure as you confess to your partner and to God any wrong thoughts, attitudes and feelings so that they do not become actions. James 5:16 says, "Confess your sins to each other and pray for each other so that you may be healed." We are better together when we confess our sins and pray for one another.

Action Item: Are you entertaining thoughts that could get you into trouble? Talk to God about them and use your journal. You might also consider who you could ask to beome your accountability partner in this area.

Prayer: *Lord, thank You that You daily forgive us of our sins and purify us from all unrighteousness. I ask You to see my every thought and help me to take captive those thoughts that are not pleasing to You. Amen.*

Karen Ferguson
Houston, Texas

take a deep breath

*If we confess our sins, he is faithful and just and will forgive us
our sins and purify us from all unrighteousness.*

1 JOHN 1:9

As a young Christian at First Baptist Church in Jacksonville, Florida, my Sunday School teacher taught us the skill of "spiritual breathing." She explained that confession of sin should be as natural and spontaneous as breathing. When a bad thought comes, we confess it, ask forgiveness and breathe in God's forgiveness and strength—all in one breath!

The fact is that Satan plays hardball with us. He doesn't want us to just have a bad hair day; he wants to destroy our very lives. The Bible says that he "comes only to steal and kill and destroy" (John 10:10). It's his nature to be the one to lead us into temptation and then stand as our accuser when we give in to the temptation. He does it ever so subtly by planting thoughts such as, "It's not hurting anyone" or "No one will ever know" or "Those people really don't know you. You don't have a problem; they do." The one he uses with me the most is, "You deserve this," a little personal pleasure that comes from overeating.

So what can I do about it? The answer: be quick to confess and take every thought captive. Don't let your thought life get out of control. Unconfessed sin is only more ammunition for the enemy of our souls to use against us.

An old pastor friend of mine says it this way, "You can't keep the birds from flying around your head, but you can keep them from building a nest."

Action Item: Practice the skill of spiritual breathing for the entire day—bad thoughts out, God's grace in!

Vicki Heath
First Place 4 Health Associate Director
Edisto Island, South Carolina

we are loved

*In him we have redemption through his blood, the forgiveness of sins,
in accordance with the riches of God's grace that he lavished on us
with all wisdom and understanding.*

EPHESIANS 1:7-8

When I think of the word "lavish," I think of extreme generosity. A dear friend of mine gave me a sixtieth birthday party just a few weeks after our daughter Shari's death. A party was the last thing I wanted at the time, but I was touched at the love she lavished on me that day, and it was sweet to be with friends and family who loved me.

Another meaning to me for the word "lavish" is over the top of all my expectations. Our daughter Lisa brings us food for our freezer when she cooks for her family. She certainly doesn't have to do this, but when she does, she lavishes Johnny and me with her love.

We serve a God who lavishes us with love and grace. First John 3:1 says, "How great is the love the Father has lavished on us, that we should be called children of God! And that is what we are! The reason the world does not know us is that it did not know him." When we ask Jesus to come into our hearts, God begins a lifelong process of lavishing us with His love and grace, because of Jesus' shed blood on Calvary's cross. It is humbling to know that God knows everything about me and He knows every sin I will ever commit. He knows when I will run back to Him and ask for forgiveness and when I will continue in my own stubborn willfulness for a time.

Because God is all-wise and understanding, He knows that without His love and grace, I am not capable of doing anything that will bring Him glory. His lavish love and grace compel me to become the person He created me to be.

Action Item: God has lavished you with His love and grace so that you are able to give it to someone else. Who needs your lavish love and grace today?

Carole Lewis
First Place 4 Health National Director
Houston, Texas

172

I'm working on it

In him we have redemption through his blood, the forgiveness of sins,
in accordance with the riches of God's grace that he lavished on us
with all wisdom and understanding.

EPHESIANS 1:7-8

The Scripture verses came last week for Carole's new book *Better Together.* I have done everything in my power to ignore the ones on forgiveness, but my conscience will no longer allow me to ignore them. First Place 4 Health seems to choose the verses I need the most and keep them in front of me. Mind you, I know that God is at work in this matter.

We have a neighbor who called me about three weeks ago, saying some hateful and uncalled-for things about my husband. I know the man is not capable of understanding that he himself is slow in thinking and working. I tried being nice, but he made it very difficult, so I chose to ignore him. He called again and made things worse. I thought about not answering the phone when he called, but that did not seem to please God.

The next time the man called, he acted strange and mysterious, but happy, as if nothing had ever happened. I'll have to admit that the man has improved my prayer life. God has been patient with me, but I have not been patient with the man. Last night, I asked God to forgive me as I work hard at forgiving the man. God has lavished His love on me so much lately, and I do not want to disappoint Him!

Asking forgiveness is hard because we have to admit that we would rather strangle the person than forgive him (or her). That is not God's way. If we are to be at peace, we must forgive. So tonight, I am trying hard to totally forgive the man.

Yes, I am starting to feel a peace that passes all understanding as I write this. Our God is good. Our witness must show it too!

Prayer: *Abba Father, thank You for covering me with Your love. May the man in question see Your love in me.*

Betha Jean McGee
Wall, Texas

173

frosted with grace

*In him we have redemption through his blood, the forgiveness of sins,
in accordance with the riches of God's grace that he lavished on us
with all wisdom and understanding.*

EPHESIANS 1:7-8

I always think of cake frosting when I hear the word "lavished." I'm not a psychologist, but I think it's some kind of godly transference or something. Frosting was my strongest weakness when I came to First Place 4 Health. I kept an open can in the fridge and scooped out a spoonful every time I walked by. I'd just keep it in my mouth like a lollipop, letting it slowly dissolve as I went about my business. I always had at least six back-up cans in the cabinet for emergencies.

I knew I was making progress in First Place 4 Health when I was able to actually throw the unopened cans in the trash! I *did* allow myself to finish off the open one in the fridge, however. Talk about idol worship! I continued to sniff it all the way to the basket, mourning its death with every painful step. I had to get the bag right out of the house, too, so I couldn't change my mind and rescue the new ones that were screaming at me from under their foil seals.

Once I chose God's strength over my frosting weakness, and I asked forgiveness for letting it come before Him in my life, He gave me this analogy: I pictured God up there with a giant silver frosting spreader, with grace being the frosting, of course (with a slight chocolate buttercreme scent . . .), and He's just spreaaaadin' that stuff over us like a sweet glaze, so much that it just puddles up all over the place until we are swimming in it. No fear of drowning in this cake plate, no-sir-ee.

Now I have received wisdom and understanding to know that I can give up my frosting addiction for Him and, in return, He will give me back as much chocolate-scented grace as I want, because He has *way* more than six cans.

Action Item: What are some habits and priorities you need to change in order to put God in His proper first place?

Prayer: *Father, I pray for those who are still caught up in the denial of their addictions, and I ask You to lead them into a clear reflection of themselves so they can repent, return and receive Your forgiveness and lavish grace. Amen.*

Jeanne Deveau Gregory
Chatham, Virginia

His grace is enough

*In him we have redemption through his blood, the forgiveness of sins,
in accordance with the riches of God's grace that he lavished on us
with all wisdom and understanding.*

EPHESIANS 1:7-8

Don't you just love the grace of God? His grace brought me into His family, and His grace has never left me since that day as a 12-year-old girl when I asked Jesus into my heart.

Even though we go through times of suffering in this life, God's grace is working the entire time. My husband Johnny's battle with stage 4 prostate cancer has been going on since 1997. When Johnny was diagnosed, he was given about two years to live. God's grace has kept him alive and has permeated our relationship since the day of his diagnosis.

We are experiencing a time now where Johnny's PSA, the indicator of the severity of his cancer, is spiking like it did in the beginning. A rising PSA, while on hormone therapy, indicates that Johnny may be growing resistant to the hormone therapy. God's grace is so powerful that Johnny is feeling better right now than he has in months! He has more energy and stamina, and we are both amazed that this could be true.

Our job is to lay every trial we go through at the feet of our God, knowing that His grace is all over that trial. As I said in my book *Hope 4 You,* I have learned that there are three things that restore hope when our hope meter is low. Those three things are praise, thanksgiving and faith.

With Johnny's PSA at 51.7, I could be very afraid for our future, but instead I am taking every opportunity to praise and thank God. He knows our future and understands our anxious hearts. As I praise Him and thank Him for His goodness and grace, He builds my faith and I can confidently trust Him with our future.

Prayer: *Dear Lord, Your grace is sufficient for my every need today. Fill me with praise and thanksgiving today so that my faith grows in proportion to my need.*

Carole Lewis
First Place 4 Health Director
Houston, Texas

175

our inheritance

*In him we have redemption through his blood, the forgiveness of sins,
in accordance with the riches of God's grace that he lavished on us
with all wisdom and understanding.*

EPHESIANS 1:7-8

My mom passed away this past summer, and I had some time to reflect on the idea of inheritance. My mom did not have much in the way of valuable earthly goods to leave us, but she did leave a lot, nonetheless. My favorite thing she left me is her sense of humor. Mom always could find a way to laugh at just about anything! I inherited my sense of humor from her, and I have always loved it that I am like her in that way.

Jesus, when He finished His earthly ministry, went to be with the Father. Jesus died basically a poor man, a pauper. He had very little family left; He never married—had no children. He did not own property. He even had to borrow a grave in which to be buried. He did not leave a lot of earthly inheritance, but He did leave us with redemption and forgiveness—and a lot more:

Peace: "Peace I leave with you; my peace I give you. I do not give to you as the world gives. Do not let your hearts be troubled and do not be afraid" (John 14:27).

Power: "I tell you the truth, anyone who has faith in me will do what I have been doing. He will do even greater things than these" (John 14:12).

His presence: "I will ask the Father, and he will give you another Counselor to be with you forever—the Spirit of truth. . . . But you know him, for he lives with you and will be in you" (John 14:16-17).

His good name: "My Father will give you whatever you ask in my name. Until now you have not asked for anything in my name. Ask and you will receive, and your joy will be complete" (John 16:23-24).

Victory: "In this world you will have trouble. But take heart! I have overcome the world" (John 16:33).

I am careful to be grateful for all I have inherited and not squander a bit of it!

Action Item: Make Ephesians 1:7-8 personal by filling in the blank, "In Him I have _____."

Vicki Heath
First Place 4 Health Associate Director
Edisto Island, South Carolina

answer to my prayers

During the years from 2008 to 2010, my life suffered several huge losses. My only daughter moved to California unexpectedly, and she quit college her senior year. I lost a job that I loved. My father became very, very ill. The stock market crashed and we lost most of our retirement. My father-in-law had a stroke and lost his speech and the use of his right side. All of these losses took a toll on my heart and on my life in ways that were devastating.

I am a Christian, so I know that God is in control, but after each loss, I became more convinced that I deserved these punishments for past sins. I became depressed and gradually quit having my quiet time and withdrew into a shell. I sat for hours on the couch watching television and eating my pain away. I've never been a big television watcher, but I became a couch potato deluxe and gained lots of weight. The more weight I gained, the less motivation I had to do anything with my life. I woke up one day and realized that I was a useless slug, and I desperately needed help to get out of the pit.

BEFORE

AFTER

I cried out to God and begged Him to help me get a grip so that I could once again walk in peace and joy with Him. I confessed my sins of complacency and gluttony and begged for forgiveness. We have a God who hears our prayers and takes joy in answering them. The very next Sunday, in the church bulletin, there was an ad for a new Bible study called First Place 4 Health. I knew immediately that this would be the answer to my prayer, and it has been.

Our group has worked through four Bible study books now, and all four of them have been exactly what I needed in my journey to healing. The daily studies are not too long, but are so very meaningful and helpful. I've lost 30 pounds in 9 months, gained a group of Christian sisters who are on this same journey to wellness, and I am loving my sweet Jesus so much. My morning quiet time is precious and life changing. His blessings are fresh and new every morning.

This past month, I lost my baby sister in a tragic death. I just thought I knew what pain was. My heart is broken, and the guilt and sorrow want to take over again, but with Jesus by my side, and the support of my Christian sisters, I will not go back to that pit of depression. I am so grateful to the First Place 4 Health program for providing the Bible studies that lead Christians through the difficulties and heartbreaks of life in a healthier way.

Gale Dupriest
Stephenville, Texas

Notes

1. Beth Moore, *Praying God's Word* (Nashville, TN: B&H Books, 2000).
2. Rick Warren, "I Am Free," Integrity's Hosanna Music, 1989, © Integrity Music, Inc.
3. "Facts on Induced Abortion in the United States," Guttmacher Institute, January 2001. http://www.guttmacher.org/pubs/fb_induced_abortion.html.

MONTH 9

HONOR

true love

Be devoted to one another in brotherly love. Honor one another above yourselves.

ROMANS 12:10

Johnny's cancer has been the vehicle that God has used to teach me the true meaning of this verse. The word "devotion" means "ardent love and affection." We already had been married almost 40 years before Johnny's diagnosis with stage 4 prostate cancer in 1997. You would think that after that many years of marriage, I would certainly know about love. After his diagnosis, I discovered a deeper level of love than I had ever known before—a love that I would describe as "ardent love and affection."

I have thought about this phenomenon many times, and what I have realized is that I had been living my life as if I would always have Johnny with me, and I took for granted the love we shared. When faced with the prospect of not having Johnny with me, my love became devoted. Nothing is too much trouble for me if it will help Johnny or please him in any way. I am never too tired or too busy, because I have learned what devoted love means: it is to honor him above myself.

I am thankful for Johnny's illness because without it, I might never have learned to have a "devoted love." I am truly blessed to have learned to honor Johnny above myself.

I believe that most of us go through life loving many people but not to the point of loving them above ourselves. This verse is saying that this is the way we are to love everyone. When we honor another person above ourselves, we go the extra mile without giving it a thought. We can't do enough for that person because of the "ardent love and affection" we have for them.

What would happen in our world if every believer practiced this verse? Unbelievers would come to Christ because of this kind of love. Marriages would be healed, wayward children would come home, and broken friendships would be mended.

Prayer: *Dear Lord, I thank You for working in my life to teach me the true meaning of this verse. Teach me to love others with a devoted love that puts them above myself.*

Carole Lewis
First Place 4 Health National Director
Houston, Texas

177

a vow of devotion

Be devoted to one another in brotherly love. Honor one another above yourselves.
ROMANS 12:10

This verse reminds me of wedding vows and what they mean. When you love someone, honor and devotion rise to put your marriage partner's needs above your own. You are called to do something bigger than yourself. I was privileged to witness my parents' love and devotion to one another when my mother was diagnosed with Alzheimer's. As the disease progressed, I remember hearing my father talk about how he had promised to love, honor and cherish Mother in sickness and in health as long as he would live.

My father had severe back and heart problems and was unable to stand or walk for long distances without use of a walker or motorized wheel chair. Many days he was in great pain. When Mother needed specialized care and had to move to a special care facility, Daddy drove twice a day so that he could take her to the dining room to eat lunch and dinner with her. He could barely walk himself, but he pushed his beloved wife, whom he called Babe, in a wheelchair so that they could share mealtime together. He watched over her and cared for her. He demonstrated love and devotion to her in many ways.

Love does not give up when things get difficult. When we go through difficult times, love has the opportunity to grow deeper and sweeter. We reflect what is truly in our hearts if love lives there. Love perseveres. Love gives oneself to another. That's the kind of love our heavenly Father, through His Son Jesus Christ, has modeled to us.

Action Item: Ask the Lord to help you do something bigger than yourself. Acknowledge your need for Him to come in and take over your emotions and thoughts to help you love others with true devotion. Record your prayer in your journal.

Prayer: *Lord Jesus, come in and reign over my emotions and thoughts so that I can reflect Your love in all that I do.*

Connie Welch
First Place 4 Health Networking Leader
Keller, Texas

178

we can do it

Be devoted to one another in brotherly love. Honor one another above yourselves.
ROMANS 12:10

"I can do it!" These words bring laughter to my heart and a wonderful memory. I was given the opportunity to participate in a First Place 4 Health Wellness Retreat; and as an extra blessing, my 72-year-old mom went with me. What could be more amazing than spending time with my mom in a beautiful setting like Round Top, Texas! She grew up on a farm in Virginia, and walking along the gravel roads made us both feel as though we had stepped back in time.

One Sunday afternoon, we went with a few other ladies on a bike ride. I thought I saw clouds in the distance, but no one seemed deterred. When we were a good distance from the ranch, the rain started. First it was a drizzle, but it quickly turned to a downpour. There was nothing to do but pedal back as rapidly as possible.

I was instantly concerned for my mom, and then we saw our rescuers. Someone sent a car for us, and they went straight to my mom. I felt a sigh of relief until I saw that she did not get into the car. I quickly got their attention and asked why they didn't pick up my mom. The response was, "She said, 'I can do it!'" I didn't know if I wanted to laugh or cry. But I do know that we got back safe and sound, with no sniffles, and with a happy memory. Mom and I rode back through the rain together, singing songs and encouraging each other to keep going. I'm glad we didn't take the car ride.

On that trip, I learned a little more about my mom's strength—not only physically, but socially, emotionally and spiritually. Little did we know that shortly after that Mom would enter a new season of life as my dad, her husband of 52 years, passed away. She had to learn many new things, and she is still adjusting; but with God's help she knows she can do it. I am so grateful to have a godly mom to learn from, walk alongside and love in her latter years.

Action Item: Are you still a learner? What can you learn from your parents either now or through some of your past experiences together?

Linda Seagears
Gainesville, Virginia

179
my friend margie

Be devoted to one another in brotherly love. Honor one another above yourselves.

ROMANS 12:10

Some of you may remember the song "Margie" from the 1940s. One line in the song says, "Oh, Margie, you've been my inspiration, Days are never blue." I have a friend Margie, who was definitely my inspiration when I totaled my car in Searcy, Arkansas, the summer of 2010.

Margie and I grew up in a small town near Searcy and were best friends throughout all of our school years. When we both married and began our families, I moved to a larger city and eventually to Houston, Texas, while she settled in Searcy. My mother also lived in Searcy, and that summer I had rushed to her bedside when she suddenly became ill.

Margie and I had stayed in touch through Christmas cards and updates from our families, but we reconnected after my husband went to heaven, and I made annual trips to Searcy alone to visit my mom. Each year, we arranged to set aside a day to get together with our other childhood friend we called Sissie, who is also now in heaven. Those were wonderful days of reminiscing and renewing our friendships. Sissie had amazing memory recall and kept up with all of our school friends, giving updates as we talked throughout the day.

Although Margie was caring for her elderly mother the summer of my accident, she also began to care for me and my mother. She came to the emergency room after my accident and was by my side as I had staples put in my head. She brought books to read and fresh vegetables from her garden, cooked meals and prayed for both of us as we recuperated. Margie's life was full, but she honored our friendship above her own life and demonstrated "brotherly love" through a very difficult time. We both were saddened when I left to bring my mother to live with me in Houston. However, my "days were never blue" because of the prayers of my First Place 4 Health family and my friend Margie.

Prayer: *Thank You, Lord, that You lead us along life's journey, bringing just the right people into our lives at just the right time. Thank You for shining Your light of brotherly love through friends during the dark times.*

Pat Lewis
First Place 4 Health Assistant to the Director
Houston, Texas

friend of honor

Be devoted to one another in brotherly love. Honor one another above yourselves.
ROMANS 12:10

One of the most memorable weeks of my life was in October 2004. A friend invited me to join her on the trip to Round Top, Texas, for the First Place 4 Health Wellness Retreat. At the time, I was on disability retirement, with limited income. Little did I know how God would bless my life for taking a gigantic leap of faith. He blessed me with some of the most awesome friends, delightful memories and life-changing moments!

The memory of one particular day will forever be emblazoned in my heart and mind—the day I met Jean Wall, who, as a result of her compassion, would become a precious friend. I'll never forget the moment I began walking from the back of the Inn House. As I reached the end of the gravel path, I considered turning back. Only a short distance farther and I was questioning if I would live through this walk, as this was my first attempt, after many years, to walk any distance!

Suddenly, Jean Wall appeared and began a conversation. As we arrived at the Inn House, Jean told me that she had to continue her walk as she was training for a marathon in her home state of Washington. She had many miles to walk, yet she made the decision to encourage me to finish walking my first mile in many, many years! Jean Wall had clothed herself with compassion, kindness, humility, gentleness and patience!

Our friendship has grown deeper these last few years as we have shared tough times as well as times of great blessing, joy and spiritual growth in both of our lives.

When we make the effort to devote ourselves in brotherly love, and we honor another above ourselves, God will bless us in ways we could never imagine!

Prayer: *Lord Jesus, may I be devoted to another in brotherly love and honor others above myself, because You demonstrated that kind of love to me and to the whole world when You died on the cross for our sins.*

Stephanie Rhodes
First Place 4 Health Networking Leader
Arlington, Tennessee

love and acceptance

Accept one another, then, just as Christ accepted you, in order to bring praise to God.

ROMANS 15:7

You have probably heard the saying, "God loves you just the way you are, but too much to let you stay that way." This is a witty saying, but I think that we often insert our own name where God's name appears in the saying: "Mama loves you just the way you are, but too much to let you stay that way." "As your wife, I love you just the way you are, but too much to let you stay that way."

This verse is telling me that God wants me to accept others unconditionally, just as Christ accepted me, and this would mean that my only job is to love them, and leave the changes to God. Love is powerful, and true acceptance of another person is a sign that we trust God to work in that person's life just like He has worked in ours.

As a First Place 4 Health leader for 30 years, I have seen many different types of women in my classes. There are women who know so much about losing weight that you wonder why they are there at all. Then there are women who say rude things to others in the class; women who complain; and women who try to monopolize the class discussion.

Thankfully, these women are few and far between, but the lesson I have learned over the years is that these women need total acceptance, and if they can't get it in my class, where will they get it? It is the most beautiful thing to see how love and acceptance allow God to work in a person's heart to make the necessary changes. To see one of these women begin to blossom and bloom is, without a doubt, the most rewarding part of being a leader.

If you and I accepted one another just as Christ accepted us, people would be knocking down the doors of our church to get in, and our First Place 4 Health classes would be overflowing with people praising God for the unconditional love and acceptance they have found from us.

Prayer: *Dear Lord, help me today to accept others as You have accepted me so that my life will bring praise to You. In Jesus' name, amen.*

Carole Lewis
First Place 4 Health National Director
Houston, Texas

accepted, sins and all

Accept one another, then, just as Christ accepted you, in order to bring praise to God.
ROMANS 15:7

When my mother called to tell me that my brother was in trouble again, and he was in jail facing a long sentence for sex crimes, I wasn't surprised. I told her it didn't concern me, as he was no longer my brother. My biggest fear at the moment was that my friends would find out that the man in the news headlines was my brother. Shame and anger kept pride intact until the morning Mother called to say my brother had been born again. A local minister had gone to visit him and said Johnny had made a profession of faith.

This was too hard for my mind to comprehend, but God started in on my selfish pride and picked away until I began to earnestly seek guidance through Scripture. The book of Romans is filled with great verses, but this verse jumped out at me. God had forgiven my brother, and Jesus had died for him as much as He had for me. Accepting my brother as a believer didn't mean that I had to condone his behavior; but I had to love and accept him just as Jesus loved and accepted me.

One night in choir rehearsal, God nudged me with a powerful punch. He wanted me to tell my story; but fear of rejection, ridicule and shame crept in. Finally, I could not sit still, and I asked the choir director if I could say a word. Once the words left my mouth, they spewed forth with an urgency that surprised me, and the whole story tumbled out.

At the end, the choir sat silent, but then they applauded, and afterward so many came to offer hugs, love and prayers. They accepted me because they loved me and knew that my brother's behavior had nothing to do with me.

Accepting one another, sins and all, is no more than Jesus would have done, and still does. Because of pride, I almost missed the opportunity of having a great crowd of prayer warriors. Johnny's sins are forgiven; he is a child of God, and I praise God for His faithfulness.

Action Item: Is there someone in your life who needs forgiveness or acceptance from you? Go to that person and offer your love and forgiveness. If there is someone from whom you need to seek forgiveness, go to that person and seek their forgiveness. God will reconcile all relationships when you seek to do His will.

Martha Rogers
Houston, Texas

183

safely accepted

Accept one another, then, just as Christ accepted you, in order to bring praise to God.
ROMANS 15:7

Most every group, class or organization has one person who makes people laugh, who keeps things humorous and likes to clown around. Some leaders enjoy this while others find that it detracts from the overall focus of the lesson. Often when a person is always acting in an extroverted manner, there is something going on within that he or she is trying to cover up.

Recently, when my class began gathering and members were chatting about their week while others were weighing in, our jovial member came in; and the moment we asked how she was, she burst into tears. Her entire body was racked with sobs as she shared how she had just attended the funeral of a long-time friend and former co-worker. The pain she felt traveled through each of us as we wrapped our hearts around hers. She cried herself out in the safety of our First Place 4 Health group, knowing that we cared and accepted her the same way as Christ accepts us.

In First Place 4 Health, we share similar goals, and as we come together each week, we become responsive to one another's needs. We develop sensitivity toward each other and our hearts are made tender when another is hurting. The Christian love we show is compassionate, and we are humbled as we set aside our own set of problems and focus on a sister or brother in Christ who is hurting.

We may need to be reminded that we all have hurts and pain and require a safe zone in which to release them, all the while knowing that we will receive encouragement and love in the process. The Holy Spirit can soften strong personalities through the love of Christian sisters and brothers.

Action Item: Do the members in your group feel safe enough to express hurts and pain? What might you do to encourage someone who is acting uncharacteristically quiet or loud? Ask God to give you the right words or actions to accept the person with godly love.

June Chapko
First Place 4 Health Networking Leader
San Antonio, Texas

184

misfits: wanted!

Accept one another, then, just as Christ accepted you, in order to bring praise to God.
ROMANS 15:7

After about 40 years of rambling around in the desert of the world, looking for the Promised Land of love and acceptance, it was purely God's hand that finally pointed me in the right direction. I am blessed to have found a few places, like my First Place 4 Health groups and some rare churches, where I believe the good folks are on the right track or at least they seem to be getting this part right: I have felt welcomed. I have felt loved. I have felt missed when I wasn't there. I have felt listened to. I have felt laughed at (in a good way!). I have felt comforted and supported, included and encouraged.

I *haven't* felt judged, talked about behind my back (in a bad way!), avoided, snubbed, insulted or unimportant. I haven't felt like I was sitting in someone else's seat, was talking too loudly or taking too long in the bathroom. I haven't felt like I wore the wrong thing, arrived too late or too early, or shouldn't be opening the refrigerator. I haven't felt used. Did I mention that I haven't felt judged? It is hard to freely and openly praise God when fiery arrows are flying at you from all corners of the room, or at least you *think* they are. You might be jumping around all right, but not for the right reasons!

I think the common thread and the recycling fuel that makes their whole world turn in the right direction is that people are not afraid to be themselves when they are not judged; and when they are not judged, they feel accepted for who they are; and when they feel accepted for who they are, they can in turn treat others that same way; and pretty soon you have a whole church that feels loved and accepted and can't wait to come on in and praise God! *Woohoo!*

After all, what exactly *is* "normal," anyway?

Action Item: How can I make the groups I belong to more accepting of everyone so that we can praise God together with our whole hearts and minds?

Prayer: *Lord, what a smorgasbord You bring to the table—the crazier the better! I don't know why we strive so hard to conform to the wrong way when You made us just the way we are supposed to be. Help us to revel in each other's differences and see them as the many facets of You!*

Jeanne Deveau Gregory
Chatham, Virginia

the power of pause

Accept one another, then, just as Christ accepted you, in order to bring praise to God.

ROMANS 15:7

One word comes to mind when I think about how Christ accepts us, warts and all: "unconditional." He came to love the unlovely, even when others insulted and rejected Him. He did the unimaginable and loved us anyway. No one could ever accept and love us unconditionally like He does. Jesus sees in us what we cannot see in ourselves. He looks past the flaws and weaknesses. He looks beyond our selfishness to that diamond in the rough.

Accepting others who are different from us can be a real challenge. But there is a way to meet this challenge with victory. You can respond to others with Christ's love by doing it for Him, not for yourself. Pay attention to your thoughts the next time you are faced with the challenge of accepting someone. If someone says something to hurt your feelings, do you snap back in retaliation? We have the choice to either react or respond to others; there is a difference between the two. Most of the time, reacting is snapping back without thinking, and with our emotions out of control. Responding is taking that pause moment to think about what we are going to say before it leaves our lips, being under the Holy Spirit's control.

That pause moment gives us the time to filter our actions through God's Word. Responding means that we can relate to others the way Jesus did. This does not mean that we embrace sin. Christ loved the sinner, not the sin. Holding grudges and resenting other members of the Body separate us from the will of Christ. Accepting one another promotes unity and bonds us together. It makes the Body of Christ stronger. And this brings honor to God. Do others see Christ in you?

Action Item: You will probably have an opportunity this week to take a pause moment. Will you *react* or will you *respond*? Rely on His Spirit and His Word to give you the help you need; and record in your journal how the week went.

Prayer: *Lord, please help me respond to others with the same love and acceptance that You give me.*

Connie Welch
First Place 4 Health Networking Leader
Keller, Texas

186

God honors honor

"Honor your father and mother"—which is the first commandment with a promise.

EPHESIANS 6:2

Ephesians 6:3 tells us what the promise of the preceding verse is: "That it may go well with you and that you may enjoy long life on the earth." I believe there is a profound truth here much greater than we can see on the surface.

It is easy to honor parents who love Jesus and who love you. It is not so easy to honor parents who don't know Jesus and who don't know how to love you. In my book *Hope for You,* I tell a story of Karen, whose mom became a raging alcoholic. At Karen's dad's funeral, Karen's husband invited her mom to live with them. Karen was furious because she didn't even like her mom. But her mom moved in, and within two months she accepted Jesus, and her life was radically changed.

Jan Coates's story in my book *Give God a Year* is a striking example of God's miraculous emotional healing demonstrated when Jan's mom accepted Jesus. Jan suffered tremendous physical abuse as a child, and her mom ended up living on the streets as a bag lady. Jan honored her mom by looking out for her and buying her a coat and gloves during a freezing winter. Jan's mom accepted Jesus at a Salvation Army Rescue Center and God healed both Jan's and her mom's hearts.

I have a dear friend who was devastated by her parents' divorce when she was a teenager, and she has not had a close relationship with either parent for years. My friend began praying that God would show her how to honor her parents, and she is seeing miracles happen right before her eyes. God is restoring "the years that the swarming locust has eaten" (Joel 2:25).

When we are able to lay down our hurts and our anger and our bitterness over a less-than-perfect childhood, our God comes in mightily to heal and restore us.

Prayer: *Dear Lord, teach us what it means to honor our father and mother, and help us do it so that You can do the healing work that needs to be done in our lives. In Jesus' name, amen.*

Carole Lewis
First Place 4 Health National Director
Houston, Texas

through the eyes of love

"Honor your father and mother"—which is the first commandment with a promise.

EPHESIANS 6:2

As we grow up, our relationship with our parents changes. As children, we are very dependent on them. But as we become adults and parents ourselves, we begin to see our parents from a different perspective. The eyes of our heart are enlightened, and we get to know our parents better. We have the opportunity to become friends.

Our relationship changes again as our parents age and we become their caregivers. It honors the Lord when we give honor to our parents in how we treat them and relate to them. He didn't say in His Word to honor our parents "when we feel like it" or "when it's convenient."

I know that for some it may feel difficult to honor their parents, much less be friends. But God's Word tells us that honoring them is a commandment with a promise. The dictionary references honor as respect. When we show lovingkindness to our parents, that is also respect and honor. Honor should not fade just because circumstances are difficult. In 1 Corinthians 13:4-8, we are told how we are to love each other just as God loves us. May we hold up the mirror of these verses to our hearts and see if honor is reflected there.

I am reminded of a sweet picture of an adult child holding the hand of her elderly parent who is holding the hand of our heavenly Father. As children, our hands are held out to our parents as we learn to walk. But when they are old, we hold their hands. I have a treasured memory the morning my dad passed away of us holding hands. From our hands to our heavenly Father's heart, love never fails and never dies; and neither does honor.

Action Item: Read 1 Corinthians 13:4-8 and look at these verses about love in the context of showing honor toward your parents (if your parents are no longer living, show that honor to a significant elderly person in your life).

Prayer: *Heavenly Father, thank You for giving me the gift of wonderful parents. Help me to honor and respect them by living 1 Corinthians 13:4-8. Help me to remember that by honoring them, I honor You.*

Connie Welch
First Place 4 Health Networking Leader
Keller, Texas

hey, mom, watch!

"Honor your father and mother"—which is the first commandment with a promise.
EPHESIANS 6:2

Remembering is a way to honor your parents.

I don't really remember growing up in a health-conscious family. I remember my mom teaching aerobics and First Place 4 Health. I remember taking one of her classes with some of my teammates in high school; but as far as growing up in a house that was always paying attention to our health, I don't recall. I do recall growing up in a God-conscious house, where loving God with all your heart, soul, mind and strength was a principle lived out by my parents.

I don't remember my parents talking about exercising, but I do remember their voices cheering me on from the sidelines, night after night, week after week, year after year. I remember them encouraging us to pursue sports and other activities. I remember them encouraging us to practice even when the trumpet sounded bad and the chords on the piano didn't match. They invested in us. They bought us good shoes to run the court, good instruments to make music and good gloves to make diving catches.

I remember parents who were conscious of the children God had given them and who were conscious of His desire for them to be good stewards. They disciplined me when I misbehaved, because that was good for me. They knelt and prayed over me as I slept in my bed because that was good for me. They read and proofread my papers, because that was what was good for me. They loved our hearts, our souls, our minds and our bodies, caring for each part of us.

I have memories of a house where Mom and Dad loved the Lord with all their heart, soul, mind and strength, and I think that made all the difference.

Action Item: Honor your parents by carrying on the good things they taught you—with all of your heart.

Michael Heath
English Teacher, Iraq

189

honorable children

"Honor your father and mother"—which is the first commandment with a promise.

EPHESIANS 6:2

In October 2010, my family and I were blessed to honor my parents for their fiftieth wedding anniversary in Niagara Falls, New York. It was wonderful to see so many family and friends travel from Florida, Texas, North Carolina and throughout New York State to show their love and celebrate with us.

As I reflect back on my childhood, I remember attending confirmation classes where we would study and memorize parts of the catechism and Bible verses. The fourth commandment was, "Honour thy father and thy mother: that thy days may be long upon the land which the LORD thy God giveth thee" (Exodus 20:12, KJV). As a child, this was not my favorite verse! I didn't want to always have to obey their rules or face the consequences of my disobedience. I'm sure that I also provoked them to anger a time or two. And if I didn't honor them, would I really not live long on the earth? It just didn't seem fair.

Growing up, I remember the importance of keeping God in our daily life by going to church and Sunday School with my family each week, attending a Lutheran school, praying together before and after each meal and reading *Little Visits with God* with prayers each night before bed. I also witnessed the sacrifice my parents made to honor and care for their parents as they grew older and needed assistance in everyday living.

Now that I am married with three beautiful daughters, God has shown me what a blessing it has been to have Christian parents who loved and cared for me and set a godly example for me to follow. Although I live 1,600 miles away and miss my mom and dad, I talk with them almost every day and am able to visit them for several weeks each year. Whether I live a short or a long life on this earth, I pray that my life brings honor to God in all that I do.

Action Item: What can you do today to bring honor to God? What can you do today to honor your parents or their memory?

Prayer: *Dear Lord, thank You for kind, loving parents. Help me to always show You the love and honor and respect You deserve as I also honor them.*

Sandy Miller
Houston, Texas

a fractured childhood

"Honor your father and mother"—which is the first commandment with a promise.
EPHESIANS 6:2

I often wondered how I could obey this command. How could I honor my alcoholic father and the mother who uprooted me, tearing me from family and friends after their divorce? Some people have parents who make honoring them easy, while others, like me, try to forget painful memories.

God met me in my pain after my divorce. I came to Him in tears asking for help in raising my three children. It was then that God showed me that my parents deserved my respect in spite of their flaws. I made many mistakes as a parent, but I want my children to respect me as their mother. I can do no less for my own parents, even though they have long ago passed away. I could not have known back then the difficulties they were going through in their marriage. I wasn't capable as a child to understand adult situations or the tremendous strain that financial woes could play on an already shaky marriage.

When I became a mother in an abusive marriage, I discovered how difficult it was to make good choices and how children can get shortchanged in the struggles. Divorce changes people, and children must adapt. I certainly desire that my children respect me as their mother, so I must forget about self, remembering that God chose my parents and expects me to honor them even in memory.

Action Item: You may be dealing with the difficulty of honoring parents who you perceive to have failed you. Ask God to give you a forgiving heart to honor the two that He chose as your parents. If you have/had loving, godly parents, take time today to show them honor and respect.

Prayer: *Dear Lord, help me remember that You chose the two people who would give life to me. Cause me to look to You as my Parent and draw on Your love to honor the parents You gave me.*

June Chapko
First Place 4 Health Networking Leader
San Antonio, Texas

renewed hope and a rewritten story

I heard about First Place 4 Health by accident, but not in God's mind. After walking with the Lord for 30 years, I had never been in the state of mind I was in that day—I was depressed! I'm usually very joyful, full of faith and expectancy, but not now. I was taking antibiotics and all sorts of prescriptions, but my body was not responding.

The doctor ordered a blood test, which came back with news of high blood sugar. I needed to be on a strict diet and medicine for diabetes. My weight was at an all-time high—258 pounds—and I'm only 5 foot 2. Between my weight, ongoing sickness and now diabetes, my prayers seemed to be hitting a brick wall.

BEFORE

AFTER

While sitting at my computer, a friend sent an email saying that I was on her mind and in her prayers. I wrote her back and admitted that for the first time in my entire life, I felt hopeless. "I need a divine intervention, and soon," I wrote. When I hit "send," my phone rang.

It was my daughter, Tara, calling to see if I would baby-sit for her on Friday mornings for 12 weeks while she went to a class. I asked what kind of class she was taking. She said First Place 4 Health, a Christian weight-loss program. I started to tear up with the thought that divine intervention had come. I paid for baby-sitting and joined the class with her.

The day we walked through the doors for the meeting, the leader handed me the book *Renewing Hope*. I broke into tears. God knew—He was very aware of my hopelessness and was waiting for the day that I would begin to walk in the purpose He had for me.

I attended a few sessions of First Place 4 Health and was one of the biggest losers. I decided, after coaxing from my leader, to start a class in my area. The first class met in my home, then the doors opened to meet at a church, where we had several sessions; and now my home church has taken our group as one of its ministries.

My physical history was written in my family bloodline. My dad had high blood pressure and diabetes; and after years of poor health, he died from arterial sclerosis—clogged arteries associated with a life of excessive food choices. I've always been overweight, tried every diet plan and quick-fix scheme imaginable, only to ride the roller coaster of lose and gain, over and over again. But now I am coming into a balanced lifestyle emotionally, mentally, spiritually and physically. God is setting me free!

We sing a song at our church, "I am royalty, I have destiny, I have been set free, I'm gonna change history!" While singing it one Sunday, God began to show me my life: "You are the King's kid—royalty; you have destiny—a purpose I created you for; I am setting you free to set others free, and your history has been changed!"

God has used First Place 4 Health to free me from my obsession with food. He has healed me, and I'm now off high blood pressure medicine after 25 years! I am no longer diabetic, and I have gone from a size 24-26 to a 12-14, and have shed 82 pounds. My history has been rewritten!

I read this statement from my Bible study *Giving Christ Control*: "God uses the weakest areas of our life as a platform to exhibit His power." I never thought I would praise God for a testimony of obesity, but I rejoice in His wonder-working, re-creating story of my life! I am humbled and grateful for the divine intervention of First Place 4 Health. It has changed my life and afforded me the joy of seeing Him rewrite the history of the lives of many others as well.

Jackie Lapouble
New Orleans, Louisiana

MONTH 10

GODLINESS

191

extra grace required

No one has ever seen God; but if we love one another,
God lives in us and his love is made complete in us.

1 JOHN 4:12

My former pastor, Dr. John Bisagno, wrote a powerful book called *Love Is Something You Do.* "Love" is a powerful word, in that it has the power to change us as we practice it.

Most of the time, I find that I must make a deliberate decision to love someone who is unlovable. While it is easy to love people who love us back, it is quite hard to love people who do not love God or us.

Over the years of leading First Place 4 Health classes, I have been able to observe the transforming power of love. I have had many women join who needed to be loved more than anything else. These women are easy to spot because they test you to see if you will reject them like so many others have in their past.

I silently name these women EGR (Extra Grace Required) and begin praying about how to reach their hurting hearts. They thought they came just to lose weight, but as they receive unconditional love from our class, God begins to heal their deep hurts and the emotional pain that had kept them from ever having real victory in the weight-loss area.

First Corinthians 13 tells us what godly love looks like, and the book of 1 John tells us how to walk it out. Without the power of God's love living inside us, it is impossible to love others as God does. As we practice loving others, God's love is made complete in us. There is an old song that says, "They will know we are Christians by our love," and that godly love is something sadly lacking in our world today.

Action Item: Is there someone in your life who is difficult for you to love? Ask God to begin loving that person through you and see the miracle that is sure to happen.

Carole Lewis
First Place 4 Health National Director
Houston, Texas

192

love enough for the world

No one has ever seen God; but if we love one another,
God lives in us and his love is made complete in us.

1 JOHN 4:12

I grew up with an inferiority complex. I had very few friends, and I was mostly afraid of people and their opinions of me. Then I met the Lord. I received His love and forgiveness for my sins. For the first time in my life, I experienced unconditional love. Someone cared deeply for me despite my many character flaws.

I prayed for the Lord to deliver me from selfishness and fill my heart with love for others. He has abundantly answered my prayers. My heart is overflowing with God's love. He brings people into my life for me to love and care for. He has blessed me with opportunities to minister in His name. He has provided funds so that I can help those in need.

God's love has changed my life. He has given me the treasure of several Christian women friends who love me unconditionally, and I feel the same about them.

The world has nothing to compare with the love of God. We can be free from fear and worry when we open ourselves to the love of the Holy Spirit within us. We know that God causes all things to work together for good when we love Him and allow Him to fill us with His love. His Spirit and His Word provide all we need to live out His love in the world.

When we show the love of God to others by our attitudes and actions, they see God in us and are drawn to that love. The love of God will change the world if we allow it to overflow onto everyone He sends into our daily lives.

Prayer: *Dear Lord, thank You for Your love, which fills our hearts and overflows to others. Thanks for every opportunity to show that love to others. Thank You for using us to show Your love to the world.*

Karen Baker
Eagle Point, Oregon

193

I call Him the "shapeshifter"

No one has ever seen God; but if we love one another,
God lives in us and his love is made complete in us.

1 JOHN 4:12

The cool thing about being the Shapeshifter is that not only is God ready, willing and able to shift the shape and transform *our* hearts, minds and bodies, but He shifts the shape of His *own* image. I don't think He stopped at burning bushes and talking donkeys.

When I read the opening words of 1 John 4:12, I chuckle—because I see *Him* when I see *them*—the faces of my church family, many of whom I have come to know and love dearly through our First Place 4 Health program. The image shifts from one into another and another so fast that my brain cannot contain all the images:

Sometimes His locks are curly blonde, sometimes He prefers a 'fro.
Sometimes He comes in colors too—what to expect? I never know.
Sometimes His eyes are brown or blue, or perhaps a different hue.
Sometimes He's nearly in the grave, sometimes He's almost new.
Sometimes He towers over me, sometimes I feel so tall;
But in His image He created them, and His love defines them all.

I don't find the definition for "godliness" in a dictionary (no offense, Mr. Webster). But I find it in a wordless compilation of faces of those through whom He has acted out its meaning. As they live out godliness for me through their selfless love, humble acts of service, patience and forgiveness, grace and mercy, willingness to admit their wrongs and their seeking to trust God with all that they are and all that they have, I see God in a myriad of faces.

Action Item: Who has God placed in your life to teach you about godliness? Thank God for them today and write them a note to tell them so.

Prayer: *Lord, thank You for the people You have sent into my life to show me by example what is meant by "godliness." Help me to be the same kind of example in my sphere of influence. Thank You for sending Your saints into my life so that I can truly see Your face. Amen.*

Jeanne Deveau Gregory
Chatham, Virginia

194

doctor love

No one has ever seen God; but if we love one another,
God lives in us and his love is made complete in us.

1 JOHN 4:12

Once upon a time, in a land far, far away, lived a young girl who did not know that God is love, or that all her answers about love could be found by reading a Book that contained Genesis through Revelation. In fact, she didn't even know where to find Genesis and Revelation. One day, she bumped into a book called *Living, Loving and Learning*, written by Felice Leonardo "Leo" Buscaglia, PhD. *Ah!* she thought. *There is someone else out there who knows that something essential is missing in this cold, cold world, and actually cares.*

He had other books, too, and she hungrily read more of them. Her outlook on life began to change, mostly because she began following his example of leaping out of bed in the morning, stepping to the window and proclaiming, "Thank You, God, for this beautiful day!" Then she started sharing smiles, and then hugs.

According to Wikipedia, "Buscaglia worked actively to overcome social and mental barriers that inhibited the expression of love between people. . . . The profundity of his subject, however, almost invariably struck a responsive chord for many in an area frequently regarded as deficient in their lives, and by 1998, his books had reached 18 million copies in print in 17 languages." Leo Buscaglia left this cold world quite a bit warmer when his big heart stopped beating on June 12, 1998. If one former young girl had anything to say about it, 1 John 4:12 would be prominently displayed on his memorial marker.

Action Item: See how many smiles you can bring to faces today as you give freely smiles of your own! After you try that, upgrade to hugs. Write what happens in your journal. Then write a follow-up one week later. Make note of any improvements you see in your relationships as you make a difference in people's lives, and in your own!

Prayer: *Dear Lord, now I know that You wrote the Book on love, but I thank You for Your servant Leo Buscaglia and for others who dedicate their lives to bring love back into this cold, cold world.*

Jeanne Deveau Gregory
Chatham, Virginia

spreading His love

No one has ever seen God; but if we love one another,
God lives in us and his love is made complete in us.

1 JOHN 4:12

The other day, when I drove into our carport, my next-door neighbor's son-in-law walked up to me to tell me that our neighbor had a stroke while Johnny and I were in California at the doctor. We have lived in our townhouse for eight months, and I have talked with this man several times as we were coming and going, but I had never met his wife. His wife, who is 83, has two jobs; so she had always been at work when I talked with her husband.

I had just come from my office where I picked up some copies of my newest book *Hope 4 You.* I was in a hurry to wash my hair for a party that evening, but I felt the prompting of the Holy Spirit to take a copy of the book next door and give it to the wife. I argued in my mind for a few seconds and then grabbed a book and went next door.

What a blessing awaited me! The family was all there, and this man's wife, without a doubt, was one of the sweetest Christian women I have ever met. She was thrilled to have the book and said that she would read it while sitting at the hospital and then pass it on to her family to read. When she found out that I directed First Place 4 Health, she said that her daughter had been in the program at our church! What a small world!

I went to the party with unwashed hair, but I received a huge blessing and was used by God to love on a hurting family.

Action Item: Is there someone you know who needs your love today? Pray and ask God what He would have you do. Then do it! God will bless you and the other person as well.

Carole Lewis
First Place 4 Health National Director
Houston, Texas

196

when we call

Know that the LORD has set apart the godly for himself;
the LORD will hear when I call to him.

PSALM 4:3

In 1981, Dottie Brewer founded the First Place program. One night, Dottie was returning home from a trip to Dallas to talk with a possible publisher for the First Place program. Dottie was involved in a car wreck and her car caught fire, but her door would not open. Dottie cried out, "God, help me!" and out of nowhere a man appeared, dressed in white, opened her door and helped her out of the car. Dottie believed it was an angel because, as people began showing up to help, the mysterious man was nowhere to be found. I loved it when Dottie said, "I sure was glad that God and I had such an intimate relationship that when I called out to Him He knew my voice."

All of us who know Jesus personally have the same assurance as Dottie that God hears us when we call to Him. I will never forget sitting in the family room at the hospital the night our daughter Shari died after being hit by a drunk driver. When the chaplain told us that Shari was gone, the room was so quiet you could hear a pin drop. After a few moments, I lifted my eyes and said, "God, if You don't help us, we are not going to make it." God's peace flooded the room at that instant and we were able to make it through that awful time wrapped in His arms of love.

My son-in-love, Jeff, who is very shy by nature, was able to speak at Shari's memorial service. Jeff spoke eloquently, and it was obvious that God was speaking through him. Jeff's sister, Yvonne, who Shari led to Christ, also spoke publicly for the first time and brought God glory with her testimony of His love and grace.

Prayer: *Dear Lord, thank You for hearing us when we call to You. What a privilege to be set apart for You!*

Carole Lewis
First Place 4 Health National Director
Houston, Texas

197

our chain gang

Know that the LORD has set apart the godly for himself;
the LORD will hear when I call to him.

PSALM 4:3

Jesus said that in this life we will have troubles, but it seems like some people have more than their share. I have a dear friend whose life was overwhelmed with burdens. It was always bad news. Always—until one day I heard an unfamiliar lilt in her voice: She was going to be a grandmother! *Finally,* I thought, *something good!* I rejoiced with her during the time of anticipation, but one phone call stopped me in my tracks—an emergency with the pregnancy, and both mother and child were at risk. Her voice racked with tears, she asked me to start a prayer chain.

I felt as if their very lives hung on my next move. My fingers trembled as I dialed the phone. I passed along the details as best as I could, and then for the first time in my life, I dropped to my face on the kitchen floor, begging God not to allow this one good thing to be snatched away, and to return full health to mother and child and to give the doctors the wisdom and skill to handle the situation.

I have no idea how much time really passed, but what seemed like before I could even get up off the floor, the phone was ringing again—me of little faith, of course I feared the worst. My breath caught in my throat as I said, "Hello?" The crisis had *passed*; they were both going to be *fine!* I hung up the phone in shock. It took a minute for the reality to sink in. With trembling fingers yet again, I passed along the details as best as I could! Their prayers of thanksgiving spread with the same fervency as their passionate requests moments before. I know that our Father smiles when He hears the sound of the men and women working on *this* chain gang—one I never want to escape from!

Action Item: Read about the faith of Daniel in your Bible. If you don't already keep a prayer list in your journal, start one today, and be sure to include a "date answered" column.

Prayer: *Lord, now that I know that I know that I know how instantly You hear us and can answer prayers, I trust Your wisdom in how, when and where You choose to do it. I thank You and praise You for Your mercy, love and compassion.*

Jeanne Deveau Gregory
Chatham, Virginia

198

use me up, God

*Know that the LORD has set apart the godly for himself;
the LORD will hear when I call to him.*

PSALM 4:3

Being godly! Now that is a challenge! It is my heart's desire for God to use me—all of me. This Scripture says He has set me apart for this very reason, and He expects me to be godly. After all, according to 2 Peter 1:3, He has given me everything I need for life and godliness.

There are some practical things I can do to help the process along, but one thing stands above all the rest: pay attention to my spiritual health. Jesus was a perfect spiritual person. He worshiped regularly; He obeyed God continually; and He witnessed to His friends. He was able to do this because He knew the importance of spending time with His Father. Mark 1:35 tells us that "very early in the morning, while it was still dark, Jesus got up, left the house and went off to a solitary place, where he prayed."

Life is not going to get easier or less busy. There is so much to do for the kingdom of God, and He is looking for the godly. We don't need to be running on spiritual vapors and living life at warp speed. We should be like water-filled clouds over a dry and thirsty land. Are we reapers who are too weak to swing the sickle of salvation in a world white with harvest?

Developing godliness comes but one way, and Jesus said it best in John 15:5: "I am the vine; you are the branches. If a man remains in me and I in him, he will bear much fruit; apart from me you can do nothing."

Prayer: *Father, slow me down enough to develop godliness in me, and then use me up.*

Vicki Heath
First Place 4 Health Associate Director
Edisto Island, South Carolina

199

trust Him with your heart

Know that the LORD has set apart the godly for himself;
the LORD will hear when I call to him.

PSALM 4:3

My husband's routine colonoscopy turned into multiple surgeries when a tumor was removed and cancer cells were found in the lymph nodes. There are upcoming decisions concerning chemo, and our life has changed in just two short months. My prayer in the beginning was for the tumor to be benign; that prayer changed in the second surgery to: "Please, Lord, let the cancer be contained." After the discovery of the cancer, I pleaded with God for a clear report on the lymph nodes. They found two positive nodes.

My first reaction was, "Why, Lord? Why didn't You hear my prayer?" During subsequent days and many hours in quiet time with God, I felt Him telling me, "I heard your prayer, just trust me." Each day I am learning to trust Him more. David knew he had been set apart for God, and he recorded that knowledge in God's Word. I know that I have been set apart as well. Often I fall short of God's expectations for me, but that does not prevent Him from hearing my prayers. God has a purpose in everything He allows His children to go through; and while I would rather not have had the word "cancer" change our lives, I am assured that God heard my prayer and will carry us through this valley as He continues His work in our lives.

As believers, we may sometimes feel that our prayers are floating around in virtual space and we may give up praying. We must never give up! It's because we have been forgiven that God hears our prayers. We can bring our concerns and burdens to our heavenly Father and rest in His mercy and grace. He wants His best for us because He has set us apart for Himself. Even when things look bleak, especially when the hour is dark and seemingly without hope, that is when we must trust that God is listening and will answer. The answer may not be exactly what we expected, but we can know that God is our hope.

Prayer: *Heavenly Father, I'm glad to be Your child and thankful You have set me apart and listen to my cries for help. I am so joyful that You know my heart and my doubts and questions and that You speak to my hurting heart. I trust Your answers. In Jesus' name, amen.*

June Chapko
First Place 4 Health Networking Leader
San Antonio, Texas

200

special-delivery faith

Know that the LORD has set apart the godly for himself;
the LORD will hear when I call to him.

PSALM 4:3

We are told throughout Scripture that the Lord hears us when we call to Him. A sweet illustration the Lord gave me was about the envelope of faith and His promise that He hears me. In our First Place 4 Health group, we were memorizing the Scripture Hebrews 11:1: "Now faith is being sure of what we hope for and certain of what we do not see."

At the time we were memorizing this verse, I was burdened in my heart over several issues. I could see myself writing each burden, care and concern on a piece of paper and placing it in an envelope. On the outside of the envelope I wrote out the Scripture Hebrews 11:1. I addressed it to the names of the Lord and what each name stood for. I could see myself walking up to my heavenly Father and handing Him the envelope. It was marked "special delivery, fragile, handle with care." I saw Him with His hand reached out, and in His hand I placed my envelope of faith.

Here is the important part. I had to let go. I had to give the envelope to Him. It was no longer mine, but His. As I looked into His face, I saw a smile, and He held the envelope I had placed in His hand next to His heart. With His other hand, He touched my tear-stained face and said, "There, there, child, it will be all right." I had the sweet assurance that He heard me, and my burdens were in His care. They had been transferred from my heart and hands to His.

Whenever I start to worry, I remember that I have already delivered that envelope of faith. I keep a visual reminder of that envelope where I see it often. How thankful I am that I have assurance from His Word that He hears me and daily bears my burdens.

Action Item: Make your own envelope of faith. See yourself placing that envelope in your heavenly Father's hand and hear His words spoken over you when you call.

Prayer: *Heavenly Father, thank You that I belong to You; and I thank You for Your sweet assurance that You hear me when I call.*

Connie Welch
First Place 4 Health Networking Leader
Keller, Texas

we serve a mighty God!

His divine power has given us everything we need for life and godliness through our knowledge of him who called us by his own glory and goodness.

2 PETER 1:3

What a comfort to know that I have absolutely everything I need to live out this life on earth. The day I asked Jesus to come into my life, He sent His Holy Spirit to take up residence inside of me and He has never left me. My knowledge of Him has grown through the years as I have studied and memorized His Word.

God has been so faithful to Johnny and me since 1997, when we began Johnny's stage 4 cancer journey. He guided us to our wonderful doctor and has given us the courage and strength to face an uncertain future with hope and joy. We have not had a need that He has not provided in all these years.

God has shown His mighty power in our lives since we lost our home and all of our possessions when Hurricane Ike hit in September 2008. He provided a furnished townhome, and we had everything we needed for 15 months. We didn't own one thing in that house, but it was ours to use and enjoy.

Knowing that God has given us everything we need keeps us from being afraid of the future. When we need Him, He is there. He has helped me direct the First Place 4 Health program since 1987. There have been so many times when I didn't have a clue what the next step would be, but God stepped in to lay out the plan.

It has been said that "those He calls, He equips." What comfort to know that the very instant we ask Christ to come into our lives, He begins equipping us with everything we will ever need to live this life. What a God we serve! He gets sweeter every day!

Action Item: Write in your journal about something in your life that needs God's divine power right now. Confess that you know you have everything you need, and ask God to reveal His plan to you.

Carole Lewis
First Place 4 Health National Director
Houston, Texas

202

God wants you to do it

His divine power has given us everything we need for life and godliness through our knowledge of him who called us by his own glory and goodness.

2 PETER 1:3

I used to be so afraid to pray in groups. I worked at a church, so praying in groups was common. Many times we would gather in a circle and hold hands, and I would try to rub my hands on my pants because I knew they were already getting sweaty. Everyone's prayers were so much better than anything I could say. They prayed Scripture, their words were so elegant, and they would think of so many relevant things to pray for the event or person.

As part of our small staff at First Place 4 Health, we met for prayer each week. You would think it wouldn't be as bad praying in front of those three or four ladies that I knew so well, but it was worse! To my mind they are in the top 10 of best pray-ers! How intimidating! They were very sweet and would bounce around or skip over me and act like it didn't matter, but it mattered to me.

When I began to lead a First Place 4 Health class, my co-leader always led the prayers. When she stepped down, I started leading the class with another person. As we decided who would do what, I realized that I would be the one leading the prayer at the beginning of each class. My heart raced that first time, but what a relief! It wasn't so bad after all. In fact, I enjoyed it. What a privilege to pray for those ladies and our time together that day! For so many years I had let my perfectionism keep me from that blessing.

Is fear or perfectionism keeping you from doing something you feel led to do? Are you hesitating to start a First Place 4 Health class of your own because you don't think you are good enough or have lost enough weight, or because someone else can do it better? Do you have a story to share, but don't feel like you can tell it well enough? Do you hesitate to say your Scripture each week because you might get one or two words wrong? Don't miss out on the blessing that can be yours if you take that leap. You can do it through His divine power.

Prayer: *Lord, give me the strength to follow the path You've set before me. Ease my fears and my insecurities, and guide me as I grow stronger and more confident in all I do for You.*

Lisa Lewis
First Place 4 Health Director of Events
Houston, Texas

a season of restoration

*His divine power has given us everything we need for life and godliness
through our knowledge of him who called us by his own glory and goodness.*

2 PETER 1:3

I have been in First Place 4 Health almost 17 years, and I love the program. God has taught me so much during this time. My journey has been one of losing, gaining and beginning again. But through it all, God has always been faithful!

I had severe colitis and had to go on a medical disability from teaching. I was taking four different medications just to go anywhere. I was overweight and miserable. I discovered First Place in the fall of 1993, and I started leading a group the following spring. I lost 65 to 70 pounds and was well on my way to my weight goal. Then I developed arthritis in my knee and tendonitis in my heel. I was taking Celebrex to keep moving.

In 1998, I found myself in a long "season of loss." I lost seven close family members, including both my father (my hero) and my mother. I am an emotional and stress eater, so I regained almost all of the weight I had taken off.

In 2001, I began again faithfully doing the First Place 4 Health program. God brought first Dr. Richard Couey into my life through the First Place 4 Health program and used him to teach me a plan of nutrition and fitness to fight inflammatory diseases and get rid of the arthritis. Then through our New Hope Baptist Church wellness program He introduced Dr. Gary Huber, who discovered several hormone imbalances and taught me what to do to correct them with an all-natural, healthy program. I now take no medications of any kind, not even over-the-counter meds.

I have now lost 130 pounds, 7 dress sizes and I just received the best medical test results of my entire life! God has used First Place 4 Health to teach me "everything I need for life and godliness" for His glory.

Action Item: Ask God what He wants to give you to help you in your wellness journey. He has all the power you need.

Janet Kirkhart
First Place 4 Health Networking Leader
Loveland, Ohio

204

He is the *everything*

His divine power has given us everything we need for life and godliness
through our knowledge of him who called us by his own glory and goodness.

2 PETER 1:3

I have to giggle each week as we begin our First Place 4 Health class. Everyone steps up to the scale, taking off as much clothing as possible, while mumbling over and over under their breath the memory verse they are about to quote.

Recently, this verse in 2 Peter 1:3 challenged me, and the Lord had me share this fact with the class. After all, isn't this why we come together, to be encouraged as we share the good, the bad and the godly of our journey to live a balanced life? The verse said, "His divine power has given us everything we need for life and godliness," and immediately a thought came: *So why am I not reaching my goals?* It surely wasn't His fault.

I began tracing my steps: food plan, check—food journal, check—Bible study, check—exercise, not so much—prayer time, not so good. I reasoned, *It's been crazy lately with all the busyness of life.* Suddenly, the words "life" and "godliness" popped into my mind, and I headed for my dictionary.

"Godliness: the ability to conform to the laws and wishes of God." Ouch! I hadn't been spending much time with Him, talking and getting to know His wishes, much less conforming to them! I thought, *Foolish Galatian, are you trying to attain your goal by human effort, running your race in your own strength, counting on self— the very one that got you in this shape and bad health to begin with?*

That week I meditated on the verse, spending time in His presence, getting to know Him and His Word more. Through that knowledge, you know what I realized? He is the *everything* I need to live this life and to acquire godliness.

Action Item: If you aren't meeting your physical goals, is there something missing in the emotional or spiritual realm that God can help you with? Remember, He's your everything! Do some pondering and praying, and record in your journal what the Holy Spirit brings to mind.

Prayer: *Father, forgive me for letting the busyness of life rob our time together. I love You and I want to spend my time getting to know You even more. You are my everything! Amen.*

Jackie LaPouble
New Orleans, Louisiana

nothing lacking

His divine power has given us everything we need for life and godliness
through our knowledge of him who called us by his own glory and goodness.

2 PETER 1:3

There has been much discussion through the centuries concerning the inerrancy—the perfect correctness—of the Word of God. Are the translations we read really accurate, and are they 100 percent reliable? For my sanity, I have to say yes! If I doubt what happened in Exodus, how can I have full assurance that John 3:16 is true?

With that in mind, what do we do with a verse like the one above? Do we really believe that everything—direction, guidance, power, counsel, wisdom—that we need for life and godliness is found in the knowledge of Jesus? Again, for my sanity, I have to say yes!

As we come to know Jesus more, we will gain more understanding in how to do life and how to walk in godliness. As we spend time with Jesus through prayer, Bible study and simply reading His Word, the Word becomes alive and active, and we are given insight into what we are to do that day.

Do you have a problem? God will provide the solution in His Word.

Do you need encouragement to keep on keeping on? God will provide a Scripture that will speak to that direct situation.

Do you have a wound that needs to be healed? God's Word is like the Balm of Gilead and will provide comfort and relief for that pain.

It is really up to us. God has distilled His thoughts into 66 books, and has given us through His Holy Spirit the ability to know Jesus and to know His Word. Are we willing to take the time—quantity and quality—to know Him? When we do, we can be assured that His Word is perfect and we can have everything we need for life and godliness.

Action Item: Begin today spending time with Jesus through His Word. Ask the Holy Spirit to be your Teacher and your Guide. If you are already doing that, why not ramp it up? It will never be wasted time, for His Word never comes back void.

Becky Turner
First Place 4 Health Speaker
Houston, Texas

206

nothing but the godly truth

Have nothing to do with godless myths and old wives' tales;
rather, train yourself to be godly.

1 TIMOTHY 4:7

I remember being told when I was pregnant that I could tell the gender of my child by tying a string to a pencil and holding it above my bare stomach. You were supposed to be able to tell the sex of the child by the way the pencil swung. This was an old wives' tale that has no validity in fact.

I think it is amazing that God planned from the beginning for there to be an equal number of boys and girls in this world. China, because of its one child per family policy, and because boys are favored above girls, has experienced a phenomenon of having too many boys and not enough girls for them to marry. I was pleased when my book *The Mother-Daughter Legacy* was translated into Chinese. When I asked why it was translated into that particular language, I was told that the Chinese government is attempting to give value to girls and encourage their people to have and keep more girl babies. Many girl babies are aborted before birth and many others are abandoned at birth or given up for adoption.

We can train ourselves to be godly by not relying on anything for truth but God's Word. The daily horoscope is not our guide; the Bible is our guide. Inside its pages we can find answers to everything we need. The key is to memorize Scriptures that speak truth into the godless myths and old wives' tales we have been told. In doing this, we cover the lies with God's truth.

Another way we can train ourselves to be godly is to ask God to send us someone as a mentor who is a step ahead of us spiritually. An accountability group of committed Christians is still another way to train ourselves to be godly.

Prayer: *Dear Lord, I want to train myself to be godly. Show me Your plan for my life as I dedicate myself to reading, studying and memorizing Your Word. Give me strong Christians to help me on this journey toward godliness.*

Carole Lewis
First Place 4 Health National Director
Houston, Texas

our daily bread

Have nothing to do with godless myths and old wives' tales;
rather, train yourself to be godly.

1 TIMOTHY 4:7

"You must eat a grapefruit with every meal," a well-meaning friend instructed, as she nodded knowingly. "This is supposed to really work. I read about it in a magazine." *Another magazine article spouting advice,* I thought, *from yet another so-called expert wanting to sell books providing a quick fix to rapid weight loss.*

I'd seen it all and, unfortunately, tried it all before. Grapefruits all day. Ice cream only. Liquids for breakfast, lunch and dinner. Every time I turned on the TV or stood in line at the checkout stand, I would find myself bombarded with the next great diet and health program. Some had tidbits of truth; others, well—let's just say I found myself wanting for a new program or plan. This constant seeking and searching for the ultimate weight-loss program had me flipping from one fad to another. I was caught up in the madness of myths and old wives' tales, things God's Word instructs us to avoid if we are seeking godliness.

But wait a minute . . . don't those scriptural instructions apply solely to the spiritual realm? That was a question I often pondered. I found myself compartmentalizing my life. Body, mind, emotions and spirit were different; therefore, I should treat each accordingly. Shouldn't I? Hopefully, you already know the answer to that question. Fortunately, I do too, thanks to First Place 4 Health.

Rather than treating just "one piece" of ourselves, we are to focus on becoming godlier in all areas. Godliness embraces complete health, including a healthier body. God's Word gives us all the information we could possibly need to attain maximum health in every area of our lives. We no longer need to depend on whatever myth or fad the world is currently serving up. Instead, let us fill up on the right feast: God's truth, found in His amazing Word, and the complementary godly principles implemented in our First Place 4 Health program.

Action Item: Before you spend money on the fastest-growing weight-loss fad, take time to search God's Word and your First Place 4 Health materials for answers. Remember: There is no quick fix that offers lasting, godly results.

Carol VanAtta
Troutdale, Oregon

do it again and again

Have nothing to do with godless myths and old wives' tales;
rather, train yourself to be godly.

1 TIMOTHY 4:7

A dear friend of mine was an ice dancer and spent countless hours on the rink doing the same four-minute routine again and again. I noticed that others would even break down the free dance and do a specific lift or jump that may only be 10 seconds long, dozens of times. Why? Because amateurs train until they get it right, while professionals train until they can't get it wrong.

The question before us today is, "Are we amateur Christians who do just enough to get by, or are we professional Christians who train ourselves to be godly?"

To train ourselves in godliness takes three things: knowledge, practice and coaching. Obviously, the most logical place to gain knowledge about godliness is through the study of God's Word. But we can also gain knowledge by doing life with others. Want to know what a godly spouse looks like? Go hang out with someone who models that. Want to know how to run a business in a godly way? Read a biography of a businessman who does this.

The next step after gaining the knowledge is to start practicing what we know because to know and not do is sin (see James 4:17). The key point here is that it is practice—sometimes we will nail that jump and sometimes we will fall flat on our face. But regardless, do it again!!

Lastly, we all need a coach, a mentor, an older man or woman to walk along-side of us and encourage, direct and correct. It takes a huge act of courage to be willing to be vulnerable enough to allow someone into our lives to see the good, the bad and the ugly. But when we do that, not only will we grow but also we will impact those that are around us.

So strap on those skates, grab a coach and hit the ice!! The kingdom of God is relying on us.

Action Item: In what areas do you need to shore up your training routine? More knowledge? More practice? A coach? Spend some time journaling your need to God and ask Him to show you the next steps you are to take.

Becky Turner
First Place 4 Health Speaker
Houston, Texas

"outrun" the excuses

Have nothing to do with godless myths and old wives' tales;
rather, train yourself to be godly.

1 TIMOTHY 4:7

I started running in 1987. I've participated in aerobics classes, kickboxing classes, boot camp classes, biking and other exercise options, but I always run. I heard someone say that runners run, and it's true. I've had to stop at different times due to pregnancies or illnesses, but I always begin again.

I run basically the same route every day. It's actually the same route twice. I run it once and then run it again to get my allotted miles for the day. I've found that running is as much a mental exercise as it is a physical one. As I reach the end of my first lap around, I have the choice to turn and do it again or go straight and head home.

Many days, as I reach that point of no return, my heel or my stomach will start to hurt. Or I'll think, *One lap is probably enough; I went to sleep really late last night* or *I should probably just do one; I didn't eat much dinner last night.* My mind tries to talk me out of continuing my run! However, I've learned that if I keep going, after I've gone a block or two, my heel doesn't hurt anymore! Or my stomach doesn't hurt anymore, or whatever it was, and I'm fine for the rest of the run. For a long time, I would occasionally give in to these excuses until I learned that I didn't have to. I could keep running and be perfectly fine.

I've started to recognize this mental challenge in other areas too—when I try to convince myself I deserve that slice of cake or extra cookie, or when I worry about something instead of giving control of the situation over to the Lord. I don't have to believe the lie. I can believe that "I can do all things through Christ who strengthens me" (Philippians 4:13, *NKJV*). I can believe the truth. I can do it.

Action Item: What lie are you believing? That you can't exercise? That you'll never lose weight? Write them down and then across from them, write the truth of God's Word. Believe, trust and obey, because you can do it!

Lisa Lewis
First Place 4 Health Director of Events
Houston, Texas

210

what a concept!

*Have nothing to do with godless myths and old wives' tales;
rather, train yourself to be godly.*

1 TIMOTHY 4:7

I admired our church secretary as I observed about 65 pounds melt from her body. I needed to take off about 20 pounds, but with a husband who loves to cook, especially dishes containing rice, potatoes and beef, I was having trouble staying on a diet. When Cathy offered a Bible study based on First Place 4 Health, I joined.

Over the years, I had tried the boiled egg diet, the grapefruit diet, the Atkins diet, the Jenny Craig diet, and many others. I always lost weight on them, as much as 20 pounds, but when I started back eating normal foods, I would quickly gain it all back. I even tried a vegetable soup recipe as an exclusive diet for two weeks. A friend who was a trainer had given it to me. It was healthy soup, but not a healthy daily diet. I'd heard of special herbs, drinks and food preparation methods that were supposed to help control the appetite or enhance metabolism, and I had tried some. Most of these did absolutely nothing for me. Reading the nutritional information in the First Place 4 Health literature convinced me that a lot of diet information we are given is destructive.

I hadn't realized how much worldly information, salted with myths and old wives' tales, was so prevalent in our society. It's no wonder we live in an overweight culture. Fast food places are trying to introduce healthier menus but still have a ways to go to include balance.

The Bible study emphasizing godly training helped me identify which areas of my life needed help. Replacing haphazard planning with balanced living gave me a new attitude. It became a fun challenge. I haven't reached my goal yet, and I have slipped a few times. But I am honoring my body and my health from God's perspective. What a concept! Depend on Him for wisdom instead of information gathered from unreliable sources. God has a plan for all of us, including taking care of our bodies. His plan for us is balanced living, which gives us resources to carry out His will in our lives.

Prayer: *Gracious Lord who created us and gave us life, give us wisdom to make the right choices to live a balanced life, reflective of You and Your will.*

Gigi Falstrom
Irving, Texas

211

the blessing of grace

It teaches us to say "No" to ungodliness and worldly passions, and to live self-controlled, upright and godly lives in this present age.

TITUS 2:12

The verse before this one gives us the answer to what teaches us to say no to ungodliness and worldly passions: "the grace of God" (Titus 2:11). I have heard the word "grace" described as "God's unmerited favor." This means to me that God gives me many things that I do not deserve and that I have not earned.

He gave me salvation and accepted me into His divine family because of Jesus' sacrificial death on the cross. He bestows blessing after blessing on my life just because He loves me. This alone should cause me to say no to ungodliness and worldly passions.

Since we don't get this truth easily, God also sends others to show us grace when we don't deserve it. A police officer who doesn't write me a ticket when I am stopped for speeding is showing me grace. A friend who understands when I am having a bad day and loves me anyway is showing grace.

If God has personally given us so much grace and He has sent others into our lives who show us grace, then why is it so hard "to live self-controlled, upright and godly lives in this present age"?

I believe the reason is that this body of mine will always want to do what it wants rather than what God wants. Paul said in 1 Corinthians 9:27, "No, I beat my body and make it my slave so that after I have preached to others, I myself, will not be disqualified for the prize."

Living a godly life is not possible unless you and I learn to submit our worldly passions to God and ask Him to teach us how to say no when our bodies are screaming to say yes to ungodliness and worldly passions. God's grace is ready to do just that!

Action Item: Write about the most critical area in your life in which you need to say no. Ask God to teach you, by His grace, how to live a godly life that brings Him glory.

Carole Lewis
First Place 4 Health National Director
Houston, Texas

212

worthy living

It teaches us to say "No" to ungodliness and worldly passions, and to live self-controlled, upright and godly lives in this present age.

TITUS 2:12

Have you ever wondered why some people live in joy and victory, while others live in misery and defeat? We all have the same opportunity to believe we can do all things through Christ who strengthens us, and the ones who gain victory in life are the ones who believe they can (see Philippians 4:13).

It doesn't make much difference what we do or don't do if it's not done in faith, if according to what God says is true: "Everything that does not come from faith is sin" (Romans 14:23). The point here is not that we won't do anything, but that if we don't have faith, what we do is worth nothing. If we do have faith, we can do a lot of good things and make a lot of great choices.

I now recognize that it is impossible to have any victory over life-controlling problems by simply trying harder. Programs, methods, support groups, treatments and counseling techniques will not be very successful if they are not of faith. First Place 4 Health has helped me understand the importance of how my faith makes the difference when it comes to making healthy wellness choices.

Freedom from my old worldly ways has come by believing the truth that sets me free. It has been lifechanging for me knowing how to say no to the world and yes to God. Faith can make all the difference in the world.

Action Item: How about you? Are you ready to say yes to God and know the truth that can make all the difference in your life? Begin your faith journey today by trusting in Jesus Christ as your Lord and Savior.

Prayer: *Dear Father, I praise You for the victory You brought by overcoming the world when You sent Your Son, Jesus Christ, to save us from our sin. Increase my faith and help me to be all that I can be in this present age, for Your glory. Amen.*

Sara Rainey
Colorado Springs, Colorado

self-control is God-control

It teaches us to say "No" to ungodliness and worldly passions, and to live self-controlled, upright and godly lives in this present age.

TITUS 2:12

"No" and "self-control" are words we don't like to hear. Immediately, they conjure up images of deprivation and restriction. We want the freedom to do things our way. However, having self-control and learning to say no are vital if we are to slay worldly passions and live upright and godly lives in today's world. They are also vital to developing a healthy lifestyle. While doing it our way may seem like freedom, it usually leads to restriction rather than freedom, when it causes us to make poor choices that adversely affect our lives.

Nearly everything seems to center around overindulgence of some sort in our "Have it your way society." Over-indulgence is the opposite of self-control. From gluttony and overspending to alcohol and drug addiction we see the damaging effects that living out of control has on people. It leads to destruction, disease and even death.

As followers of Christ, we should strive to live lives that are in control. If we can't control ourselves, what are we saying about the power of God that is at work within us? If our lives are spinning out of control, then why would anyone who is not a believer want to follow Christ? Self-control brings about health and restoration, which result in a healthy and fruitful life that ultimately brings glory to God.

Action Item: First Place 4 Health teaches us to develop self-control emotionally, spiritually, mentally and physically. Write in your journal ways you are seeing more self-control in your life as a result of being involved with First Place 4 Health.

Prayer: *Heavenly Father, when I am tempted by worldly passions, give me strength and courage to say no to fleshly desires and to live a fruitful and self-controlled life for Your glory.*

Joni Shaffer
Mercersburg, Pennsylvania

214

a more livable home for the Holy Spirit

It teaches us to say "No" to ungodliness and worldly passions, and to live self-controlled, upright and godly lives in this present age.

TITUS 2:12

"It" often refers to the not-to-be-mentioned elephant in the living room; but here "it" is the wonderful grace of God. Only the grace of God and His Holy Spirit working in us can teach us to say no properly and effectively, leading to godly living. A retired elementary school teacher, I realize that true learning occurs when we actively implement what is taught. God's Word teaches us how "to live self-controlled, upright and godly lives," but only as we practice living in His grace and power can we begin to grow and have victory in these areas.

We read that our body is God's temple, but it isn't livable until we begin to care for it properly. Self-control is a vital component in First Place 4 Health, yet it cannot be achieved until it is received from His grace and fueled by His Spirit. If I have faith in God to help me become healthy (self-controlled in making wise choices) but do not accept my part, how can I possibly expect any lasting results in living a godly, balanced lifestyle? My part in making appropriate changes to care for His temple is to provide *needs* for my body; God's part is to provide *power* through Christ so that I can follow through with the good plan of First Place 4 Health. A helpful reminder to me is to record on my Tracker whether my day was "Spirit-controlled" or "flesh-controlled." Implementing self-control remodels our bodies into the home He desires.

When lived by God's grace and in the Spirit's control, each day is an "upright and godly" day. It is (1) offered to the Lord, (2) well-planned, (3) filled with wise choices, and (4) producing healthy results in due time. And at the end of each day, we will hear His affirmation of our efforts that brought Him honor and glory. "Well done, child. You have shown that you care for My home by keeping it clean and pure, uncluttered and healthy. Now I can use it for My purposes tomorrow."

Prayer: *Lord, by Your wonderful grace, help me to keep my body healthy and offer it as a home that honors and pleases You every day.*

Judy Marshall
Gilmer, Texas

215

grace-schooled

It teaches us to say "No" to ungodliness and worldly passions, and to live self-controlled, upright and godly lives in this present age.

TITUS 2:12

I get this verse, I really do—I fully understand it. I even think that I have been more than a little bit helpful to others. I can encourage others to say no. I am remarkably accomplished at being able to see where others struggle with the kinds of challenges mentioned here by Paul. Trouble is, that's not the point, is it?

Helping others to appropriately say yes and no is a beautiful thing. It might even qualify as discipling under certain circumstances. But *helping others* to live a self-controlled life can never substitute for *living* a self-controlled life. Pointing out the faults and failures of others will never resolve my faults or failures. I love the gospel songwriter's perspective on this: "Not my brother, not my sister, but it's me, Oh Lord." Can I get a witness?

Paul is speaking to Titus about the process of learning to live like Christ. That's the subject being taught and hopefully learned. One small additional question should be asked and answered. This verse launches with Paul saying, "It teaches us." So, what is "It"? Verse 11 tells us. "It" is grace. The unmerited and undeserved favor of God reminds me that I am made in the image of God and I should live up to that high calling.

So grace is teaching, ever teaching, and in the end, I learn. I learn and I am changed.

Prayer: *Lord, help me today not to focus on other peoples' faults and failures but on those that are in my life in which You want me to grow. Help me to remember the gift of grace and undeserved favor that You have given me and live in a way that reflects Your image. Amen.*

Robin Heath
Pastor, Edisto Beach Baptist Church
Edisto Island, South Carolina

INSPIRATIONAL STORY

more than I could imagine

As I looked in the mirror, I knew I had to do something drastic about my weight. The dial on the scale was moving very close to 200 pounds. I had tried several diets, but nothing seemed to work. I was aware that a group in our church had begun a program called First Place 4 Health, and on checking it out, I discovered it to be a healthy solution with no dieting involved; and it not only was for weight problems, but it paid attention to the mind, soul and spirit as well.

After four years of the program's healthy eating plan, beginning a regular exercise routine and spending time daily in God's Word, I lost 40 pounds. Receiving encouragement from the ladies in our group and being accountable to them weekly all began with Matthew 6:33: "Seek first the kingdom of God and His righteousness, and all these things shall be added to you" (*NKJV*).

God's plan for my life was certainly different than any I could have imagined. Four years after beginning First Place 4 Health, I met a new friend at church. Two

BEFORE AFTER

months later, she found out she had to have a kidney transplant, and I was honored to donate one of mine to her. The doctors had been concerned about my age, but they discovered I was healthier than most of the donors who were much younger.

I have been a part of First Place 4 Health for 10 years now and have kept my weight off, but I realize I still need the encouragement and accountability that it provides. A verse that seems to fit so well with my healthy lifestyle is Ephesians 3:20, paraphrased this way: "My plan for you and everything I desire to do in your life is beyond what you could hope for; it is beyond what you could dream. I am able to do this as you put your trust in Me and allow the power of My Spirit to work within you."

Marjorie Kirkpatrick
Omaha, Nebraska

MONTH 11

PRAYERFULNESS

216

the privilege of
praying for others

Pray in the Spirit on all occasions with all kinds of prayers and requests.
With this in mind, be alert and always keep on praying for all the saints.

EPHESIANS 6:18

I absolutely believe that the only reason my husband, Johnny, is still alive today is because of the prayers of the saints for him after he was diagnosed with stage 4 prostate cancer and given a maximum of two years to live. Our First Place 4 Health family has diligently prayed for Johnny all these years (since 1997), and Johnny is still with me today.

Each Christmas, I send out a photo card of Johnny and me. The reason I do this is because I hope and pray that our friends will place this picture somewhere as a reminder to pray for us.

In the past, when I received a request for prayer, I would promise to pray and then I would forget. I don't ever want to do that again, if I can help it. I have learned that prayer is a powerful tool, and I try to pray immediately when I receive a request for prayer. It doesn't matter if I know the person personally or not, God calls me to pray. If the request is in an email, I write a prayer when I reply. If the request is received by telephone, I pray for the request before we hang up. There are so many people and situations that need our prayers today. It is our job to be alert to the needs and to stop and pray immediately.

Prayer is also a gift that we can give to our pre-Christian friends. We can be quick to pray when they are sick or have a need in their family. By doing this, we earn the right to talk with them about our faith in Christ and ask them to accept His free gift to them.

Prayer: *Lord, I want to be a person of prayer. Teach me how to pray without ceasing for my brothers and sisters in Christ.*

Carole Lewis
First Place 4 Health National Director
Houston, Texas

217

everywhere prayer

*Pray in the Spirit on all occasions with all kinds of prayers and requests.
With this in mind, be alert and always keep on praying for all the saints.*

EPHESIANS 6:18

I took one of those spiritual gifts inventories and discovered that it was extremely helpful. I scored high in the areas of administration and shepherding. That was no real surprise. What was extremely helpful to me was identifying the weakest of all the gifts—intercessory prayer! How could that be helpful? I had always had a difficult time staying focused during my quiet time when it came to praying. I always found myself getting distracted, and I would usually just give up. I have always had the desire to be a great prayer warrior but could not seem to make it happen.

I finally sought the advice of a good friend, someone who knows me quite well. She said I would have much more success if I went for a walk or did something active as I prayed. She suggested that I use exercise as an extension of my quiet time and try praying that way. Now I have great success and am no longer plagued by guilt and shame because I could not keep my promise to pray for my friends and family.

The apostle Paul told the Ephesians to "pray in the spirit on all occasions" and for me, that means any occasion, whether I am driving in my car or taking an afternoon stroll. It keeps me alert and I am keeping my prayer promises for all the saints.

Action Item: Take a walk today and meet the Lord outside—praying for the saints as you go.

Vicki Heath
First Place 4 Health Associate Director
Edisto Beach, South Carolina

218

daily battle prayer

Pray in the Spirit on all occasions with all kinds of prayers and requests.
With this in mind, be alert and always keep on praying for all the saints.

EPHESIANS 6:18

The First Place 4 Health Bible studies taught me how to pray and how to memorize Scripture, and I am so grateful for the truly amazing difference both of these habits have made in my life.

I learned the prayer (see below) based on Ephesians 6:10-11,13-18 in one of the studies. I "woke up" when I read, "The devil will not stay around when the Word of God is being spoken." I practiced the prayer every morning, acting out the parts.

As God's timing would have it, soon after thoroughly memorizing the prayer, a family crisis temporarily took me away from all my Bible study and Sunday School leadership roles. The prayer proved to be absolutely lifesaving for me. I prayed it every day, even when days were so hectic that all I could do was place my hand on the prayer.

When I was able to return to First Place 4 Health, I testified to the power of praying God's Word and "performed" the prayer for my group. Afterwards, through tears, I told my precious classmates that they had been the saints mentioned at the very end of my daily battle prayer.

Prayer: *Dear God, today I want to be strong in the Lord and in Your mighty power. I will put on the full armor of God so that I can take my stand against the devil's schemes. I will stand firm with the belt of truth buckled around my waist, with the breastplate of righteousness in place and with my feet fitted with the readiness that comes from the gospel of peace. In addition to all this, I will take up the shield of faith, with which I can extinguish all the flaming arrows of the evil one. I will take the helmet of salvation and the sword of the Spirit, which is the Word of God. And I will pray in the Spirit on all occasions with all kinds of prayers and requests. With this in mind, I will be alert and always keep on praying for all the saints.*

Beth Serpas
Houston, Texas

219

what a difference!

*Pray in the Spirit on all occasions with all kinds of prayers and requests.
With this in mind, be alert and always keep on praying for all the saints.*

EPHESIANS 6:18

I have started a prayer journal many times with the best of intentions only to give up after a few days. I wanted to have an effective prayer life, but it never seemed to work for me. It really bothered me, because the people I admired the most were faithful in journaling.

Carole Lewis often talks about how she has kept a prayer journal for years. When she is writing a book, she often looks back into her journals to be sure that her memory is correct about some incident or person she is writing about. One day, we were talking, and I expressed my frustration to her about my difficulty in keeping a journal. My handwriting is so awful that sometimes I cannot read what I wrote the day before. I told Carole that I wished I could do my prayer journal on my computer, and she said, "Why not?"

Now I look forward to sitting down at my computer and pouring out my heart to my heavenly Father. I can type much faster than I can write, and I can read it when I am done. I put the date and where in the Bible I am reading that day. Then I talk to the Lord. From time to time, I print it out and put it in a notebook.

Every day when I start to read my Bible, I open my prayer journal and read what I wrote a year ago. It is amazing how some things that seemed so overwhelming at the time turned out to be so unimportant. Other times, I see how God has done an amazing thing in my life. It is so affirming to see how God has worked in my life over the course of a year. It also reminds me of things that have happened in the lives of others so that I can share a word of encouragement with them.

Action Item: Why not try keeping a prayer journal by hand or by computer? I promise you that it will change your life.

Prayer: *Father, thank You for allowing me to bring everything to You, no matter how small or how large. I pray that You will bless Carole for encouraging me to start my prayer journal.*

Dee Matthews
First Place 4 Health Networking Leader
Sugar Land, Texas

miracles still happen

Pray in the Spirit on all occasions with all kinds of prayers and requests.
With this in mind, be alert and always keep on praying for all the saints.

EPHESIANS 6:18

Since I began in First Place 4 Health, I was diagnosed with Crohn's disease. It can be an extremely painful disease, with many unpleasant symptoms, including severe fatigue. There is no known cure for Crohn's, and as the pace and responsibilities of my growing family increased, I held out little hope of ever being able to keep up with them.

One day while I was having my quiet time with the Lord and meditating on Isaiah 53, I was struck by the end of verse 5: "By his wounds we are healed." I remember like it was yesterday that He said, "You know, you've never asked Me to heal you." It was like being struck! Whether because I had prayed for years for the Lord to heal my father and instead the Lord took him home, or whether I believed I deserved this illness for years of not treating my body as the temple of the Holy Spirit, I had, in fact, never asked the Lord to heal me.

I don't want to miss out on a single thing that Christ shed His blood to give me! Beginning that very day, I started asking the Lord to heal me. I asked my family and some of my First Place 4 Health friends to join me, and we began petitioning the Lord together. A hope began to burn within me. Hope makes it easier to be patient in affliction. Whether the Lord healed me or not, I knew He was able! Daily I petitioned Him in prayer, and for reasons that I don't know this side of heaven, the Creator of the universe healed my body in an instant!

Not only is there no sign of Crohn's within my body, but there is no scar tissue remaining either. My doctors can't explain it, but I know! I, my family and a faithful band of prayer warriors know that God gave us hope as we patiently asked for the miraculous—and got it!

Prayer: *Lord God Almighty, what have I given up hope on that You desire to bless me with? Please renew my hope. Enable me to be faithful in prayer and patient as I wait on You to reveal Yourself mighty in the midst of my circumstances. In Jesus' name. Amen.*

Karrie Smyth
Brandon, Manitoba, Canada

before we even ask

Therefore I tell you, whatever you ask for in prayer,
believe that you have received it, and it will be yours.

MARK 11:24

When Johnny and I moved to the bay in 1997, we lived in a very small house. It had one bathroom, and you could see the back of the house from the front door. Our bedroom was part of the back porch where the table and chairs resided for eating meals.

In 1999, when it became apparent that my mom could no longer live alone, we began to pray for a bigger home. One day soon after we began to pray, we were out our golf cart on a Sunday afternoon and spied a "For Sale by Owner" sign on a fence. The house was built in 1960, and was absolutely perfect for our needs. The only bedroom that had a wheelchair accessible bathroom was the one that was perfect for Mom. This bedroom was on a separate air conditioning unit so it could be kept warmer than the rest of the house.

Within two weeks, we were the proud owners of the house and lived there until Hurricane Ike destroyed it in 2008. It had served its purpose in our lives and had provided many happy memories with family and friends over the years and we were privileged to live there. My mom was able to live the last three years of her life in a beautiful, peaceful place that was close to the house on the bay that she and my dad had owned for years. She spent many hours on the pier, enjoying the water and the sound of the sea gulls, even though she was steadily declining mentally due to dementia.

God knows our needs, but He wants us to ask Him to provide for them. I just love it that He has already answered before we even speak! We can know that there is no such thing as coincidence in the life of a Christian. Our Father is the best father possible!

Action Item: What do you need today? Ask God and believe He heard you; I promise He did!

Carole Lewis
First Place 4 Health National Director
Houston, Texas

multiple blessings

*Therefore I tell you, whatever you ask for in prayer,
believe that you have received it, and it will be yours.*

MARK 11:24

For years, I wanted a contract for one of my novels. I already had written several Bible studies and stories or devotionals for various compilations, and even a story in a novella, but nothing in novel form. I voiced this desire several times over the years, and one of my First Place 4 Health members started praying for me and my writing.

When Carole Lewis introduced us to *Give God a Year,* I decided to try it and see how God would work. In January 2009, I made a list of things for my part and then God's part. One of the things on my list for God was to get a contract for a novel. I didn't share the list with anyone, but did my best at keeping my end. I didn't always succeed, but I didn't give up.

With the prayers of Dee Matthews, and several other friends, and my new commitment, I had confidence and believed that God would honor my request. What happened that year is a testimony to God's faithfulness and how He answers the prayers of His children.

In June 2009, on my seventy-third birthday, I received a call from my agent that Strang Communications wanted to offer me a contract for a book proposal she had sent them. After accepting the offer, I received a contract for not one, but four books all based on the one proposal we had sent them. God had not only answered our prayers, but He had blessed me four times over.

We are on this journey together, and when we share our heart's desires with others who then pray for and with us, it becomes sweet music to God's ear. We rejoice with each other in triumphs, and we cry together in heartache. God hears and sees it all, and blesses us beyond measure for our faithfulness to Him and our belief in His answers.

Action Item: Make a list of ways God has been faithful in answering your prayers. Then write a prayer of thanksgiving for the many blessings He has given you.

Prayer: *Heavenly Father, may our prayers today be sweet music to Your ears as we trust and believe in Your answers.*

Martha Rogers
Houston, Texas

223

healing the hairline crack

Therefore I tell you, whatever you ask for in prayer,
believe that you have received it, and it will be yours.

MARK 11:24

Have you ever had a ceramic vase that was beautiful and still didn't hold water? I have a Polish pottery teapot that was given to me by my daughter. It is lovely, and I have tried to use it several times without success. "Why?" you ask. It has a hairline crack around its base and it leaks every time I pour liquid into it. The funny thing is that every once in a while I try again, without success, to get it to hold water.

A cracked pot—that's what I was for more years than I want to count. I look good at first glance; I look like a leader, but I don't hold up under scrutiny. That is, until I found First Place 4 Health.

I would rather fail a class or drop an entire college program than ask for help or admit that I was in over my head. I would rather turn my back on a commitment if there was the slightest opposition, whether warranted or not. I didn't even want to call First Place 4 Health headquarters or other First Place 4 Health leaders to ask for help. It has been a real lifelong source of frustration for me, my family and for those to whom I had committed.

That's how I know that my being a leader of First Place 4 Health is truly from the Lord. He has kept me going through three and a half sessions where nine of us have a net loss of 194.4 pounds. But the greatest proof of the Lord's leading was at our last Victory Celebration where we had tears and confessions, testimonies and laughter, along with multiple times of spontaneous prayer. I am very excited about the movement of the Holy Spirit within our little church, and it's all through First Place 4 Health!

Remember the Emotional Mapping exercise? It works . . . in God's timing. He has started to seal up that hairline crack in my spirit. I *can* be used for God's glory. Maybe you can too.

Prayer: *Lord, You are great and gracious; You love us and are merciful to us; You forgive our sins and heal our infirmities; You teach us how to have a relationship with Yourself and others; You are kind and gentle with us. May You, Lord, be all we need for the trials of today.*

Pauli Lewman
Midvale, Idaho

God does the impossible

Therefore I tell you, whatever you ask for in prayer,
believe that you have received it, and it will be yours.

MARK 11:24

During my first session of First Place 4 Health, I'll admit that I didn't exercise much at all. I fully embraced other parts of the program, like the food plan, daily Bible study and Scripture memory, but I held on to my lifelong hatred of exercise. Oh, I had my reasons: my back hurt, I didn't like sweating, I didn't have time, and the list of excuses went on and on. My prayer partner encouraged me to think outside the box to find creative ways to incorporate exercise into my day. I tried, but all the while I held on to my negative attitude about exercise.

During my second session of First Place 4 Health, I realized that although I had asked God to help me exercise more, I had never asked Him to help me *want to* exercise. I stepped out in faith a little bit further and asked Him to give me a *love* for exercise! Whoa, is that even possible? Could I ask Him for that? Could He really change my whole attitude? Well, of course He can. He is Almighty God, right? He set the sun and moon and stars in place and conquered death, and He lives inside me!

So for several weeks the only prayer request I shared with my group was that God would give me a love for exercise. After an initial chuckle (because they knew how much I hated it), they agreed to pray, and so did I. And week after week, God was changing me from the inside out. I actually did begin to desire exercise. When I started First Place 4 Health, I would have *never* thought that was possible. But with God, all things are possible.

Action Item: What have you never before thought of asking God for in prayer? Ask Him today, and keep asking. Is it possible that He's just waiting for you to ask? Then He can display His awesome power in you to accomplish what seems impossible!

Barbara Bright
Columbus, Ohio

225

I gave God a year

Therefore I tell you, whatever you ask for in prayer,
believe that you have received it, and it will be yours.

MARK 11:24

In October 2008, Carole Lewis challenged us at the Wellness Retreat in Round Top, Texas, to "Give God a Year" to do what only He could do in our lives. We were asked to pray and write on a card "God's part"—what you want God to do this year. We were then to write on a second card "my part"—what you need to do this year.

Throughout the year, I continued to pray for my needs and prayed for wisdom to follow and obey what God wanted me to do. Here are some of the requests:

1. I asked God to help me reach my healthy weight goal. In July 2009, I reached my healthy weight, and by July 2010, I reached my ideal weight goal. I now wear a smaller size then I did as a teenager.

2. I asked Him to help me get more physically fit and healthy to serve Him longer and better. This past year, I received the best medical test results that I have ever had. God has healed the colitis that doctors said could not be healed. He healed the arthritis and tendonitis and now I can go up and down stairs and exercise. I do not have to take medications of any kind. I feel better and younger than I did 20 years ago!

3. We have asked God to grow our wellness ministry at New Hope Baptist Church (NHBC) to reach our community for His Kingdom. Our First Place 4 Health classes have grown. He has given us several opportunities to tell our story of what He is doing in our lives.

Three of our First Place 4 Health members here at NHBC have now committed to the "Gve God a Year" challenge. I am seeing God do amazing things in their lives as they pray and obey.

Prayer: *Dear God, thank You for answering my prayers in such an awesome, wonderful way. You have given me more than I could have imagined, and I give You all the praise.*

Janet Kirkhart
First Place 4 Health Networking Leader
Loveland, Ohio

God always provides

Do not be anxious about anything, but in everything,
by prayer and petition, with thanksgiving, present your requests to God.
PHILIPPIANS 4:6

I received an email from my dear friend Jana Tornga, letting me know that both of her parents had been diagnosed with Alzheimer's disease. I answered Jana's email by asking for more information and wanted to share her reply with you. May it build your faith today as it did mine.

> Mom and Dad used to live in the house across from us. On January 1, 2009, they moved in with Roger and me, and we began to rent their home. We thought at that time we were moving them in with us because of their financial state; however, we soon discovered their financial state was because of much deeper issues!
>
> After 18 months with us, it was apparent they needed more care than we could provide at that time. We inquired about assisted living quarters for them because we felt we had no other options. About that same time, my sister, Julie's, 20-year-old daughter moved in with a friend, and her room became available. With busy lives and family commitments, Julie and Jim were unable to be actively involved in the care of the folks but would occasionally come for a visit if we were out of town for the weekend. All of a sudden, they wanted the folks to move in with them!
>
> They were going to remodel their son Jimmy's room for the folks. They added a door from that bedroom to the bathroom, and they enlarged the width of the bathroom by a foot to accommodate Mom's wheelchair. Just like that, Mom and Dad were able to move into Julie and Jim's home, and God provided the care they needed!

God is always right on time to provide our needs when we present our requests to Him with thanksgiving.

Prayer: *Dear Lord, You are faithful to take care of Your children. Help me not to be anxious about anything today and to bring every need to You and then wait for Your perfect answer.*

Carole Lewis
First Place 4 Health National Director
Houston, Texas

227

a safe place

Do not be anxious about anything, but in everything,
by prayer and petition, with thanksgiving, present your requests to God.
PHILIPPIANS 4:6

My husband, Nick, recently went for his first routine colonoscopy. The doctor discovered a precancerous polyp too large to be removed at that time and advised it be removed soon through a laparoscopic procedure. He scheduled an appointment a week after my return home from the First Place 4 Health Wellness Retreat. I encouraged Nick, reminding him that I had that procedure done successfully. Before I left for Wellness Week, we discussed it again, acknowledging the doctor's conversation that *if* they couldn't remove the polyp through the laparoscopic procedure, Nick would then have to undergo a more invasive surgery. We didn't linger on the subject, hoping he wouldn't have to face that possibility.

Wellness Retreat is a restorative time when I meet with God and allow Him to heal me of hurt, pain and worry. I spent quiet time in prayer, asking Him to calm my anxious thoughts—thankful that I was in a safe place covered by His grace and surrounded by the love of Christians who care. I presented my request for my husband's pending surgery to my small group. I had faith that each of them would pray unceasingly for Nick's physical and spiritual health. When I returned home, my spirit was lifted knowing that God is in control. No matter the results of the surgery, God is faithful and will never let me down.

Action Item: What is going on in your life that is causing you anxiety? Begin in your prayer closet presenting your request with thanksgiving to God; seek out friends who will be faithful to pray, and ask them to intercede on your behalf. Having done those things, have faith in our God who never fails!

Prayer: *O Lord, help me to give You my anxious thoughts, heavy burdens and cares that weigh me down. Show me those who will walk beside me in prayer. When I have done those things, help me trust You with the outcome.*

June Chapko
First Place 4 Health Networking Leader
San Antonio, Texas

the perfect anxiety prescription

Do not be anxious about anything, but in everything,
by prayer and petition, with thanksgiving, present your requests to God.

PHILIPPIANS 4:6

I type medical reports for a living and I'm saddened by the number of reports I type daily in which the patient is struggling with severe anxiety. It has become an epidemic, affecting people of all ages. I certainly understand feeling anxious. I would often find myself struggling with anxious thoughts and was called a "worry wart" by others. If there was nothing to worry about, I would find something to worry about!

I used to even feel anxious every time I decided to eat healthy and lose weight. I would obsess about how long it would be before I fell off track again and went right back to my old habits. I worried about failing before I even got started. Yet, the more I studied the Bible the more I realized that fear was the opposite of faith. Scripture tells us not to be anxious about anything.

I still find myself giving in to that old "worry wart" mentality at times, but I've learned that anxiety is a sign that I'm not praying and trusting God. When I try to fix things myself rather than allowing God to work them out, it causes anxiety and fear to take over. God wants us to come to Him by prayer and petition, with thanksgiving, and lay our requests before Him.

What a wonderful privilege it is to be able to take all of our burdens and anxious thoughts to our heavenly Father. Life is filled with stress and anxieties that are real and unpleasant, but God will give us peace and calm in the midst of any storm. We need to stop worrying and start praying, because prayer is the perfect anxiety prescription!

Action Item: Are anxious thoughts weighing you down? Write a prayer to God casting your burdens on Him and asking Him to fill you with His perfect peace.

Prayer: *Heavenly Father, when anxious thoughts weigh heavy upon my heart, help me to remember that peace is found in You alone.*

Joni Shaffer
Mercersburg, Pennsylvania

229

do what you *can* do

Do not be anxious about anything, but in everything,
by prayer and petition, with thanksgiving, present your requests to God.

PHILIPPIANS 4:6

Not long ago, I was having an anxious moment—a moment when I was filled with frustration and wanted to scream. Out in our back pasture, I was overwhelmed with a huge mess that seemed impossible to clean up. All that was in my sight were broken tree limbs, weeds to be pulled and rocks everywhere.

I was feeling hopeless, discouraged and full of anxiety. As I surveyed all that needed to be done, I started to pray and gave my anxiety to the Lord. In the quietness of that pasture, I heard the Shepherd speak to my heart, "Instead of looking at what you can't do, look at what you can do." I immediately thought, *Yes, I have two hands and an able body. I can pick up rocks, limbs and pull weeds.*

I diligently started in one area and started to make rock piles, wood piles and weed piles. Some were small and easy to pick up. There were heavier ones embedded into the ground that took more effort and strength. As I worked, I prayed and asked the Lord to show me lessons He wanted me to see through each task. I thought about how this represented habits and obstacles in life that work as stumbling blocks as we work toward living a lifestyle that is honoring to Christ.

To accomplish what needed to be done, I had to give my anxiety to Christ so that He could show me that what once was impossible was now possible with Him. What was once disarray was now transformed, and that not long ago my anxiety blocked the possibility of seeing progress. I felt the Lord remind me that He can do this in every area of my life. Those stubborn weeds of unhealthy habits and the stumbling rocks in my life can be made over by the Master if I am willing and work along side of Him to do the things to cultivate a healthy lifestyle.

Action Item: Pause when you are anxious and ask God to turn your anxiety inside out, and pray beyond the obvious. Thank Him for what He has prepared ahead.

Prayer: *Lord, thank You for taking my anxiety and for showing me that with You all things are possible.*

Connie Welch
First Place 4 Health Networking Leader
Keller, Texas

2 3 0

both burden and blessing

Do not be anxious about anything, but in everything,
by prayer and petition, with thanksgiving, present your requests to God.

PHILIPPIANS 4:6

September 28, 2009, just 22 days old, our baby Luke was diagnosed with a rare (1 in 50,000) genetic skin disease called Epidermolysis Bullosa. Our lives were forever changed that day and we began to see life differently. I will never forget sitting in the small room in the dermatology clinic in Texas Children's Hospital listening to words I never thought I would hear in my lifetime. "Your baby will be a special-needs child." Words so gracefully and gently spoken by sweet Dr. B, yet so harsh and painful to hear. Luke's hands and feet were covered in blisters; we wanted so badly to hear that they would all go away, but instead we heard the opposite. His blistering would continue and likely worsen. He would endure pain throughout his life and his disease would inhibit him in many ways. In short, he would not be "normal."

After much discussion, Dr. B left the room. It was a surreal moment for us. We were dazed and confused. Why? Why us? Why Luke? Why are there awful illnesses in this world? Why an innocent baby?

As we left the doctor's office, it was as if things were moving in slow motion. We were filled with worry and concern. What was wrong with our precious baby? What is this disease and what is Luke's plight? Is he going to be okay? As our walk continued, we began to notice the many sick children waiting to visit their doctors. These children were so terribly sick, many literally fighting for their lives. This put things in perspective for us.

As we watched a child in a wheelchair wheel by, every body part strapped down, hardly coherent to the world around him, Greg said something to me that I will never forget. "Luke could have it so much worse . . . we could have it so much worse." He was right. We are blessed. We are thankful for our precious, wonderful son. I knew Luke was going to be okay. God has given us the peace He promises that surpasses all understanding. With prayer comes peace.

Prayer: *Lord, thank You for this wonderful life You have given us. I pray You take the burdens of our hearts and carry them for us. Help us remember that You know what is best for us, and show us that You hear our cries. Amen.*

Melissa Jones
Houston, Texas

leave everything with God

For the eyes of the Lord are on the righteous and his ears are attentive to their prayer, but the face of the Lord is against those who do evil.

1 PETER 3:12

Our God is all-seeing and His eyes are always on us. His ears are all-hearing and he hears us when we pray. So what do we do when confronted with evil deeds and evil people?

Peter tells us, "Do not repay evil with evil or insult with insult, but with blessing because to this you were called so that you may inherit a blessing" (1 Peter 3:9). Because the face of the Lord is against those who do evil, we can be confident that His eyes see and His ears hear when evil is done to one of His children. God is the righteous judge and His punishment will always perfectly fit the crime.

If we live a righteous life, God will take care of those who wish us harm. And even if it takes some time, we learn valuable lessons through the process. Either way, these trials are for our good and for God's glory.

Becoming a mature Christian is realizing that not everyone in this life wishes us well. We know we have reached maturity when this fact no longer threatens to destroy us. I spent so many years wanting everyone to love me that it was hard for me to believe that some people didn't have my best interests at heart. There are those we meet along life's journey that have their own interests at heart, and they often wound people to accomplish their desires.

Knowing that the face of the Lord is against evil removes the burden for our need to repay the evil. It prevents us from allowing unforgiveness and resentment to build a fortress in our minds and hearts.

God's plan is that we should bless others when they do evil against us and we will also then inherit a blessing. Bless and be blessed today.

Prayer: *Dear Lord, thank You for seeing everything and for hearing my prayers. Help me leave judgment to You, knowing that You are against the evildoer but You still desire for them to turn to You.*

Carole Lewis
First Place 4 Health National Director
Houston, Texas

232

for our good

For the eyes of the Lord are on the righteous and his ears are attentive to their prayer, but the face of the Lord is against those who do evil.

1 PETER 3:12

God used this verse in a vivid way in my life recently. I was driving home from Brookings, South Dakota, with my First Place 4 Health friend. We had spent the weekend at the Hope 4 You event where we were blessed to hear all the victorious testimonies and inspiring speakers.

My friend and I were chatting nonstop about all we had learned and experienced. As we came to a small town, the speed limit was 30 mph. I slowed down, but I was not as attentive as I should have been. I mistakenly sped up too soon. A policeman was waiting and pulled me over to write a ticket. At the last minute, he received an emergency call and had to depart. Whew! I was saved. God is so gracious and merciful to spare me the ticket I deserved.

As I continued the drive, I pondered a new understanding. The Lord's eyes are on me because He sees me as righteous and not the sinner that I am. God's eyes watch even when I'm doing something wrong. Like a good parent, He does not look away when I need correction. His love takes every opportunity to teach me that abiding within limits is designed to keep me safe. Even when I think I am obeying, I can still be wrong.

I can apply that concept with my First Place 4 Health endeavors. When I think I am eating the proper amount, it will work against my goals to success if I have not measured for portion control. When I am tempted to not record on my tracker honestly, I need correction to acquire a pure heart to obey in truth.

I need to remember that the Lord's limits are for my own health and protection. I thankfully praise Him for a weight loss of 80 pounds. More importantly, He has heard the prayer of my heart to renew my mind and set me free to love Him unto obedience.

Action Item: Ponder a recent time when God disciplined you personally. What new insight does He desire for you to learn? What change does He desire for you? Pray for His help to be transformed.

Mary Kloek
Minneapolis, Minnesota

233

God's ears

For the eyes of the Lord are on the righteous and his ears are attentive to their prayer, but the face of the Lord is against those who do evil.

1 PETER 3:12

Since beginning First Place 4 Health in February 2010, I have made a daily decision to put Christ in first place and to love Him with all my heart, soul, mind and body. Through daily Bible study and prayer, I am learning what it looks like to seek His righteousness and am becoming more like Him. I don't know how the Lord's eyes manage to follow all of us around to find those who are righteous, but I trust His promise that when He does find His children trying to do things right, His ears are attentive to their prayers.

One of the features of my body that I really don't like is my ears. They are not all that big, but they don't lie down against my head. Once, when I was walking with some of my First Place 4 Health ladies, I started talking about my ears and they said they had not noticed them. I said, "Sure." Well, as we were walking, the sun was going down and I said, "See, look at my shadow." They looked and all started laughing.

When I was growing up as a little girl, the TV show *The Flying Nun* (Sally Fields) was popular. My ears, I thought, might work kind of like the nun's hat she wore on her head. My ears were also compared to Dumbo, the flying elephant. I can assure you that my ears have never gotten me off the ground, but I'm grateful that God has big ears, and my prayers have gotten off the ground right into His big ears and into His big heart because His ears are attentive to my prayers.

Prayer: *Lord, thank You for the way I am fearfully and wonderfully made. Help me to continue to seek You daily, learning more about who You are and the plans You have for me. Thank You for hearing my prayers. Amen.*

Vickie Martin
Stephenville, Texas

God and you: better together!

For the eyes of the Lord are on the righteous and his ears are attentive to their prayer, but the face of the Lord is against those who do evil.

1 PETER 3:12

What is better together—milk and cookies, mom and dad, praise and worship or . . . ? My choice for "better together" is Google and Round Top Retreat Center. Bet you are saying, "strange," but allow me a moment to explain.

It was late summer and I was praying about my yearly week away for spiritual growth, so I went to my trusty friend Google and entered "spiritual retreat centers." Up came Round Top Retreat Center, so I clicked on it and started reading what it offered. Partway down the page under "events" was something called Wellness Retreat, with a link to First Place 4 Health, which described it as "a week away that would minister to the four-sided person—mental, physical, spiritual and emotional." It sounded like what I needed, so I sent my money and prepared for something I knew nothing about but believed God had ordered.

Upon arriving, I was weighed and given a pedometer. Within 24 hours, I had been poked, prodded and tested in every conceivable way and given 1,400 calories a day to eat. But I had also been given prayer, support, encouragement, new friends and a place called Round Top Retreat Center that is an anointed place to get away and let God do His thing in your life.

It is one month later, and I am still riding the wave of God's grace and encouragement. Four wonderful women in my church are joining a book study with me of *Give God a Year* in preparation for our First Place 4 Health Bible study to begin in early 2011. I am humbled to say that I have lost 14 pounds thus far and am excited to write down everything I eat in CalorieKing. Now it is time to tackle exercise, and quiet time with God. I am encouraged by Carole Lewis and her transparent love for everyone, but especially for God.

So, what is better together? It could be Google and Round Top, or First Place 4 Health and Wellness Retreat, but ultimately, I believe it is God and me or God and you! Thanks be to God for His indescribable gift of grace!

Prayer: *Thank You, Lord, that Your eyes are always on us and Your ears are attentive to our prayers. What great plans You have for us when we call upon Your name.*

Linda Snow
Houston, Texas

look who's listening

For the eyes of the Lord are on the righteous and his ears are attentive to their prayer, but the face of the Lord is against those who do evil.

1 PETER 3:12

Anyone who's been a parent understands this verse completely. As a parent-to-be, you spend nine full months waiting, hoping and anticipating the birth of your child. At the end of those months, the child is born and then the fun begins.

It doesn't take much to amuse and entertain a new parent, especially when it's your first. A little cooing, the wiggling of a hand or foot and especially the crying; each of these and a hundred other visually or audibly noticeable events will capture the eyes and ears of mom and dad.

I once knew a first-time father who shot five complete rolls of film (maybe 150 pictures) of his baby daughter's left pinkie! Now that's attentive (or perhaps obsessive)! Peter says that God is like that, attentive, looking and listening. How might our prayers be impacted by knowing that He's looking and listening?

Perhaps we begin our prayers with the idea that He is aware of our circumstances. We focus more on seeking direction and less on trying to convince Him that things are really tough or painful or hard. Maybe we free ourselves to do more of the listening part of prayer (it is conversation, after all, and not mere monologue).

Possibly, we are more promptly and more audibly thankful because we know that He sees and knows how His mercies (and not mere good fortune or random circumstance) have been new each morning, including this morning. As you spend some time in conversation with the Lord today, know this, He's looking and listening, so . . . pray.

Prayer: *Lord, I know that You are aware of my circumstances. Please show me Your plan and direction for my steps. Help me to focus on You and not my circumstances.*

Robin Heath
Pastor, Edisto Beach Baptist Church
Edisto Beach, South Carolina

INSPIRATIONAL STORY

an ever-closer walk

As pastor of Southeast Baptist Church in San Antonio, Texas, I have slowly, over the years, inched my way up in pounds. The potluck dinners, the low activity level and the stresses of the ministry have all contributed to my unhealthy state. I have tried all my life to lose the weight and keep it off.

For better health reasons, I decided to join First Place 4 Health to see if it would work for me. As I began my new lifestyle to mold myself into a better emotional, mental, spiritual and physical person, I was surprised to see the weight begin to come off. It was hard to believe that I could go through each day without being hungry and yet see the pounds drop. At the same time, I found myself becoming even more disciplined in my Bible study, devotional time and exercise habits. Even as a pastor, I was being drawn closer to God than I had been in a long time. My stress level began dropping. I found myself having a new attitude toward the everyday strains of the ministry. I found myself repeating verses of Scrip-

BEFORE
AFTER

ture that would help me through problem situations. Scripture memory was never my forte, but God has opened my eyes to a completely new way of honoring Him.

Now, 24.2 pounds lighter after my first 12-week session in First Place 4 Health, I have so much more energy and feel spiritually, emotionally and mentally stronger than I have ever been. My new lifestyle has affected the church members as well. They ask me how I am losing all the weight. I give God all the glory and tell them that without God's help I could not have done it. I have prayed that God would help me change my lifestyle so that I could become stronger in all four areas of life, and He has truly been faithful to help me complete it.

This is only the beginning for me. Yes, I still need to lose at least that much more weight, but I am looking forward to continuing my closer-than-ever walk with Him. I praise Him now for what I know He is going to help me accomplish.

Pastor Jerry Cosper
Southeast Baptist Church
San Antonio, Texas

MONTH 12

OBEDIENCE

radical love

The entire law is summed up in a single command:
"Love your neighbor as yourself."

GALATIANS 5:14

The other day I was talking with a friend who said to me, "When I came to Christ, I hated myself, so it was easy to love others as I loved myself." She went on to say that after losing her third job she was forced to look at the common denominator in all three job losses, which was her attitude and treatment of her co-workers.

I believe this verse is talking about a basic love for ourselves that is wired into our DNA. We feed ourselves so we are to feed our neighbor who is hungry. We dress ourselves so we are to give clothes to those who need them. We have a roof over our heads so we are to help those who don't have a place to live.

The friend I was talking about in the first paragraph is a totally different person today than she was when she came to Christ 15 years ago. God has taught her that she is worthy of love, and she has accepted His love to such a degree that she desired to walk out this verse in her daily life.

In the book *Radical*, David Platt invites you to encounter what Jesus actually said about being His disciple, and then obey what you have heard. After this friend read the book, she began looking for someone who needed a place to live so that she could share her extra bedroom.

We serve a God who loves everyone, and He is asking us to do the same. He wants us to be His arms, eyes and ears in this fallen world. We can reach out to help a harried mother at the grocery store or on the plane. We can stop to visit with an elderly neighbor who is lonely. We can share Jesus with friends who don't know Him personally.

His command to "love your neighbor as yourself" is something we can begin doing today.

Prayer: *Dear Lord, I pray for eyes to see and ears to hear opportunities to put this verse into practice today. May I come to truly love my neighbor as myself. In Jesus' name, amen.*

Carole Lewis
First Place 4 Health National Director
Houston, Texas

237

my helpful neighbor

The entire law is summed up in a single command:
"Love your neighbor as yourself."

GALATIANS 5:14

I have a friend who has been following the First Place 4 Health plan for several years. She shared the food plan with my mother and me about four years ago. I was very successful in losing weight just with the food plan. I lost almost 40 pounds and was able to keep that weight off for almost a year. This was quite an accomplishment for me as I have fought my weight since I was a teen and have gained and lost so very many of the same pounds

I have tried many diets since First Place 4 Health and have lost weight, but every time I gained back the lost weight and more. I remembered this plan and contacted my friend to find out if she still had the food plan. She said yes, and she also had a couple of really good books written by the director of First Place 4 Health that she felt would be very helpful. Well, she was right! One of the books she gave me was *Back on Track*. I was like a sponge—this book spoke volumes to me. It was exactly where I felt I was struggling in my life; I just did not have my priorities in order.

Back on Track speaks of Wellness Retreat at Round Top, Texas. I looked online and found out that it was coming up very soon. I made arrangements to attend the Retreat and it was the best decision I could have made for myself. Wellness Retreat allowed me to get my priorities back on track!

My neighbor (friend) loved on me that day by sharing with me the tools that allowed her to be so successful over the past few years. I've come to realize that my struggle is not just with weight; when you get your life in balance, things just fall into place!

Prayer: *Lord, thank You for putting people in our lives that help us find the course that You would have us follow. Help us to continually seek to live our lives in balance.*

Melissa DeRosier
Roswell, New Mexico

ready to love others

The entire law is summed up in a single command:
"Love your neighbor as yourself."

GALATIANS 5:14

It was simple; I did not love myself! I tried to love others by being the person they wanted me to be, yet my life was in turmoil.

Carole Lewis was teaching about personalities in First Place 4 Health. I listened but could not find my personality in any of the four she described. As I was working on the assignment Carole gave us to determine our true personality, Carole looked at my paper and said, "Betha Jean, just who do you think God made you to be?" I mumbled something, and she took the paper and tore it in half! She handed me another and kept her hand on it until I promised to go home and pray that God would reveal who He wanted me to be. I was to fill out the paper and return it to her the next week.

Friday morning came and I eagerly prayed, asking God for guidance and then began marking my answers on the profile sheet. As I added up the score, I discovered I was so sanguine it hurt! In fact, those were the very words Carole had used on Tuesday. A weight lifted off me! For the first time in my life, I had an idea of who I am supposed to be. I floated to Carole's office, and with a huge smile on her face, she took the papers and said, "I told you!"

It took some time before others realized there was a distinct difference in me. There were some who would not accept the change. There are still some family members who have not spent enough time with me to see the full picture. I am happier, more carefree, and I can explain my lack of organization by stating that "God did not give me that gift." Oh, I still work on that weakness when I have time and I don't have any visitors.

My husband, Ray, died easier knowing that I had confidence in who I was supposed to be. I thank God for sending Carole Lewis to teach what God had in mind for me!

Action Item: As your members are learning new ways to be healthier physically, why not show them how to discover who God made them to be? The information is in *Simple Ideas for Healthy Living*.

Betha Jean McGee
Wall, Texas

239

monkey business

The entire law is summed up in a single command:
"Love your neighbor as yourself."

GALATIANS 5:14

If only the Good Samaritan in Luke 10 had come on the scene a little earlier, he may have been able to warn the poor man who fell in with the robbers, or even jump in to defend him.

There is a breed of deer in India that has a ferocious enemy: the tiger. Fortunately for them, however, they also have a good neighbor watching their backs. Although the deer are always alert and can pick up the tiger's scent, the tall grass makes it difficult to know exactly where he is. From their vantage point up in the trees, cute little monkeys keep a careful watch and squawk out a warning, which somehow tells the deer the location of the tiger so they can run in the direction of safety.

We can learn some lessons from the little monkeys: Arrive early to get the best seats (make the most of being in the right place at the right time); don't let differences or language barriers get in the way of going out on a limb for a neighbor; and it's not always a bad thing to monkey around in somebody else's business.

The monkeys don't know if the deer will get to safety, but at least they do their part. We won't always see the outcome of our efforts either, but we can pray for guidance and be listening for the promptings of the Holy Spirit and then just be obedient and trust God to handle the results.

Action Item: How can I use what God has taught me through experience and pain to help others avoid some pitfalls? Who are some people I see heading for danger but I have been afraid to squawk out a warning?

Prayer: *The Serenity Prayer adapts well to this context: Lord, grant me the serenity to accept the things I cannot change, the courage to change the things I can, and the wisdom to know the difference. Amen.*

Jeanne Deveau Gregory
Chatham, Virginia

2 4 0

Jesus' hands and feet

The entire law is summed up in a single command:
"Love your neighbor as yourself."

GALATIANS 5:14

One morning, my one-year-old daughter and I went shopping for birthday gifts for my son who was turning 10 that next week. As we returned home, we found fire trucks and police cars surrounding our home. Our house was engulfed in flames. The firefighters worked hard to save our home, but we lost virtually everything in the fire and our house was completely destroyed.

Later that evening, my husband and I went back over to the house to assess the damage. It was all gone. Clothes, toys for our three children, ages one, four and nine, dishes, everything. As we stood in the driveway in shock, a car drove up. It was a neighbor two streets over with a bag of clothes for our children and a booklet of free McDonald's Happy Meal coupons. We had never met before that moment. A few minutes later, another neighbor walked over and brought a bag of toys. Other neighbors, some we knew, some we didn't, began to come by to ask if there was anything they could do for us. In the midst of such devastation, what blessings!

The blessings continued over the next few weeks. My husband's parents graciously opened their home to us as we tried to figure out what to do next. My son's preschool class held a "toy shower" for him to replace some of the toys he had lost. Members of my First Place 4 Health family gave us towels and things for the kitchen.

So many people put themselves in our position and went out of their way to take care of us. They truly lived out this verse.

Prayer: *Lord, help me to always be thankful during the hard times for the blessings in my life: the people that care, the little things that make the load lighter, and the truth of Your Word that is lived out through the people around me.*

Lisa Lewis
First Place 4 Health Director of Events
Houston, Texas

241

walk it out

This is love: that we walk in obedience to his commands. As you have heard from the beginning, his command is that you walk in love.

2 JOHN 1:6

A friend of mine was devastated a few years ago when she and her husband learned that their son was embracing a homosexual lifestyle. The son moved into his own apartment and soon became involved in a relationship with another man.

Our First Place 4 Health family walked through a time of grief and despair with this woman and her husband, and lifted the entire family in prayer. Today, the circumstances have not changed, but my friend and her husband feel the call of God to begin working with other families who are in their same situation. Talk about a 360-degree turnaround!

God understands our love for our children, and even when circumstances work out differently than we desire, He comes in and works on our hearts until we begin to see the situation as He sees it: hate the sin but love the sinner.

Johnny and I experienced the same kind of feelings when our daughter Shari was killed by an 18-year-old girl who made the decision to drive while drunk. In order for us to walk in love, we had to forgive this girl, and we did. Unforgiveness and bitterness can be the tools Satan uses to keep someone from turning to Christ in their desperate time of need.

There are situations where it is virtually impossible to walk in love without the love of Christ doing it for us. If you find yourself in a situation where it seems impossible to "walk in love," why not begin praying for God to love the person through you? As you pray this prayer, you will see a miracle take place, and before long, you will understand what His command to "walk in love" is all about.

Prayer: *Dear Lord, I want to walk in obedience to Your commands, and You have commanded me to walk in love. Teach me what this means in my own life and help me walk it out. In Jesus' name, amen.*

Carole Lewis
First Place 4 Health National Director
Houston, Texas

242

encouragement in the walk

This is love: that we walk in obedience to his commands. As you have heard from the beginning, his command is that you walk in love.

2 JOHN 1:6

We are commanded in Scripture to walk in love, and we're also told what that looks like: "We walk in obedience to his commands." How are we doing with loving Him in this way? I don't know about you, but sometimes I have a hard time obeying the commands I find in Scripture. While I know they are not "suggestions," sometimes I treat them like they are.

How am I doing with Jesus' command in Matthew 22:37 to "love the Lord your God with all your heart and with all your soul and with all your mind"? Or His command in John 13:34 to "love one another"? Sure, some times are easier than others. It's easy to love others when they are lovable. And it can be easy to love the Lord in all the areas of my life when I am surrounded by others that do that too. But, what about the times when it's just me and God—and I have a chance to obey Him or not, and nobody knows it but me? These are the times when I am reminded how much better we are when we do life together.

Because of my commitment to the First Place 4 Health lifestyle, my health is restored and I have balance in my life. I have lost a total of 152 pounds on First Place 4 Health. And I have certainly found some lifelong friends within First Place 4 Health. Even in a practical sense, we walk and run together. It's an encouraging time that leaves me physically, spiritually and emotionally encouraged. It's a physical act we do together that mirrors walking through life together. I know that I can call or text them in a time of temptation and potential weakness (that may or may not even relate to food), and they will respond with an affirming word that gets me through that moment.

Action Item: If you do not have people with whom you are walking through life, connect with someone this month that can be there for you. Better yet, find someone who needs you to be that person in his or her life. We truly are better together.

Sarah Mielke
First Place 4 Health Networking Leader
Louisville, Kentucky

2 4 3

what a Friend!

This is love: that we walk in obedience to his commands. As you have heard from the beginning, his command is that you walk in love.

2 JOHN 1:6

In July 2004, I attended the First Place Leadership Summit at Houston's First Baptist Church in Texas. On Saturday, we were invited to Carole Lewis's Galveston home. There we were given the opportunity to take a boat ride and sit on the pier to watch the sunset.

My mission was to ride in a boat for the first time in more than 25 years! My friend Sheila Meadors and I headed to the pier with great anticipation. As we began to walk across, I came to a screeching halt! Sheila asked, "What's wrong?" My response, "There's no railing on the pier past the first six feet. Go ahead. I'm going back to the house before anyone sees that I'm afraid to cross the pier."

Not quite halfway to the house, I heard someone yelling, "Steph, where are you going?"

I admitted to Bev Henson that I was afraid of heights. She said, "I'll help you, let's go!" She stretched her arms out, and said, "Hold on to my arms or my shoulders, and focus on the back of my head. Do not look up or down or to the right or left. Keep your eyes focused ahead. We can do this together, without falling!" Bev obeyed God and walked in love to help someone along the way.

What an illustration! We must obey His commands and walk in love, keeping our focus only on Him and trusting Him. We are not alone! He will help us to face our fears, provide someone to share in our journey and help us up when we fall. What a friend we have in Jesus!

Prayer: *Lord, make me a blessing to someone today. Help me to rely on You to show me the way. Thank You for the times You pick me up when I fall. Thank You also for the times when I am weary and You pick me up and carry me! Thank You for being my Savior!*

Stephanie Rhodes
First Place 4 Health Networking Leader
Arlington, Tennessee

244

keep walking, no matter what

This is love: that we walk in obedience to his commands. As you have heard from the beginning, his command is that you walk in love.

2 JOHN 1:6

We often made the trip from San Angelo to Houston—but this one was different. Ray was going to be a patient at MD Anderson. His cancer was rare and terminal. We would be staying near the hospital at a cousin's home. Ray had been a member of First Place 4 Health while living in Houston, but he was not active after moving to San Angelo. I was an active member of First Place 4 Health in San Angelo and also in Houston.

Some days were longer than others—some nights shorter—but we found that the First Place 4 Health Bible studies we were involved in and the Scriptures we learned made things easier. One of the nicest surprises was the number of cards he received, not only from friends he had made in Houston, but also from my group at home. Just about the time I thought I was going to hit rock bottom, I would find a note in the mailbox from my group encouraging me and stating their love and concern for me. Some of Ray's visitors at the hospital were friends he had made in First Place 4 Health. Ray became an outstanding warrior for Christ, and to this day, I firmly believe that part of it was due to the love shown to him—Christ's love.

Being a member of First Place 4 Health is about more than losing weight and getting healthy. It is more than Bible study and memorizing verses. It is more than attendance; it is lifting others up in prayer and love. Yes, some things are just better together!

Action Item: Reach out in love to those members in your group who are in need of encouragement today and lift them up in prayer and love.

Betha Jean McGee
Wall, Texas

245

He who began a good work in you

This is love: that we walk in obedience to his commands. As you have heard from the beginning, his command is that you walk in love.

2 JOHN 1:6

I've always been able to shed a few pounds when I needed to, but one day I slipped into my little black dress to find it wasn't so cute. On an impulse, I jumped in the car and stopped by a company that guaranteed weight loss "rapidly" for almost $1,000. As I was *rapidly* leaving, I dialed my church friend Carole Lewis and she graciously allowed me to start her First Place 4 Health class as a latecomer.

My plan was conceived; I would join, lose the weight and otherwise be invisible in the weekly Bible study. After all, I attended Bible studies regularly but enjoyed my time alone with God, not with a room full of ladies. God had a different plan. He lovingly began to point out areas of disobedience in my life, particularly pertaining to people.

I attended my first class, and within a week, I had lost a few pounds. Carole began to engage me in conversation during the class time. I slowly realized that God had commanded me in 2 John 1:6 to walk in love. "Commanded"—what a strong word! God did not make a suggestion. He is commanding me, and I began to ask myself how in the world could I love others if I practiced not becoming involved with them on a personal level?

The months have moved along and God continues to work in my heart. God is showing me how to incorporate loving Him enough to simply act in obedience and trust that His way is the best. Our sweet God in heaven has shown me how much stronger we are in Him when we spend time together to glorify His name.

The weight-loss has not gone as quickly as anticipated, but my heart has grown exponentially—I know He is in control, and when He starts a good work in me, He will see it through to the end!

Action Item: I challenge you to allow God to work in you. He only requires a willing heart.

Janice Mayes-Clayton
Houston, Texas

speaking God's love language

Whoever has my commands and obeys them, he is the one who loves me.
He who loves me will be loved by my Father, and I too will love him
and show myself to him.

JOHN 14:21

The verse above is one that I memorized when I joined First Place in 1981. God has used this verse twice in my book writing as a verse He desires for us to practice in our lives. The first time was in 2002, when I began writing *Back on Track*. I was sitting in my chair where I have my time with God, when I felt the Holy Spirit impress on me what the core of the book would be: believe, trust and obey. The Scripture that was brought to my mind for "obey" was John 14:21.

God is trying to teach me and you that His love language is obedience. He cannot give us all that He desires for us until we learn to obey Him. There are many Scriptures that tell us that if we love God, we will obey Him.

This verse surfaced again as I began writing *Give God a Year* in 2008. The theme for this book was "Pray and Obey." When I protested that I had already used this verse in *Back on Track*, the Holy Spirit gently spoke to my heart and said, "Well, you still haven't learned it!"

I am learning that the reason God commands us to obey Him if we really love Him is because He wants to bless us, and He can only do that when we walk in obedience. When I am walking in obedience, it is easy to eat healthy foods and to exercise. Writing is also easy because God can use an obedient child to write His Words.

When I am disobedient, everything grinds to a screeching halt. It is hard to pray and even harder to obey. The beautiful thing about our God is that when we run back to Him to say we're sorry, He meets us with open arms of love and says, "Let's begin again."

Action Item: Write about your areas of disobedience and ask God to give you a willing heart to obey. As you begin walking in obedience, God will show Himself to you in ways you never dreamed possible.

Carole Lewis
First Place 4 Health National Director
Houston, Texas

247

to love Him is to obey Him

*Whoever has my commands and obeys them, he is the one who loves me.
He who loves me will be loved by my Father, and I too will love him
and show myself to him.*

JOHN 14:21

What motivates us to be obedient to the ways and promptings of the Lord? In my early years as a Christian, it was to avoid God's punishment. My concept of God was that He was mean and just waiting for me to mess up. I tried to obey His laws to avoid His punishment, but I must tell you, fear is not a great motivator!

As I grew, I came under the influence of many godly people. One such person was my Sunday School teacher, Ms. Rhea. She was the senior high girls' teacher at First Baptist Church in Jacksonville, Florida. She challenged us to love God with all of our heart, soul, mind and strength and to be obedient to all He calls us to do. She challenged us to memorize 1 Corinthians 13—the love chapter. Of course, I wanted to please my teacher (being a people pleaser), and I was obedient to memorize the entire chapter. I was obedient to the things of God because I wanted her to be proud of me. I was being obedient for the reward of her approval.

It's been years since I was in that senior high girls' class, but I have never forgotten 1 Corinthians 13. Funny thing about God's Word: it endures forever. It's the gift that keeps on giving. I have finally come to understand what that first verse really means: If I have a gift but I do not have love, I am but a "sounding brass or a clanging cymbal" (*NKJV*).

As I have come to know the Father, He and I have developed a deep love relationship. It is now out of my love for Him that I am obedient. I have come to the understanding that obedience is His love language. If I love Him, I will keep His commandments—not to avoid punishment or to receive reward—but purely out of love. To sustain this kind of love I spend time with Him every day. I still need to know He loves me! He continues to lavish His love upon me, day after day.

Prayer: *Father, thank You for Your great love for me. I choose to love You back and demonstrate that love through my obedience to You. It's not so hard when You do it for love!*

Vicki Heath
First Place 4 Health Associate Director
Edisto Beach, South Carolina

248

attitude adjustment

Whoever has my commands and obeys them, he is the one who loves me.
He who loves me will be loved by my Father, and I too will love him
and show myself to him.

JOHN 14:21

"Obedience"—the very word is enough to make some of us cringe! We recall our childhood and being required to obey and bend to someone else's will. The rebellious spirit would sometimes raise its head and we would become angry and defiant. But for others of us, it was a quiet rebellion of the heart.

My rebellious spirit was a quietly rebellious spirit for the most part. I saw what my brother's outward rebellion got him (a spanking!) and I decided that was not for me. As I grew older, I would comply on the outside, while on the inside my attitude really needed adjusting!

In college, with the help of a wonderful friend named Amy, I was able to start to work on this rebellious spirit that was lurking in the background. Through her kind guidance, I began to see that my pride and lack of compassion toward others was just as sinful as outward rebellion. Through that time in my life, the Lord faithfully taught me that the way to show Him that I love Him is through obedience, on the inside as well as on the outside.

As I became involved in First Place 4 Health, this concept became even more solid in my life. God laid on my heart that loving Him involved *all* aspects of obedience, even to the point of obedience in what I choose to eat or how I choose to spend my time. I am called to obey His commands, no matter what. Even if the dessert or the buffet is all-you-can-eat, I am still called to be self-controlled and alert. When I see others praised when I "deserve" it more than they, I'm still called to be humble and only focused on what God has called me to do. And when God sees that obedience, He knows that I love Him.

Prayer: *Loving and faithful Lord Jesus, forgive us for our rebellious spirits. We know they cause You grief. Change our heart attitudes to desire to be obedient because we want to show You love in the way that You desire.*

Kathlee Coleman
First Place 4 Health Networking Leader
Santa Clarita, California

when it's true love

Whoever has my commands and obeys them, he is the one who loves me.
He who loves me will be loved by my Father, and I too will love him
and show myself to him.

JOHN 14:21

"Love" is a word that is tossed about freely in Christian circles. We talk about how much we love the Lord, but do our actions line up with our words? Scripture says we show our love for God by obeying His commands. It's not enough just to know what the Bible says. It's doesn't really matter how much Scripture we memorize or how many times we have read the Bible from front to back if we are merely hearers of the Word and not doers of the Word.

We live in a time when we have more knowledge of Scripture than ever before due to our easy accessibility to Bible studies, radio and Internet resources. We are often rewarded for how much we know, but knowing and applying that knowledge are two very different things. It's easy to say all the right things, but our actions will always speak louder than our words. Too often our heads are full of knowledge while our hearts are empty and void of true love.

What an awesome blessing we receive when we choose to obey. In John 14:21, Jesus says, "He who loves me will be loved by my Father, and I too will love him and show myself to him." The promise in that verse should be enough to cause us to desire to walk in obedience to God's Word. Blessing always follows obedience. We will see God work in our lives when we apply what we learn in Scripture to our daily lives.

Action Item: How much do you love God? List in your journal some ways you are showing your love by obeying Scripture. Are there areas on which you need to work? List those also, along with a prayer asking God to help you obey His Word.

Prayer: *Heavenly Father, I so desperately want to be one who hears Your Word and obeys it. Help me to be faithful and obedient to Your Word.*

Joni Shaffer
Mercersburg, Pennsylvania

2 5 0

get the point

Whoever has my commands and obeys them, he is the one who loves me.
He who loves me will be loved by my Father, and I too will love him
and show myself to him.

JOHN 14:21

My beginning with First Place 4 Health was in a 1994 newspaper clipping. In reading it, I knew it was God's answer for a weight-loss program with a spiritual emphasis. After my first session, my first thoughts about First Place 4 Health were that it's 95 percent spiritual and 5 percent weight-loss. I felt led by God to lead a group. During the next few sessions as a leader, I struggled with my weight and emotional issues. I realized that I was an emotional eater without accountability.

Then God brought Janet Kirkhart and me together. We are best friends and accountability partners. God has blessed us over the years with opportunities to lead classes, travel and host events together. However, there were times when I would "disappear." During those times, I was being rebellious and disobedient to God. He let me struggle and be miserable until I got His point, which was to obey! Realizing that I did love Him and want to be obedient, I would call Janet and begin again.

Does God keep bringing you back to the same point over and over again? If so, He's trying to tell you something. He will continue until you get the point. It may be to obey, mend a relationship or stop doing something wrong. Whatever it is, listen and He will tell you.

This is what He has done in my life. He brought me back to the same people and place to serve. After many years in and out of First Place 4 Health, I'm back where God wants me. Also, after many years with no physical change, God and I have lost 30 pounds in three months—120 to go.

By my obedience to His commands, I show Him my love. This allows His love to flow through me to others, making us better together.

Action Item: Has God brought you to the same point again and again? What is it? What will you do? Obey or not?

Prayer: *God, I thank You for Your patience and grace and for bringing me finally to the point—to obey. In Jesus' name I pray, amen.*

Shirley Anneken
Cincinnati, Ohio

251

an everlasting love

My command is this: Love each other as I have loved you.

JOHN 15:12

My mom lived with Johnny and me the last three years of her life. She came to live with us after suffering some small strokes that left her with dementia. My mom was my greatest hero in this life and it was so difficult to see her declining by the day. I spent about six months trying to "fix her" until a dear friend, who was also our senior adult minister at our church, gave me some great advice. "Carole," she said, "love her just the way she is; you cannot fix what is wrong with her."

This is pretty good advice for life as well. I am not going to change anyone, but God can work miracles in that person's life when I love that person as God has loved me. How has God loved me?

- He forgives my sins.
- He helps me up when I fall.
- He encourages me to be better than I believe I can be.
- He walks with me through life and carries me when I cannot walk at all.

God taught me so much as I walked through those three years of caregiving with my mom. There were times when it was so hard that I had to leave my mom's side and cry out to God for help. Her helplessness, when she had always been my greatest helper, was harder to endure than I ever could have imagined. God used her helplessness to show me that I am just as helpless when it comes to living life without His help. He used one of the most difficult times of my life to draw me to Himself. He helped me every step of the way, and my mom is now in heaven with Him.

Prayer: *Dear Lord, thank You for using life's difficult times to teach me how to love and trust You. You have loved me with an everlasting love—may I love others the same way. In Jesus' name, amen.*

Carole Lewis
First Place 4 Health National Director
Houston, Texas

252

the oil factor

My command is this: Love each other as I have loved you.

JOHN 15:12

I'm on a mission to bake Christmas cookies for our cookie exchange. I love cookie exchanges so that I can give out a variety to my family, friends and neighbors to express how much I love and appreciate them. It is a way to be intentional with an important lesson I learned at First Place 4 Health—to love one another like Christ loves us.

Cookie baking has never been my specialty; however, the years of raising kids helped to perfect one kind—the sugar cookie. I think I have it down to a science and the reason is due to the oil factor.

Oil is the key to several things: Oil makes the car run smoothly, makes dry hair shine and makes sugar cookies that melt in your mouth. Granted these are different kinds of oils, but oil just the same. Oil lubricates, moisturizes and is superb in cookies. Without oil, a car motor would burn up, dry hair would remain dry and cookies would crumble.

You probably knew all this, but did you know that oil anoints? In the Bible, a person was anointed to show that God had chosen him to do a special job. My favorite example was when Mary took a beautiful jar of perfume, made primarily of oil, and poured it over Jesus' feet. This seemed extravagant because it was worth a year's wages, but for Jesus, it was a sign of amazing love.

As I ponder the oil factor, I reflect on how, like precious oil, our love for Christ should be extravagant because of the love He showed us so long ago.

Action Item: Think about how you can show extravagant love to others this Christmas.

Prayer: *Dear Father, thank You so much for the gift of Your Son, Jesus Christ. Help me to obey Your commandment to love others like You have loved me. Amen.*

Sara Rainey
Colorado Springs, Colorado

parenting class 101

My command is this: Love each other as I have loved you.

JOHN 15:12

In June 2009, I weighed 250 pounds. Not only did I need to lose weight, but I also needed to get right with God. The Lord revealed how disobedient I was spiritually. Having been obese all my life, God convicted me and I joined First Place 4 Health. What began as a weight-loss journey became a lesson in love and obedience to my heavenly Father and my earthly father as well.

I wasn't working due to a seriously ill child and a father who was diagnosed with Hodgkin's lymphoma and kidney cancer. Both my son and my father required so much nursing care that my time with the Lord went astray.

My father and I never had a close relationship. His standards were almost unattainable. What he didn't know was that the harder he pushed me the more I despised him. I loved my dad, but I didn't like him. He suffered from severe depression. Due to his criticisms, I felt like I couldn't meet his standards. My father was the valedictorian, a trained concert pianist, and was college educated with a master's degree. I had very high expectations to live up to. After my father and I got into another disagreement, I recall emphatically stating to my mother, "I will take care of you, but never Daddy!"

Being the RN of the family, however, it was natural for me to take on the caregiver role. As treatments began for my dad's kidney cancer, it appeared that my dad had no side effects from the chemotherapy. Then after receiving two treatments, he almost died. I was awake for days with no sleep. I spent countless hours at his bedside arguing with the physicians that his death was imminent. I prayed like I have never prayed before. God revealed in that moment that I was not loving nor honoring my father through Christ's eyes. I was judging him selfishly through the eyes of his child. God restored our relationship as father and daughter. Through this experience I also have a deeper relationship with my Father God.

Prayer: *Lord, I ask You today to reveal to me those in my life who need to be loved by me just as You have loved me. Please teach me to love others the way You love us. In Your precious and holy name. Amen.*

Rachel Dennis
Lancaster, Ohio

food for thought

My command is this: Love each other as I have loved you.

JOHN 15:12

Seeing others fully committed to wholeheartedly obeying the Lord Jesus in every area of their lives always challenges me and inspires me. As I examine my own heart and mind, I find myself asking: Am I willing to say yes to God—whatever He asks of me? Am I willing to say no to the things that displease or dishonor Him?

In John 4, Jesus has just told the woman at the well that only He can quench her spiritual thirst: "Everyone who drinks this water will be thirsty again, but whoever drinks the water I give him will never thirst. Indeed, the water I give him will become in him a spring of water welling up to eternal life" (verses 13-14).

She responds to His invitation and receives this life-giving water, calling everyone in her village to come and do the same. But as this miraculous spiritual transformation is taking place, Jesus' disciples have their mind on—what else—food! They fuss at Him because He hasn't eaten anything in hours.

Jesus tells them, "My food . . . is to do the will of him who sent me and to finish his work" (John 4:34). After studying this verse for awhile, I wrote my own paraphrase: "What nourishes me and fulfills me and strengthens me is to do God's will—to walk in obedience to His Word and His calling on my life, and to accomplish the work of His kingdom. Obedience. This is what truly satisfies my soul hunger."

Now when I am tempted to disobey God by turning to food to meet my spiritual and emotional needs, I often remember this verse. I remember how good obedience feels—how beautiful it looks in my life and the lives of those around me. And I'm inspired to choose what is better (see Luke 10:42).

Action Item: Where do you find nourishment and strength? Memorize John 4:34 for those times when you feel tempted to take what will be an ultimately unsatisfying and unfulfilling choice. Choose what is better!

Prayer: *Lord, may my body—this temple—become a living testimony, a visible reflection of the reality that Jesus is all I need.*

Christin Ditchfield
Christian author and speaker
Osprey, Florida

loved completely

My command is this: Love each other as I have loved you.

JOHN 15:12

Picture for a moment that you have been given a beautifully wrapped gift. It was given out of love, wrapped in grace and tied with a bow of mercy. You unwrap the box to find two extraordinary gifts: a pair of worn dusty sandals and a towel. These are Jesus' sandals, and they walked all the way to Calvary. You wonder how these sandals could be in your size, but to your surprise you find that one size fits all. This gift reminds you that you have been asked to walk in Jesus' sandals in obedience each day. The second item, the towel, was the one that Jesus used to dry the feet of those He washed. He walked in obedience. He walked in our shoes. He washed out of love.

Obedience wrapped in love is the sweetest gift of Jesus that we can give to others. It is putting Jesus' love in action by walking in His ways. Remember that Jesus not only washed His disciples' feet, but He dried them as well. He completed the job. Jesus always completed everything the Father asked Him to do, being obedient even to the point of suffering death on the cross. He loved us completely and took our place so that we could be forgiven. He sacrificed Himself for us and became the Lamb.

When Jesus faced those with hardened hearts, He loved them in spite of themselves. In the same way that He did not turn away from His disciples' calloused and tired feet, He commands us not to turn away from calloused and tired hearts. Loving others is a command, not an option, and we are to love them in the same way that Jesus loves us.

Jesus reassures us that if we remain in Him, He will remain in us (see John 15:4). In this way, we are able to do something that we could not normally do on our own. By drawing on Jesus' strength, we can walk in obedience and love others completely, even when it is difficult to do and the challenge is before us.

Action Item: Imagine yourself wearing Jesus' sandals and towel around you today and do a kind act for someone who needs an extra dose of grace.

Prayer: *Father, thank You for loving me so completely. Help me to love those You place in my life with Your unselfish love and devotion. Amen.*

Connie Welch
First Place 4 Health Network Leader
Keller, Texas

submitting to authority

Submit to one another out of reverence for Christ.
EPHESIANS 5:21

I have a dear friend who says, "Submission is when you give in when you don't agree. If you agree, then it is agreement, not submission." Given this definition, it seems that this verse is admonishing us as believers to submit to one another.

One of the things I love best about the First Place 4 Health program is that we are in a small group with like-minded people who are all endeavoring to give Christ first place in our lives. Yet I believe our groups would be even better and stronger if we practiced the truth of this verse.

I have learned submission by working with my trainer, Donna. When we first began working together, I quickly found out who was the boss. One morning, early in our friendship, I told Donna that I was so sore from the previous workout that every time I had turned over in bed, it had woken me up. Donna cheerfully replied, "Well, let's get to work!" I submitted to her knowledge and authority, and at the end of our hour together, I felt so much better that my soreness was almost gone.

Another day, I tripped over a piece of exercise equipment and turned my ankle. Donna had me lie down on a bench while she ran for an ice pack. When the pack was on my elevated ankle, Donna said, "Cross your arms over your chest and do some crunches." When I protested, Donna said, "There's no reason to waste time. I have ice on your ankle."

I love Donna so much that I willingly submit to her authority in my life. I believe that the truth of Ephesians 5:21 is that as believers, we need to cultivate friendships with other believers who are ahead of us on some level. It might be spiritual, mental, emotional or physical. In my relationship with Donna, I acknowledge that she is way ahead of me in strength training, so I submit to her, knowing that she will not hurt me in any way. The secret is to submit "out of reverence for Christ," and it will be easy to "give in when you don't agree."

Action Item: If there is an area of your life that needs help from someone who is further down the road than you are, call that person today and ask him or her to mentor you. Be ready to submit to this person "out of reverence for Christ."

Carole Lewis
First Place 4 Health National Director
Houston, Texas

honoring Christ

Submit to one another out of reverence for Christ.

EPHESIANS 5:21

"Submit." That word will raise the eyebrows of most human beings. It's not generally a word that fills us with a warm fuzzy feeling. If we are honest, we typically equate submitting with doing something we don't like to do or with having a tyrant rule over us.

Choking down submission is a large pill to swallow. But when we look at it through the eyes of Scripture, it is all about imitating Christ. When we submit, we love each other in a deep way by considering others before ourselves. We have many different kinds of relationships, but with each of them, we should have that same attitude of being honoring, loving and respectful.

As a wife, I love and respect my husband. He is my best friend and my sweetheart. We are considerate of each other. My husband is a man of honor, and I respect his role as my husband and head of our home. He is a leader with a servant's heart. His consideration for our family and me makes it easy to follow him.

But what about those relationships where we do not get along? We can still be imitators of Christ. We can show others respect, honor and have a good attitude because we are doing it for Christ. We can respect the position of authority that person holds even if we have a problem with his or her personality or the decisions that he or she makes.

Of course, God is our highest authority, and our first allegiance is to Him. If the person who is in authority over us is enticing us to sin and break the law, then we have to draw the line and take a stand. We have a spiritual and moral obligation to obey God's Word. But our good attitude of respect, honor and consideration will be a witness for Christ. It will speak volumes to someone who needs a relationship with Him.

Prayer: *Lord, please help me in all my relationships to be honoring and considerate so that others will see Your Son reflected in my attitude.*

Connie Welch
First Place 4 Health Networking Leader
Keller, Texas

how's that working for you?

Submit to one another out of reverence for Christ.

EPHESIANS 5:21

There it is in all its glory, the dreaded *s*-word—"submit"! There was a time in my life when just reading that word made my skin crawl. "Submit? You have to be kidding me. I am my own boss, and no one can tell me what to do." Then I had to ask myself, as Dr. Phil says, *How's that working for you?* It wasn't!

My unwillingness to submit had wreaked havoc in my life in relational, financial and, ultimately, spiritual ways. I was just always so amazed that I had these ridiculously hard bosses until, finally, the Lord revealed to me that the common denominator in all of these bosses was me!

Slowly, I began the process of changing and truly walking in submission. Oh, it was a two-steps-forward-and-one-step-back adventure, but as Beth Moore says, "In any math, that is still progress." There were many times that I was sitting down on the outside but standing up on the inside. However, as I studied the Word and sought counsel, I learned that submission is a gift and that the authorities placed over me are there for my protection (see Romans 13:1-5).

This became abundantly clear when I was the executive director of a ministry. A major decision for the organization had to be made, and I was truly torn between the choices and what was best for the ministry. As I sat in the boardroom and listened to the discussion, I was relieved that the burden of the decision would rest on the entire board and not on me. I trusted their authority, and I could walk in full assurance for whatever path we took as an organization.

My level of submission to the authorities (and, by the way, this includes the Department of Transportation that posts the speed limits) is in direct proportion to my submission to God. If I am not submitting to them, then I am not submitting to Him!

Action Item: Make a list of all the authorities in your life. Then, on a scale of 1 to 10, ask yourself how they would think you are doing in submitting to them. If you are falling short, start submitting to them today, even if you are just doing it on the outside.

Becky Turner
Houston, Texas

submit to others' needs

Submit to one another out of reverence for Christ.

EPHESIANS 5:21

Oftentimes when we hear the word "submit," we think of it in military terms. Submission infers rank and demands complete obedience to the highest-ranking person in the room. While that is a facet of submission, there is much more to it. We can see this in the life of Jesus, who is our example, and how He demonstrated submission.

Of course, no one outranked Jesus. He was God, and His title of "King of kings" and "Lord of lords" was still in effect during His three years of public ministry on earth. Thus, His model of submission was not based on authority, but on needs.

The woman at the well had a need, and Jesus changed His agenda to meet her need (see John 4). Two blind men cried out to Him as He was making His way through the towns and villages, and He stopped what He was doing to heal them (see Matthew 9:27-38). The people were hungry, but instead of demanding that they go and get food for themselves (and for Him), He fed them (see Luke 9:10-17). Only once did Jesus submit to another based on authority—the night He was in the Garden of Gethsemane and cried out, "Not my will, but yours be done." This was an act of submission to the authority of the Father.

We see the act of mutual submission demonstrated in healthy, Christ-centered marriages. The husband will submit to the needs of his wife—*I'm not sure why she needs to redecorate the living room again, but here we go.* The wife will also submit to his authority—*I disagree with this, but I will submit in honor of his position.*

Whether we're submitting to a need or to an authority, it's an act of love. If we're going to love someone, then we will submit to him or her. Our submission will constitute part of the relationship.

Action Item: To whom in your life do you need to submit to meet their needs? An elderly neighbor? A challenging co-worker? A mother-in-law who is negative? Ask God to reveal a need in these people's lives, and then make a plan to meet that need.

Becky Turner
Houston, Texas

260

a tough pill

Submit to one another out of reverence for Christ.

EPHESIANS 5:21

I'll never forget the first thing I volunteered to do when I moved to Virginia and joined my church: organize a "One Day Fun Day." I had heard a lot of talk on the subject, but nobody had the time that summer to head it up. I decided this was something I could do, so I called a meeting for anyone interested in helping out.

As had been my prior experience whenever a bunch a women got together, I expected lively debates, differing opinions and varied personality clashes. However, I was taken by surprise when I asked for ideas and everyone just stared at me. Not one to be comfortable with pregnant pauses, I waited as long as I could and then began suggesting a few ideas of my own. Their heads started bobbing like dashboard dogs, but still nobody was talking. I tried some communication tips I had heard somewhere in an attempt to draw them out. We moved up to one-word responses. I started wondering if I had inadvertently stepped into a filming of *The Stepford Wives*. Maybe they were trying to figure me out? Maybe they couldn't understand my accent? Maybe the cat really got their tongues?

The most outspoken one in the bunch finally gave me a clue when she said, "Just tell me what you want me to do—I've gotta go!" Apparently, they had taken my invitation literally. They had come to "help out." They had not come to debate, discuss, waste time or otherwise run the show. They thought that is what I wanted to do. I soon learned that this was a room full of godly, self-sacrificing women who were content with being Jesus' hands and feet and doing whatever needed to be done, including "submitting to one another out of reverence to Christ."

Action Item: In what areas do you have trouble submitting to another? What is one step you can take toward this process?

Prayer: *Lord, submission can be a hard pill to swallow. Thank You for sugar-coating it with the examples of my sweet, godly sisters who do it with such grace. I pray for those who need to see this lived out in their lives, and I pray for the wisdom and grace to live it out for them. Amen.*

Jeanne Deveau Gregory
Chatham, Virginia

INSPIRATIONAL STORY

a new creation

I believe I finally understand this program. I started First Place 4 Health in 2004, and I took off 20 pounds the first 12-week session. I did not stay with the program, and about a year later, I gained the weight back. I was not as successful the second time I tried it. The third and fourth time I did the program was in 2005 and 2006—again not with a lot of success. I felt like such a loser, because I was unable to get rid of the weight again. I never stayed with First Place 4 Health a full consecutive year, but I participated in about four 12-week sessions over a three-year period.

I am so grateful to God that He did not give up on me. He is so faithful. I guess I am just very thickheaded and stubborn, so it takes a lot of shaking to finally wake me up. This time at First Place 4 Health has been very different. I truly believe that I understand the concepts so much better and I am finally learning to surrender it all to God more of the time. I am changing little by little in all four areas of my life.

BEFORE   AFTER

Physically, I am exercising more and actually learning to enjoy it; I realize it is a gift that I give to myself. Exercising and listening to the memory verses on the Bible study CD has helped me a great deal.

I had to give away most of my size 2X clothes, and I am getting sizes large and 12, which is really fun. I had to cut back on my medication because my blood pressure was getting too low.

I am eating healthier and really enjoying the good foods. I plan good meals and choose to do better things for myself than eating. Carole Lewis says, "When wondering what to do, just do the next right thing." This saying has helped me greatly when wondering what I need to do next. I have lost 43 pounds and I am more at peace with myself.

Mentally, my focus is on Jesus. I realize that I am worth taking care of and that God loves me and desires good things for me. I no longer believe the counterfeit liar who tells me his way is better. I have believed his lies too long and I know it is such a deception. I remind myself that food cannot solve my problems but only add to them. Food cannot comfort me; only Jesus can. He knows everything about me and loves me despite my failures and faults—just as I am.

Emotionally, I am not wavering and inconsistent as I was before. I am not blaming others for why I am not taking care of my body. I am the one who has the power to decide to exercise and to eat healthy. When I feel hungry, angry, lonely or tired, I look to Jesus and pray about it instead of stuffing my feelings with any old food.

Finally, and most important, my *spiritual life* is so improved. I feel closer to God and turn to Him when I need His help. The Bible studies are so great. Reading my Bible every day, working the Bible study and learning more about His will and desires for my life are changing me. This is the greatest part of the program. When I focus on how much God loves me and wants good things for me, it makes me love Him more and desire to please and honor Him.

As an onion skin is peeled away layer by layer, so my God is working with me. I am so grateful to all the ladies in the Grace Covenant First Place 4 Health group. They have been so encouraging, which is another part of this great program. Every week as we gather to go over proper nutrition and share the Bible study, we also encourage and pray for each other. We will help each other finally to be victorious over our flesh and arrive at the place God has for each one of us. As Jeremiah 29:11 says, " 'For I know the plans I have for you,' declares the LORD, 'plans to prosper you and not to harm you, plans to give you hope and a future.' "

In 2 Corinthians 5:17, Paul says, "Therefore, if anyone is in Christ, he is a new creation; the old has gone, the new has come!" May we all enjoy the journey to becoming new creations in Jesus!

Justine Poplaski
Brewerton, New York

contributors

Ruth Alderman, Rock Hill, South Carolina
Month 5 Inspirational Story

Shirley Anneken, Cincinnati, Ohio
Reading #250

Rachel Aranda, Houston Texas
Reading #3

Emily Ardolf, Fairmont, Minnesota
Reading #18

P. J. Bahr, Rapid City, South Dakota
Readings #14,143

Karen Baker, Eagle Point, Oregon
Reading #192

Helen Baratta, Oakdale, Pennsylvania
Reading #89

Jan Blankenship, Medford, Oregon
Reading #38

Jeannie Blocher, Germantown, Maryland,
Readings #5, 67, 115,

Barbara Bright, Columbus, Ohio
Reading #224

June Chapko, San Antonio, Texas
Readings #112, 117, 183, 190, 199, 227

Mary Chin, St. Charles, Illinois
Readings #95, 100

Beverly Cody, Bastrop, Texas
Month 2 Inspirational Story

Kathlee Coleman, Santa Clarita, California
Readings #53, 122, 248

Jerry Cosper, San Antonio, Texas
Month 11 Inspirational Story

Rossanne Day, Granbury, Texas
Month 3 Inspirational Story

Rachel Dennis, Lancaster, Ohio,
Reading #253

Linda Derck, Shamokin, Pennsylvania
Reading #34

Melissa DeRosier, Roswell, New Mexico
Reading #237

Jewel DeWeese, South Boston, Virginia,
Reading #15

Christin Ditchfield, Osprey, Florida,
Reading #254

Betsy Dunn, Henry, Tennessee
Reading #140

Gale Dupriest, Stephenville, Texas
Month 8 Inspirational Story

Gigi Falstrom, Irving, Texas
Reading #144, 210

Pam Farrel, El Cajon, California
Reading #124

Karen Ferguson, Houston, Texas
Readings #28, 79, 87, 147, 169

Mike Friedler, Rochester New York
Reading #119

Jeanne Deveau Gregory, Chatham Virginia
Month 1 Inspirational Story, Readings
#13, 24, 45, 47, 58, 70, 83, 94, 149, 155,
158, 165, 173, 184, 193, 194, 197, 239, 260

Colleen Hammond, Kingsley, Pennsylvania
Month 4 Inspirational Story

Diane Hawkins, Houston, Texas
Readings #99, 167

Megan Heath, North Charleston,
South Carolina
Reading #92

Michael Heath, Iraq
Reading #188

Robin Heath, Edisto Beach, South Carolina
Readings #205, 215, 235

Vicki Heath, Edisto Beach, South Carolina
Readings #9, 48, 55, 68, 103, 128, 160,
170, 175, 198, 217, 247

Geni Hulsey, Houston, Texas
Reading #148

Kay Jarrell, Odessa, Texas
Reading #57

Melissa Jones, Houston, Texas
Reading #230

Margaret Keaton, Montague, Michigan
Month 6 Inspirational Story

Diane Marie Kanode,
Elizabethtown, Pennsylvania
Reading #52

Janet Kirkhart, Loveland, Ohio
Readings #23, 44, 154, 203, 225

Marjorie Kirkpatrick, Omaha, Nebraska
Month 10 Inspirational Story

Mary Kloek, Minneapolis, Minnesota
Reading #232

Claudia Korff, Houston, Texas
Reading #73

Jenn Krogh, Kewaunee, Wisconsin
Reading #2

Jackie LaPouble, New Orleans, Louisiana
Month 9 Inspirational Story,
Reading #204

Carole Lewis, Houston, Texas
Readings #1, 6, 11, 16, 21, 26, 31, 36,
41, 46, 49, 51, 56, 61, 66, 69, 71, 76, 81,
86, 91, 96, 101, 105, 106, 111, 116, 121,
126, 131, 132, 136, 141, 146, 150, 151,
156, 161, 166, 171, 174, 176, 181, 186,
191, 195, 196, 201, 206, 211, 216, 221,
226, 231, 236, 241, 246, 251, 256

Lisa Lewis, Houston, Texas
Readings #32, 109, 133, 142, 202, 209, 240

Pat Lewis, Houston, Texas
Readings #22, 60, 93, 102, 110, 179

Pauli Lewman, Midvale, Idaho
Reading #223

Martha Marks, Houston, Texas
Reading #54

Judy Marshall, Gilmer, Texas
Readings #59, 214

Vickie Martin, Stephenville, Texas
Readings #168, 233

Dee Matthews, Sugar Land, Texas
Readings #114, 219

Sandy Matthews, Houston, Texas
Reading #43, 82

Janice Mayes-Clayton, Houston, Texas
Reading #245

Janet McCluskey, Attleboro, Massachusetts
Reading #129, 140

Nan McCullough, Reston, Virginia
Reading #33

Lucinda Secrest McDowell,
Wethersfield, Connecticut
Readings #118, 134, 138

Betha Jean McGee, Wall, Texas
Readings #7, 30, 37, 77, 84,
120, 135, 172, 238, 244

Sarah Mielke, Louisville, Kentucky
Reading #242

Sandy Miller, Houston, Texas
Readings #75, 189

Debbie Norred, Lynn Haven, Florida
Reading #107

Donna Odum, Heber Springs, Arkansas
Reading #104

Justine Poplaski, Brewerton, New York
Month 12 Inspirational Story

Sara Rainey, Colorado Springs, Colorado
Readings #212, 252

Susan Ray, Houston, Texas
Reading #113

Stephanie Rhodes, Arlington, Tennessee
Readings #127, 180, 243

Donna Roberts, Houston, Texas
Reading #19

Martha Rogers, Houston, Texas
Readings #65, 80, 164, 182, 222

Beverly LaHote Schwind,
Fairfield Glade, Tennessee
Readings #40, 72

Linda Seagears, Gainesville, Virginia
Reading #178

Beth Serpas, Houston, Texas
Readings #27, 90, 97, 137, 218

Joni Shaffer, Mercersburg, Pennsylvania
Readings #62, 213, 228, 249

Kendra Smiley, East Lynn, Illinois
Readings #20, 123

Karrie Smyth, Brandon,
Manitoba, Canada
Readings #10, 29, 220

Linda Snow, Houston, Texas
Reading #234

Deb Stark, San Antonio, Texas
Readings #4, 88

Krista Taylor, McKenzie, Tennessee
Reading #74

Becky Turner, Houston, Texas
Readings #12, 35, 139, 153, 162, 163,
205, 208, 258, 259

Carol VanAtta, Troutdale, Oregon
Readings #17, 25, 50, 130, 159, 207

Jean Wall, Bremerton, Washington
Reading #64

Connie Welch, Keller, Texas
Readings #8, 39, 42, 78, 85, 98, 108,
125, 145, 152, 157, 177, 185, 187, 200,
229, 255, 257

Priscilla Works, Medford, Oregon
Month 7 Inspirational Story,
Reading #63

join first place 4 health today!

The First Place 4 Health Kit contains everything members need to live healthy, lose weight, make friends, and experience spiritual growth. With each resource, members will make positive changes in their thoughts and emotions, while transforming the way they fuel and recharge their bodies and relate to God.

Member's Kit Contains:
- First Place 4 Health Hardcover Book
- Emotions & Eating DVD
- First Place 4 Health Member's Guide
- First Place 4 Health Prayer Journal
- Simple Ideas for Healthy Living
- First Place 4 Health Tote Bag
- Food on the Go Pocket Guide
- Why Should a Christian Be Physically Fit? DVD

978.08307.45890
$99.99 (a $145 Value!)

The First Place 4 Health Group Starter Kit includes everything you need to start and confidently lead your group into healthy living, weight loss, friendships, and spiritual growth. You will find lesson plans, training DVDs, a user-friendly food plan and other easy-to-use tools to help you lead members to a new way of thinking about health and Christ through a renewed mind, emotions, body and spirit.

Group Starter Kit Contains:
- A Complete Member's Kit with Member Navigation Sheet
- First Place 4 Health Leader's Guide
- Seek God First Bible Study
- First Place 4 Health Orientation and Food Plan DVD
- How to Lead with Excellence DVD

978.08307.45906
$199.99 (a $256 value!)

www.firstplace4health.com